Pat Thomson, PSM, is Associate Professor in the School of Education at the University of South Australia. She is well-known for her innovative work as principal of disadvantaged schools in Adelaide. She has also worked in education policy and speaks regularly at conferences in Australia, North America and the UK.

D1235434

STUDIES IN EDUCATION
General editor: Bob Lingard

Answering Back: Girls, Boys and Feminism in Schools
Jane Kenway and Sue Willis with Jill Blackmore and
Léonie Rennie

Australian Education: Reform or Crisis?
Anthony Welch

*Constructing Critical Literacies: Teaching and Learning
Textual Practice*
Sandy Muspratt, Allan Luke and Peter Freebody

Markets in Education
Simon Marginson

*The New Work Order: Behind the Language of the New
Capitalism*
James Paul Gee, Glynda Hull and Colin Lankshear

Page to Screen: Taking Literacy into the Electronic Era
Edited by Ilana Snyder

Masculinity Goes to School
Rob Gilbert and Pam Gilbert

Rethinking Gender in Early Childhood Education
Glenda MacNaughton

SCHOOLING THE RUSTBELT KIDS

Making the difference in changing times

Pat Thomson

ALLEN&UNWIN

First published in Australia in 2002
Copyright © P. Thomson 2002

All rights reserved. No part of this book may be reproduced or transmitted in any form or by any means, electronic or mechanical, including photocopying, recording or by any information storage and retrieval system, without prior permission in writing from the publisher. The *Australian Copyright Act 1968* (the Act) allows a maximum of one chapter or 10% of this book, whichever is the greater, to be photocopied by any educational institution for its educational purposes provided that the educational institution (or body that administers it) has given a remuneration notice to Copyright Agency Limited (CAL) under the Act.

Allen & Unwin
83 Alexander Street
Crows Nest NSW 2065
Australia
Phone: (61 2) 8425 0100
Fax: (61 2) 9906 2218
Email: info@allenandunwin.com
Web: www.allenandunwin.com

National Library of Australia
Cataloguing-in-Publication entry:

Thomson, Pat.
  Schooling the rustbelt kids: making the difference in
  changing times.

  Bibliography.
  Includes index.
  ISBN 1 86508 685 1.

  1. Socially handicapped children—Education—Australia.
  2. Educational equalization—Australia. I. Title.

379.260994

Typeset by Midland Typesetters, Maryborough, Victoria
Printed by South Wind Production (Singapore) Private Limited

10 9 8 7 6 5 4 3 2 1

for the Paralowie mob, 1985–1997
and in memory of Jean Blackburn,
mother of the Disadvantaged Schools Programme

Contents

Series editor's foreword

There is something remarkably different about the transformations the world is currently experiencing. Theorists such as Stuart Hall use the term 'New Times' to refer to these social, economic, political and cultural changes, characterised by simultaneous differentiation and fragmentation and homogeneity and standardisation. Others speak of globalisation to capture the essence of these changes. Globalisation refers to the increased interdependence of nation-states and to the more porous boundaries between them. It also refers to the compression of time and space resulting from the information technology revolution and the availability of rapid transportation. We also see more flows of ideas, peoples, monies, images and so on around the globe. In many ways, and certainly for the more privileged, the world is now experienced as one place. Politically, globalisation has witnessed the dominance of neo-liberal economic policies. No one is able to escape the impact of these changes because they shape the material and cultural conditions of existence within which we must now interpret our lives and construct our futures. No study of education can afford to overlook the ways in which globalisation might serve to define the conditions of pedagogic work and the possibilities for doing justice through schooling. The challenge facing educational systems and educators is to understand these New Times and to respond ethically, strategically, effectively and pedagogically. It is these educational challenges that form the basic premise of the books in this series.

Pat Thomson's *Schooling the Rustbelt Kids* deals explicitly with these issues in a theoretically creative and empirically informed fashion. More specifically, this study considers the impact of globalisation on the work of schools and educators in a disadvantaged locale in one Australian city. The analysis deals with the effects in schools serving this community, particularly on the work of principals and teachers, as well as on young people's experiences of schooling. The study is also located within a consideration of the interplay of State and Federal educational policy developments that are framed to varying degrees by neo-liberalism. The book works in a most sophisticated, but engaging manner across the terrains of theory, including the work of Pierre Bourdieu, Arjun Appadurai and Edward Soja, empirical evidence constructed from a number of 'disadvantaged schools', and the emergent policy and practice contexts. The study intelligently reinforces the aphorism that there is nothing as practical as good theory.

Thomson utilises Appadurai's argument that the global and the local meet each other in 'context productive' and 'context generative' ways. The former refers to the effects of globalisation and their mediation through state policy regimes, while the context-generative elaborates the potential for local actors to reconstitute the global in vernacular ways. The optic of the state here usually works with an aggrandised conception of the knowledge of the policy maker and a mistrusting, disrespectful, diminution of the practical knowledge of pedagogues. Thomson tellingly demonstrates the negative fall-outs from neo-liberal policy regimes that have become almost hegemonic and which restrict the possibilities for generative local practices and result in the deeper 'marbling in' of poverty in particular locales. She shows how contemporary policy discourses about 'risk' and 'school effectiveness' decontextualise the work of schools and teachers. This thinning out is also evident in the 'literacisation' of educational policy and in relation to the morphing of the Federal government's Disadvantaged Schools Program, a progressive policy child of the Whitlam era, into a Literacy program for Disadvantaged students. While providing a critique of these developments, Thomson makes some interesting suggestions for a way forward in policy terms and for new system/school and school/community relationships. Despite globalisation, schools remain very localised institutions.

Schooling the Rustbelt Kids will be of interest to sociologists of education, educational policy sociologists, students interested in the application of contemporary theory and methodologies in educational research, and to educators and parents in disadvantaged schools. There are also lessons for policy makers and politicians committed to ensuring some homology between the rhetoric of social justice in education and the reality of actual practices and outcomes. This is a book that ought to be read by all those interested in understanding the ways inequality works in New Times and what might be able to be done in policy terms, in principled principalships and through productive pedagogies. In the post-September 11 era, that ought to include all of us, for it is readily apparent that the growth in inequality within and between nations is unhelpful in doing justice in schools and in creating the future most of us would want to see.

Bob Lingard
Series Editor

First words

This book is based on research undertaken as part of doctoral study (Thomson, 1999a). The major corpus of evidence consisted of taped conversations with 36 school principals, a body of photographic material, a variety of officially produced and public statistical data and existing research literature. In addition, I used my own experiences of working in disadvantaged schools and neighbourhoods from 1971–97, and of working as a policy activist in a range of Australian state and national forums over the same time span. I have continued to read about disadvantaged schools and to have conversations with people still working in them and these have been critical in ensuring that this book is as up to date as I can make it.

The methodological approach I have taken is based in a view of research as writing (Richardson, 1994; 1997), and the production of knowledge as occurring in and through language (see Thomson & Wellard, 1999). The transcripts of conversations, documents I collected, and stories and poems I wrote as part of this research were therefore subjected to a range of narrative analyses (e.g. Riessman, 1993), discourse analyses (e.g. Fairclough, 1994) and deconstructions (e.g. Lather, 1991). I have endeavoured to make obvious through the construction of this book my view that those who were interviewed did not speak 'the truth', any more than I do, although all of us have been truthful and our stories do have some veracity. Both the original thesis and this book are what I describe as a policy sociology with literary leanings. I have been informed and encouraged in this by recent scholarly debates about the textual representation of research (Denzin, 1997; Ellis & Bochner, 1996; Stronach & MacLure, 1997). Readers will find this text to be primarily, but not exclusively, naturalistic. I have used some writerly devices that are not conventionally found in studies of this kind. For example, in the first chapter I invent two hypothetical children. They do not exist, but they are not simply fiction: these stories are grounded in my research and they carry the theorisation of the production of educational disadvantage that underpins the remainder of the book. The fourth chapter about school discipline and welfare begins with an imaginary script for a film that has and will never be made, but could be, because all of the dialogue is taken from actual interview transcripts and published writings. And, while the particular rustbelt kids and schools in this book are in Adelaide, South Australia, I often refer to 'the city'. I do this because I want to recreate how, as a researcher, I came to see my home-town as a new and unfamiliar place, in which I re-searched for explanations about how and why it is as it is today. I have used these, and other distancing, non-naturalistic textual devices, to draw attention to issues that require interrogation, not just a straightforward reading.

One of the criticisms of research on poverty, disadvantage or class is that it is 'researching down', it is an exercise by the academy that reproduces and produces dominant power relations. I have to say that that has not been my major concern in this book, as perhaps it should have been. Rather, I have been concerned about the everyday realities of rustbelt schools. The most common picture of these schools is that they are blackboard jungles and the students feral. Sometimes researchers try to avoid stigmatising representations by focusing instead on pedagogy and knowledge, or constructing the 'daily onslaught', as one principal described it, as a welfare problem or a parent–school relationship problem—and I can understand why. It is of course all of these things and more. But I have chosen to deal with what for me was, and is still for my erstwhile colleagues, a hallmark of the disadvantaged school—the time taken managing order and welfare, and the resulting lack of time and resources to do as much as might be done to change curriculum, pedagogy and school practices. I therefore run the considerable risk that my colleagues and friends will be distressed by this text, that they will see it as further stereotyping and 'othering'. I also run the risk that I have, despite censoring the most provocative stories, tended to go for the 'exotic' rather than the mundane and ordinary.

So I want to stress one point. This is not a text of blame, nor of pity. This is not the story of inadequate and badly managed schools, nor of heroic soldiers fighting the just war. This is not the story of bad or sick or irresponsible families or cultures of welfare fraud.

This is one story of disadvantaged schools, not all stories. It is told in anger at the retraction of support for families and schools that deserve better. It is told in the hope that the telling is also a form of 'narrative justice', and that the stories might contribute to much needed shifts in policy and understanding.

1 | Vicki and Thanh

Statistically speaking, the best advice we can give to a poor child, keen to get ahead through education, is to choose richer parents (Connell, 1995, p. 6).

Imagine two children about to start school. They are both five years old and are eagerly anticipating their first day. Imagine that each brings with them to school a virtual schoolbag full of things they have already learned at home, with their friends, and in and from the world in which they live.

The first child is a boy called Thanh. He lives in an extended family where he has been chatted and read to in Vietnamese and Chinese since he was very small. He has watched Australian television, visited shopping centres and worked with his family in its restaurant—doing small tasks like collecting dishes, giving out menus and change, and washing vegetables. His parents spent much of their married adult lives in separate refugee camps and were not reunited until they got to Australia. Thanh's father carried a *nguyet* (a guitar-like instrument) with him on the long walk from the town where he was born to the camp in Thailand and kept it safe until he reached his new home in Australia. When he is not too tired he plays it, and Thanh loves to listen to the traditional songs handed down through the generations. He also loves to hear his older brother and sister talk about school. His parents' formal education

1

was disrupted by the civil war, but both of them are literate in two languages and treasure books. They have worked long hours and several jobs to finally open, with the help of the hui (the community financial system), the restaurant where they now work most days and nights. Thanh comes to school with three spoken languages in his virtual schoolbag, a love of music, an understanding of the restaurant trade, a capacity to get on with a wide range of people, knowledge about Vietnam, China, Thailand and Australia and an understanding that school is important.

The second child is Vicki. Her parents are both university educated and Vicki's mother runs a small catering business at home, supplying gourmet cakes to cafes. Her father is a teacher at the local high school and is currently researching his Irish family heritage. She is the oldest child and has one younger brother. Vicki has been to both childcare and preschool and has already begun to read, much to her parents' delight. Vicki loves to help her mother and regularly plays on the family computer with the data base of recipes, customers and accounts. Vicki also has a small dog and her current ambition is to be a vet. She watches a lot of television and can sing along with all of the advertisements, much to her father's disquiet. She loves being read to at night and knows that her parents expect her to join in and comment on the connections between the illustrations and the story. She knows that when she is read to, she is expected to sit still and listen. Vicki's schoolbag consists of spoken and written English, well schooled reading behaviours, knowledge about the white colonial history of Australia, and understandings about popular culture, animals, business and the computer. Both children's schoolbags contain roughly equal but different knowledges, narratives and interests.

Thanh is going to a state primary school in a neighbourhood known to demographers as one of the poorest in the country. Vicki is going to a state primary school in a leafy, green part of town. Vicki's parents think that they will send her to a private girls' school before she starts high school. Thanh's parents hear lots of stories about the local state high schools but think that Thanh will probably go to one not too far away where there is a uniform and where some friends' children have already graduated to go on to university, a profession, a life of something other than long days in the restaurant trade. They are determined that Thanh will do his homework and work hard.

Vicki and Thanh have different life worlds yet their life trajectories are connected—and differentiated—through the school system.

HOW SCHOOLS MAKE DIFFERENCE(S)

Educational statistics suggest that these two children will probably emerge from their schooling in very different social places. Thanh and other children from localities classified as 'low socioeconomic' have much less chance of completing their full twelve years of schooling and taking up further education, and much more likelihood of being underemployed, than Vicki and her peers. Thanh, particularly if he works as hard as his parents want him to, may be one of the children who goes against the trends, because after all such trends are probabilities, not life sentences meted out to every individual. And Vicki could find herself living in a 'low socioeconomic area' one day, a casualty of an unhappy marriage cast onto the welfare system. Their actual life trajectories are impossible to predict. But Thanh is already more fortunate than many others in his neighbourhood, because even if he is not as successful in schooling as his parents would like, there is a family business and a network of business contacts who can potentially provide secure work for him.

There have been many explanations offered for the different social and educational outcomes between children such as Thanh and Vicki—children whose families have modest incomes and live in low-income neighbourhoods and those who are more comfortable and live in the wealthier parts of town. In the past, many people believed that working-class children, and children from particular races and cultures, were just less intelligent, and that somehow 'smart brains' were distributed according to the thickness of parents' wallets and the colour of their skin. Others have argued that the culture of working-class homes and neighbourhoods is hostile to school success and that working-class parents do not want to help their children do well. Research shows this to be untrue: the vast majority of parents, regardless of their bank balance, think that school is very important and try hard to help their children succeed (Connell et al., 1982).

This explanation of deficient homes and parents produced particular kinds of policy solutions. If the 'problem' emanated from homes, the policy 'solution' was to compensate for children's perceived shortages and shortcomings. One 'answer' to inequity was to educate the parents, perhaps compel them to supervise their children's homework (this is still a popular policy in the United Kingdom [Vincent, 2000]). If the 'problem' was not caused by families, but by their lack of income, then the policy 'solution' was to provide some of the resources that were not available to low-income families, such as books, visits to art galleries and museums; to provide additional tuition for particular children, often in literacy; and to provide schools with additional funds to purchase equipment and materials that were lacking in children's homes or in the neighbourhood. A few have favoured explanations that highlight the processes of schooling (e.g. Bishop & Glynn, 1999; Gillbourn & Youdell, 2000). This line of argument suggests that the 'problem' was that the different knowledges and skills that working-class children bring with them to school are not those that are important for school success. It is not the children who are disadvantaged but rather it is the school that does the disadvantaging. The policy 'solution' arising from this analysis was to change the school. Advocates of this policy approach come from both the right and the left side of politics. They believe that teachers and schools can be radically changed to make 'educational outcomes' more evenly distributed, by concentrating on changing timetabling, student groupings, teaching methods, curriculum content and school–parent relationships. Local practices and micro-interactions in the classroom are the locus of intervention.

This seesawing between resources that compensate or school processes that must change has been a hallmark of equity policymaking in many countries. But there are other ways to think about educational difference(s) and differentiation.

THE MEDIATION OF PRIVILEGE(S)

Bourdieu[1] suggests that the curriculum can be thought of as 'cultural capital'—the knowledges that are valued. Curriculum and assessment regimes are the means of creating a hierarchy of cultural capital, and cultural capital acquired through formal processes of education and credentialling becomes 'symbolic capital'. Possession of the right symbolic capital can be 'cashed in' as a down-payment on further education and jobs. The school knowledges that are at the top of the cultural capital league table are not only those required for university entrance but are also the cultural knowledges of those who are socially, economically and politically privileged and who determine what counts. In other words the rules of the schooling game are geared to perpetuate particular kinds of knowledges, thus advantaging their holders. In *Making the Difference* (1982), Bob Connell and his associates illustrate the congruence between the competitive academic curriculum and the work, life interests and cultural and social capitals of parents who sent their children to high fee private schools. By contrast, the different work, life interests and social and cultural capitals of working-class families were more often at odds with the practices of schools. Rather than a question of deficiency, Connell and his colleagues argued that educational disadvantage was about difference and power, and coined the term 'organic relationship' to describe the homology between schooling and the already privileged.

Bourdieu sees the (partial) production of privilege and disadvantage through school education as a 'practice' or a 'game'. The children who are most often successful are those who already possess, by virtue of who they are and where they come from, some of the cultural capital that counts for school success. Through the game of schooling, they acquire more. They are able to do this because they are 'at home' with both the ways in which schools operate and with the kinds of knowledges, the cultural capital, involved. They are at ease in the place called school—it is their place.

Because schooling success is both based and realised in material differences manifested as social, cultural and economic possessions, status and political power, formal education produces a hierarchy of differences, or 'distinction' (Bourdieu, 1984). Bourdieu suggests that differences between children become educational differentiation 'in the relation between familial strategies and the specific logic of the school institution' (Bourdieu, 1998, p. 19). He argues that this happens through the 'practices' of the schooling 'game', when the outcomes of grouping, assessing, categorising, promoting and ranking favour particular kinds of players. In other words, schooling is *organised* to make differences and differentiation. It is geared to produce particular and different kinds of educated persons.

Bourdieu stresses that schooling is a social institution. The ways that people can behave in the institution of schooling (Bourdieu would call this a 'field' of action) are regulated through a 'logic of practice', the sets of explicit rules and taken-for-granted ways of doing things, procedures for the allocation and distribution of material, symbolic and cultural resources, and the negotiation and balancing of the competing 'interests' of everyone involved. It is important to note that in Bourdieu's explanations of differentiation, *both* the distribution of material resources *and* the cultural and symbolic capitals produced through the logical practice of schooling are important. This is an explanation that moves beyond a binary of resources or school change to say that *both* are important.

Bourdieu's explanation also acknowledges that, because some players' interests are dominant, changing the balance of power in the schooling game is not going to be a simple technical matter. Nor will change be uncontested, since those who benefit from the game at present are positioned to work to maintain their positions of privilege. Further, he argues that the game is not strictly predictable. Bourdieu does not suggest that there is a *simple* reproduction of existing social relations of privilege by the school system, and that every child will come out of schooling with the cultural and symbolic capitals that ensure they remain in the same social and economic position as their childhood milieu. Indeed, Bourdieu stresses that schooling is *not* a determinist process. He argues that people *do* have the capacity to act. He says that children, parents and teachers

> . . . are not particles subject to mechanical forces, and acting under the constraint of causes; nor are they conscious and knowing subjects acting with full knowledge of the facts, as champions of rational action theory believe . . . [they are] active and knowing agents endowed with a practical sense, that is an acquired system of preferences, of principles of vision and . . . schemes of action (Bourdieu, 1998, p. 25).

Bourdieu's explanation emphasises that teachers, principals, system officials and policymakers do not deliberately and wilfully act unjustly towards particular children. The schooling game positions everyone involved in it to play in ways that differentiate between children and produce social difference. Adults in the school system are engaged in what might be called processes of 'mediation' of privilege, of being positioned and positioning students in the game. This positioning occurs through the actions each person takes to regulate the possession and acquisition of symbolic and cultural capitals. Some children do move 'upwards', and some 'down' by virtue of the mediation of cultural and symbolic capitals they acquire (or do not acquire) in school. It is because a large number of people are involved in these mediating practices, each of whose actions contribute to the final results, that none of them can be said to be individually responsible for the outcomes in a simple cause and effect relationship (Bauman, 1993, pp. 124-25).

Bourdieu asserts that it is the *combined* and institutionally proscribed and discursively regulated actions of all players that work (that is, use, construct, contest, alter and direct) to (re)produce socially and culturally differentiated symbolic and cultural capitals. He calls this the 'destiny effect' (Bourdieu, 1999a, p. 63). It is through the destiny effect that the social institution of schooling *contributes to* the pro-duction and reproduction of the overall patterns of social, economic, political and cultural difference, differentiation and distinction.

Bourdieu also argues that this (re)production of difference is not only *not* determinist, it is also local, contextual and historical. It changes over time. As Levinson and Holland (1996, p. 22) put it, 'Schools provide each generation with social and symbolic sites where new relations, new representations, and new knowledges can be formed, sometimes against, sometimes tangential to, sometimes coincidental with, the interests of those holding power'. Education is not just about the (re)production of the social order but also about its change.

DOING BETTER FOR VICKI AND THANH

Educational differences between Vicki and Thanh become apparent in their first year at school. Vicki is advantaged in her classroom. She feels comfortable with its rules and modes of operation. She already knows about book behaviours and is not shy about asking for help, whereas Thanh feels awkward and he is also embarrassed about his occasionally clumsy English. What he knows about restaurants and music is not necessary for success in his classroom. Even within the first few weeks Vicki starts to 'outperform' Thanh in almost everything. Thanh has a knack with numbers, his teacher says, which is what she has been told by an acquaintance in another school she can expect of 'Asian' students. There is nobody she can ask about this, and because she is anxious to help Thanh feel successful rather than out of place, she allows him to spend more time on numbers than on those classroom activities with which he is struggling.

Vicki's virtual schoolbag contains many things she is able to use in school everyday, whereas Thanh is only required to open his virtual schoolbag for arithmetic. Thanh's teacher is not unaware of this, but cannot find the time and space in her busy and crowded classroom to organise alternative learning activities for him—and all of the other individual students with their particular schoolbags, their unique interests and knowledges. As the principal brings yet another student to her door saying that her class is not yet 'full', she fears that the time she has to think about what might work better for Thanh is running out.

The probability that Vicki will do well at school and go on to university like her mother and father and that Thanh will end up in the family business are already being brought into reality through the mediating practices of schooling. Changing these probabilities is fraught with difficulty. It is neither helpful nor just to think that Thanh's educational success must come at the cost of Vicki's failure. It is neither helpful nor just to think that Vicki's success must only be measured in terms of her school credentials, because they will not prepare her for a highly gendered workforce and possible changes in family life.

Changing educational probabilities does mean that somehow, during their days and weeks at school, both Vicki and Thanh must be able to use and build on their local 'funds of knowledge' (Moll, Tapia & Whitmore, 1993). In order for this to happen, their teachers' working conditions must be such that they are able to find, use and value each child's particular configurations of knowledges, narratives and interests. Their teachers must also have a repertoire of pedagogical practices that will connect children to the knowledges that count through work with the individual and collective resources that the children bring with them (Dyson, 1997). But even this still leaves Vicki at an advantage because of the congruence between her schoolbag and the school curriculum, and her ease in the school setting.

If Vicki is successful at school and goes on to university like both her parents, her social future will be much the same as that of her parents, peers and others in her general milieu. If Thanh is to be successful, he must become a person different from the rest of his family, peers and life world. A successful school student is one who has acquired much of the dominant 'habitus', that is, ways of being in the world, as well as the cultural and symbolic capital derived from their schooling. As Bourdieu (1999b, p. 128) says, 'At the risk of feeling themselves out of place, individuals who move into a new space must fulfil the conditions that the space tacitly requires of its occupants.'

Social mobility means leaving 'your place' behind. Success for working-class children comes at a cost for the individuals concerned and their families. Mark Peel succinctly puts it this way:

> In an isolated, factory based suburb, hoping your children 'would be better than you', or 'wouldn't make the same mistakes you did' must often translate into raising them so they would want to leave. A fundamental part of the educational bargain for working class children, after all, is that they must change, become something different and better. The overt and covert curricula of the primary and high schools, even the day to day techniques of classroom teaching . . . urge working class children to become what they are not and cannot be without inventing themselves as something very different (Peel, 1995a, p. 149)

So, even if Thanh's teachers are able to eliminate the 'destiny effect' at work, Thanh will have some choice(s) and say in the matter. He may or may not choose the everyday costs associated with becoming different through school success—being seen as the 'nerd', accused of thinking he is 'too good' for his friends, suspected of regarding manual work as menial and beneath him, getting too 'uppity', getting ideas beyond his station. These common phrases, used to describe the children who become socially mobile via schooling success, are telling. The metaphor they create is of a social, intellectual ladder whose credentialling steps value school knowledges over local, traditional and practical knowledges. Children's place on the ladder becomes their 'identity', particularly if they go further then their peers and family. Somewhere here in the struggle for equity and justice in schooling there is the larger question of changing the knowledge that counts, of changing the nature of the game, of officially bringing Thanh's virtual schoolbag in from the corridor into the main classroom. Without such educational transformation, the game remains the same. As long as particular cultural capitals are valued in education, those that favour Vicki, then Thanh's teachers will have a bigger job to do, and working-class children like Thanh will have to make decisions about who—and where—they want to be.

The production and reproduction of educational advantage is complex. It is embedded in everyday micro-transactions in the classroom and schoolyard where virtual schoolbags are variously opened, mediated and ignored. In addition, the processes of differentiation between students are integral to school policies and practices, and also to the larger system. These complex relationships and operations are not usefully thought of as a series of interconnected levels of schooling, but as a shifting and changing educational ecosystem. Local change both requires and generates action right throughout the whole organism/organisation. If policymakers keep their eyes focussed on unattainable abstractions and simple top-down prescriptions for change, attempting to 'steer at a distance' the work of individual teachers and schools, then they lose sight of what is happening to Vicki and Thanh each day and each week. They fail to observe how their decisions contribute to the production of difference(s).

Recognising the difficulties in achieving more equitable changes can be depressing. When teachers have 'realistic' expectations of what they can achieve, it can sometimes mean lowered expectations, which translate into low achievement for students. On the other hand, teachers' utopian, emancipatory ideals can become heartbreaking self-realisations of futility, or alternative forms of domination and authoritarianism (see Ellsworth, 1989; Gore, 1993). The paradoxes and ambiguities around equity and justice in education are unpalatable to policymakers, who more than ever want simple and technical 'solutions', rather than slow movement against a murky tide and tugging backwash.

Thanh and Vicki's schools and teachers cannot sit and wait for shifts in the value accorded to different cultural capitals. They work in the here and now. But their capacity to effect even small changes is not the same. No matter how willing the staff and parents, the differences between disadvantaged and privileged schools are extensive. The educational mandates of sorting and selecting and producing good citizens, workers and parents operate differently. The schools are differentiated by their localities, which are differently positioned socially, spatially, economically and politically. Furthermore, they are positioned differentially by a complex educational ecosystem of supports, allocations, rules and policy frameworks.

As a disadvantged school, not only does Thanh's school have a different and bigger job to do than Vicki's privileged school, but its capacity to make change is dependent on how well the wider institutional frameworks of policy and infrastructure support it in this endeavour.

EXISTING UNDERSTANDINGS

For three decades educational sociologists, anthropologists and psychologists have been researching how it is that schools produce and reproduce unequal educational benefits, and therefore contribute to ongoing social inequities. Despite arguments that the study of 'class' has been subsumed by studies of other social processes such as the construction of gender and race (e.g. Mac An Ghaill, 1996), there are still knowledges and understandings about 'classed' schooling that can be and are assumed in this study.

This book builds on existing understandings of the following.

SCHOOLS ARE HISTORICALLY AND GEOGRAPHICALLY POSITIONED

The history of schooling in the city in which this study is set is not unlike that of other Australian cities. State Government schools were established in this city in the late nineteenth century as an alternative to the private schools which the wealthy had established, often through the auspices of churches, to educate their own children. These private schools were located in the wealthier and middle-class suburbs and in the city centre itself. Government primary schools were established in neighbourhoods right across the state and strongly reflected the particular social and cultural composition of their specific localities. The school enrolment in Catholic parish primary schools was similarly characteristic of the broader neighbourhood in which they were situated.

The importance of local geographies to schools was noted by Australian disadvantaged school researchers Connell, Ashenden, Kessler and Dowsett (1982, p. 68), who commented,

The spatial arrangement of the city itself is an important form of social organisation. How people organise their domestic life and their leisure depends partly on where they live. And where they live, in turn, depends both on the resources they personally command, and the way the city has been constructed so as to produce class separation.

Connell et al. went on to suggest that the story of the public school as a common school, where all classes rub shoulders together, was and is not materially the case, since neighbourhood schools reflect the class composition of their location.

In the early twentieth century selective State high schools (for which students had to sit an entrance examination) were established in middle-class suburbs in the city, and a little later one was established for working-class children in the western side of town. High school enrolments tended to be more diverse than that of primary schools: high schools collected together students from a broader geographical area of the city and the surrounding rural communities. A school for secondary technical education was also built at this time. By the mid-twentieth century, a system of technical high schools was established to cater for those who would not go on to university, but would enter skilled trades. A hierarchy of secondary provision was thus constructed both from locality and school type, with private schools at the top, followed by government selective high schools in the city and middle-class neighbourhoods, working-class government selective high schools and finally government technical schools.

In the postwar period, as the State's population expanded with both the baby boom and immigration, and the industrial sector and accompanying clerical and managerial sectors grew rapidly, there was increased demand for secondary schooling and for university education. As a result more technical high schools were built, and more selective high schools, and these, like primary schools, increasingly reflected their particular localities. The technical schools were also part of the overall government strategy to ensure semi-skilled labour for expanding manufacturers nearby. A layered system of educational status therefore mapped on to the expanding city's residential and industrial geographies.

By the 1970s, however, educational progressives in the public service and the government had come to believe that a system of technical and selective high schools was highly inequitable, channelling children into life choices at the end of primary school. What was required, they successfully argued, pointing to similar moves in the United Kingdom, was a State system of comprehensive schools that would combine both technical and university-oriented curriculum streams and would be strongly neighbourhood based. A system of zoning accompanied the 'comprehensivisation' of schools across the city. Only students from designated primary schools had the 'right' to attend their neighbourhood comprehensive high school; others had to take on a maze of difficult bureaucratic procedures to argue why a school 'out of zone' was preferred over their local one.

The intention of policymakers was to eliminate one of the buttresses of the educational hierarchy, that of secondary school type. While they could not change the status attached to schools in particular regions and neighbourhoods, they could, they thought, eliminate the two-tier system of secondary schools. However, such change is rarely won by fiat, and to this day narratives of 'good schools' remain attached to the old high schools, while the former technical schools struggle with their local reputations as educators of the 'dull, feral and manual' workforce.

SCHOOLING HAS AMBIGUOUS INSTITUTIONAL MANDATES

Changing the mediating practices of schooling is no simple matter. It is not just about redistributing resources, redesigning pedagogical processes, improving the performance of particular schooling actors (individual teachers and principals) and/or reforming schooling structures and cultures. Each of these is necessary—and more besides. The notion that achieving equity and justice in schooling is straightforward and can be willed top-down by policymakers or achieved bottom-up by particular schools is highly problematic. Equity is not all that counts in the schooling game.

The institution of schooling has mixed mandates (cf, Levin & Young, 1998). Schools have an ambiguous and conflicting set of outcomes they are expected to meet. They must fulfil the potential of each child; ensure that all children are active, tolerant citizens, good parents and productive workers; sort and select for higher education and employment; keep children safe and occupied while their parents are at work; improve standards; deliver a hierarchy of credentials; discipline the disruptive and prevent future social mayhem; assist the national economy . . . the list seems endless. In significant ways, the mandates and expectations pull in different directions. Consider whether it is really possible to simultaneously achieve high standards, educate all children to their fullest and give out credentials, the value of which depends at least in part on their scarcity and their capacity to rank and create hierarchy (Dorn, 1996). Sorting, selecting and distributing social and cultural capitals to those that matter are significantly at odds with ideas of equity, justice and entitlements. They move in different directions.

Sorting and selecting, and the processes of differentiation and distinction, seem to always have the upper hand.

CLASSED SCHOOLING IS AN ECOLOGICAL TANGLE

Despite the disciplinary divisions that exist within education faculties, research traditions and in schools, the processes of schooling cannot be easily separated out into neat boxes. As Nespor (1997) puts it, students become 'tangled up in school'. There has been important and careful research that attempts to tease out how it is that strands of discipline and welfare, curriculum, assessment and pedagogy, institutional practices and children, their families and neighbourhoods produce and reproduce inequities.

Research that is important to this study includes:

- Connell and his colleagues' findings that the competitive academic curriculum was a key factor in the mixed patterns of working-class students' schooling. They showed how poor attendance, sullen compliance, overt resistance and mediocre results were produced by the sorting and sifting of grading, testing, student grouping and school reporting.
- Thrupp's (1998, 1999) New Zealand school ethnography, which suggests that the aggregated cultural capitals in both the classroom and the school can be seen in the form of the 'school enrolment mix'. This 'mix' compounds the pedagogical paradox of sorting and selecting while achieving equity and justice for all, producing welfare and discipline 'problems'.
- Wexler and colleagues' (Wexler, Crichlow, Kern & Martusewicz, 1992) work which points to the institutional regimes that constitute 'discipline' and 'welfare' and, through their denial of classed, gendered and raced social relations, their role in producing anti-social identities and agency in teachers and students alike.
- The ongoing longitudinal ethnographic studies by Hill and colleagues (Hill, Comber, Louden, Reid & Rivilland, 1998),

which suggest that only some children arrive at school with repertoires of behaviours that enable them to perform in the ways expected in classrooms and thus become 'successful' learners. As well, some teachers are able to make available a wide range of positions for children to be in and learn in the classroom—while others cannot.

- Freebody, Ludwig and Gunn's (1995) documentation of how much time is spent on the maintenance of social order through the management of 'interactive trouble' in the classroom in disadvantaged schools. This has been further elaborated by Comber (1999) in her discussion of the continued tension for teachers between teaching 'literacy' and teaching 'doing school'.

- Haberman's (1991) illustrations of how to move from the 'pedagogies of poverty'—those focussed almost exclusively on discipline and welfare and those obsessed with the maintenance of order through classroom technique—to a rigorous curriculum that also engages most of the students. This occurs with/against the constraints of maintaining order.

All of these studies attempt to bridge the order–curriculum divide that is conventionally created in policy documents and to bring together broader social patterns of inequalities and the practices of schooling.

SCHOOLING SYSTEMS ARE SLOW (AND HARD) TO CHANGE

In their study of a century of US educational reform, Tyack and Cuban (1995) argue that the institutional arrangements of cohorts of students in age groupings, classes, subjects and lessons create a time-space-age 'grammar of schooling' that is only able to be changed slowly, not seismically as policymakers appear to desire. Their view is amplified and made material by careful ethnographies of school reform that show how contestation over educational changes, such as de-tracking and team teaching, are produced out of ongoing relations and micropolitics of race (Cummings, 1998; Fordham, 1996; Lipman, 1998), gender (Datnow, 1998) and class (Tittle, 1995). There are also well grounded warnings not to take up uncritically the prescriptions of school reformers or to adopt a 'one size fits all' approach to change (Bascia & Hargreaves, 2000; Datnow, 2000).

But there is also evidence that, despite the sometime opprobrium and the work involved (e.g. Neilsen, 1999), some:

- teachers can change pedagogies, curriculums and assessment practices to make tangible differences to the lives of marginalised students (Brown, 2000);
- schools can and do provide for students otherwise unlikely to succeed (Meier, 1995); and
- targeted equity programs can assist vulnerable parents to take charge of their own and their children's lives (Ames & Ellsworth, 1997).

Studies of school reform also suggest that there is an accumulating body of knowledge about the things that are important to address in educational change (Lingard & Mills, 2000; Newmann & associates, 1996) and the kinds of processes at classroom, school and system level that are conducive to reform (Fullan, 1999; Levin, 2001).

SCHOOLING IS BEING FORCED TO CHANGE

There are also indications that schooling is under more pressure to change than ever before. The development of alternative popular pedagogies (Luke, 1996), 'new' children and young people (Green & Bigum, 1993; C. Luke, 1999), the changing nature of work (Du Gay, 1996), and the growth of self-help organisations (Giddens, 1991), including home schooling, are just some of the issues that currently challenge schools, systems and teachers.

There is evidence, too, that the institutional framing of schooling, the time-space-age grammar, is beginning to change. Some schools:

- are now open at night;
- allow students to come and go as required;
- utilise information technologies so that the classroom is now a 'virtual space';
- have students engaged in learning in workplaces, outdoors, in cultural institutions such as museums, and in neighbourhood houses and further education colleges;
- allow students to take up courses of study 'above' their expected age level;
- expect that students will be able to find information outside the school and negotiate and direct their own learning.

The traditional boundaries around age, place, time and authority are perhaps already moving (Kress, 2000).

Some school systems have taken up the challenges of changing times and are using them to provoke discussion and experimentation in schools (e.g. A. Luke, 1999a, 1999b). How much these changes will produce more equitable distributions of the benefits of schooling and how much they might founder on the ongoing tussle of race, class and gender to produce exclusion and exclusivity remains to be seen.

SCOPE OF THIS BOOK

This book is only a partial tale. It is a specifically situated explanation of the workings of classed schools and the (re)production of privilege and disadvantage. This study does not rely on, or provide, simple cause and effect explanations. Nor does it propose easy or complete solutions. Instead, the examination here reveals a little more about how contemporary macro social changes and shifts are mediated (that is, moderated and negotiated) through the ongoing educational ecosystem. The result is the construction and consolidation of a familiar hierarchy of differentiated knowledges, opportunities and identities. This book adds to the existing body of literature some possibilities for situated intervention and action.

The story is told at a particular time as well as in a particular place. In Australia, the provision of schooling is the constitutional responsibility of State Governments, but there is also considerable financing of, and policy intervention in, schools by the Federal Government. In recent years, the combined deliberations of State and Federal Governments have produced some nationally agreed policies. What occurs in the city of this study and its schools is constructed by the interaction of these interconnected layers of policy. One major congruence between them is the agreement that all schools must produce better outcomes for all children because the fate of the national and state economy in a post-manufacturing 'First World' is bound up with the knowledge production capacities of its workforce (Spring, 1998; Latham, 2001).

Disadvantaged schools are thus faced with a very considerable task. They are being asked to do what has never been done before— to produce educational equality—in particular policy frameworks and in changed times and places (Thomson, 1999; Lingard, 1997). Current conservative national education policy agendas assume a hermetic seal around the 'disadvantaged school'. Previous national policy regimes in the 1970s and 1980s which allowed consideration of social and economic circumstances beyond the school are demonised (Comber, Green, Lingard & Luke, 1998; Thomson, 2001). Indeed, an ahistorical and narrow problematisation of 'disadvantage' underpinned the Federal Government approach that was in operation at the time that this study was undertaken. This is still the case. This book specifically addresses the sending off stage of social, economic, cultural and political contexts, but also suggests principles that might be used to judge present and future policy directions.

The book will show that, far from being encased in impenetrable walls with chutes leading to and from workplaces and connected by an ISDN line with the world, disadvantaged schools are in reality particularly porous places. They are indelibly coloured by particular neighbourhoods, permeated by national and global events, saturated with flows of information and images, and tangled in complex networks of social relations. The changes for better and worse in neighbourhoods, as well as in the far-reaching networks of associations and institutions that are commonly lumped together as 'globalisation' and 'restructuring', are also *in* the disadvantaged schools as children, parents and teachers, as spatially distributed material and cultural resources and as possibilities for action.

Regardless of whether socioeconomic contexts and circumstances are acknowledged or not, their effects are integral to everyday life in disadvantaged schools. Teachers contend daily with myriad contextually produced mundane and routine frustrations, achievements, sadnesses and micro-politics, and struggle to find the words to explain how it is that relentlessly focussing on learning is easier to say than to do. It is this teacher-talk about these everyday matters that has regularly been categorised by policymakers, and also by some academic researchers, as deficit, patronising and an avoidance tactic. But more often than not, this teacher-talk can equally be seen as the efforts to understand and articulate how it is that complex social, cultural, economic and political matters come together and are embodied in children's lives, and are mediated through particular teachers, situated pedagogies and the institutionally bound workings of specific schools.

This book is also concerned with how it is possible to discuss such questions, when all we have available to us is 'dirty discourse'. The words 'disadvantage', 'class' and 'low socioeconomic' are all used in this text, as are notions of equity, justice, privilege, difference and inequalities. Each of these terms is tainted and subject to considerable debate. Lack of definition in this book is a positive refusal to arrive at some kind of unsatisfactory lexical settlement, and stands as an invitation to join in debates around the tangible meanings of these words. This debate infuses, but at the same time is tantalisingly outside, the major focus and purpose of this study. This book is primarily concerned with everyday life in disadvantaged schools and how policy might be of more help.

This story begins in the city.

2 | The city

Places/regions are characterised by the nature of the social relations which link them together. And social relations, necessarily, are full of power. So uneven development is not only about unequal levels of distribution, it is about the geography of power (Allen, Massey & Cochrane, 2000, p. 51).

The city is set between the sea and a range of low hills. Imagine it as divided into four quarters. In the centre is a small mile-square grid of modest high-rise office buildings, spacious tree-lined terraces, elegant sandstone buildings of various cultural and government dispositions and gracious Victorian-era residences. Around the city centre is a substantial ring of green parklands. A torpid, muddy stream winds out to sea from the hills, through the centre of the city and the parklands. Ducks and black swans forage industriously among the reeds, while the city's residents variously stroll, jog and bicycle along the park that stretches along the entire length of the waterway. From the town centre, the east of the city blurs upwards into foothills, while to the west compact plains slope down to the coast. The north and the south straggle outwards, extending the city across the dusty coastal strip, blending through market gardens and vineyards into near-desert grain and sheep farms at each edge.

The city's population is a little over a million, sprawled out some 70 kilometres along the coastline, mostly on suburban quarter-acre blocks that constitute the popular image of Australian home life. A lot of ground is covered by relatively few people, and it seems that many of the city's residents can, for comparatively little cost, have a sizable lawn, fruit trees, room for a pool, a vegetable garden and the inevitable barbecue. The first-time visitor may take a little time to decode the city sufficiently well to articulate the finely honed social demarcations that constitute this apparent backyard egalitarianism.

Historically desirable areas (therefore price and status) were afforded by:

- the degree of incline, with the eastern suburbs closest to the hills and the foothills themselves being the greenest, leafiest and most desirable;
- access to a sea breeze and a sea view, with houses on the esplanades that stretch along the beachfront being much in demand; and
- proximity to parklands that ring the city, provided they were on the crest of the rise overlooking the plains.

In recent years, the city and anywhere close to it have become fashionable, as have any areas with numbers of houses built in the nine-teenth century. There are also new up-market housing developments with artificial lakes and cafes as their symbols of 'quality'.

The one daily newspaper regularly publishes league tables of residential housing prices, but the city inhabitants do not need this information to find out where their next move should be, merely how much it is likely to cost. Being down on your luck—being downwardly mobile—often equates, in this city, with moving to the outer northern, western or southern suburbs, living on the edge economically and socially. Everyone who lives in the city understands that where you live, your 'place' and your 'position', as in most other cities, is both material and social.

THE GEOGRAPHIES OF DISTINCTION

The eagle's eye view afforded by demographic maps confirms these residential geographies of distinction. The overall picture in the city is one of stark income polarisation.[1] The east, the southeast and northeast, inner city and foothills are home to those who have higher incomes, while there are significant concentrations of low-income people in the northwest and on the northern plains, with low-income suburbs marbled in among more affluent areas in the west and the south.

Public housing is concentrated in pockets in the west and south, and in large tracts in the northwest and north where there is significantly lower home ownership than in other parts of the city (Australian Bureau of Statistics, 1997b). Other advantages and disadvantages map together with income and housing. Higher income coincides with higher qualifications, professional and managerial occupations, more cars, better health, better school retention, high university entrance rates, and much higher levels of employment. Low income, on the other hand, correlates with lower qualifications, unskilled and semiskilled work, lower car ownership, higher rates of respiratory and circulatory disease, poor neonatal and maternal health outcomes, early school leaving, low university entrance rates, high unemployment, concentrations of single parents and welfare recipients.[2]

These are *correlates* with low income, not explanations: they are attributions of causality which take the problem to be explained as the explanation.[3] Low income in itself does not explain why it is that people with low incomes have high rates of early school leaving, but it does point to a process that requires both investigation and explanation, and to particular 'sets' of life circumstances to do with education, health, housing, work and income that are not only connected but also spatially differentiated in the city.

One of the correlates most implicated as a determinant of people's life circumstances is underemployment. The State in which this city is situated had, for some time, the second highest unemployment rates in the country (10.3 percent in September 1998) (Spoehr, 1998b) and finally reached the top of the national jobless table in February 2000, a full 2 percent higher than the national average (Australian Bureau of Statistics, 2000b). The outer north (27 percent in March 1998) and northwest (24.4 percent in March 1998)[4] have featured for over ten years in high unemployment statistics (Spoehr, 1997) and figure in the top ten locations in the country with the highest unemployment rate since the Great Depression (Spoehr, 1998b). The State has the highest levels of long-term unemployment as well as the longest average duration of unemployment[5] for adult men in the nation (see Spoehr, 1999b). When youth unemployment is factored in, the picture becomes even more stark—northern Adelaide averaged 19.4 percent youth unemployment for the period 1988-96 (Spoehr, 1998a). A national study by the Australian Housing and Urban Research Institute (Baum et al., 1999) placed the outer north and the northwest of this city at the very top of its list of most vulnerable metropolitan locations in Australia. One in five households lives below the national poverty line (Wheatley, 2000). Single people and sole parents have higher levels of poverty than the national average (Carson & Martin, 2001).

Maps constructed from data that stand for race show an overlapping picture, but one that is not a neat duplicate. While recent immigrants are heavily represented among the unemployed, there are large numbers of Australians of diverse racial, ethnic, cultural and linguistic backgrounds who are among the employed, and there are some who are quite wealthy. The north is home to the largest concentrations of people who emigrated from the United Kingdom after the Second World War: many still live in the northern satellite town that was built to house them, but now the city and its immigrant English-speaking 'other' are now seamlessly joined together. The inner west has large concentrations of people who emigrated from Greece; the northwest is home to large numbers of more recently arrived Vietnamese people; and there are clusters of Aboriginal people in both the west and the outer north. Moving beneath the big statistical picture of wealth and poverty opens up a city that is a richly diverse kaleidoscope of old and new residents, of particular racial, gender, ethnic and age groupings and finer distinctions of status.

But even at this level population categories are deceptive. Beneath labels of income, race and gender lie complexities relating to religion, urban and rural experience, political affiliation, differing connections to homelands, language and dialect, sexuality, family structure and duration of residence. In reality, what appear to be homogeneous blocks of low-income suburbs are actually discontinuous, overlapping and heterogeneous places. At the same time, however, all low-income people share the common experiences of (de- and re-) industrialisation. 'Class' in this post-industrial city is diverse, local and specific, but also common, within the shared socioeconomic space.

Maps show population patterns, but they cannot explain how they are produced by combinations of agency and policy. While some members of particular immigrant groups did (and do) choose to cluster together in the city, where they move was (and is) constrained by deliberate government intervention in the shape of the built and social environment.

PLANNED GEOGRAPHIES

This is a very planned and managed city. Suburbs for different 'classes' of people were established during its white colonial infancy. In the mid-nineteenth century the mansions to the immediate north of the city were cleaned by the women from the row-houses that were built to accommodate the male workforce for the brickworks and tanneries on the river flats. Successive generations of wharf workers in the busy port settled in cottages near the harbour while those who did clerical work in the maritime import-export trade built more sizable dwellings in adjacent streets. Lawyers, accountants and managers built even larger homes closer to town and to the beach. These niceties of neighbourhood stratification are an ongoing feature of the city.

During the long boom period after the Second World War, in a veritable blueprint of nation-building economic and social intervention, the conservative State Government formalised the historical geographies of distinction. In what was seen for many years as a model of economic success, the Government managed spectacular expansion through the 'seemingly irresistible nexus of manufacturing growth, suburbanisation and population growth through immigration' (Forster, 1986). International motor vehicle, ship-building and white goods manufacturers were attracted by the presence of ready supplies of labour, much of it from immigration, to whom they paid the minimum wages allowable. Besides cheap labour, there were other government inducements such as low cost land and cheap fuel, power and water from the State-owned utility companies. Public housing was an integral part of this overall State economic strategy.

Unlike most other States in Australia, public housing was not just intended for the poor. Large tracts of public housing were established adjacent to designated industrial areas in the northwest, the west, the north and in the south, ensuring a nearby ready supply of working-class labour for the emerging heavy manufacturing base of the State (see Hamnett & Freestone, 2000). During protracted industrial struggles in the 1950s and 1960s, it was not uncommon for entire streets of auto-workers and wharf labourers to be out on strike at the same time. Workingmen's social and sporting clubs sprang up in these localities, and their political allegiances ensured the election, to all tiers of government, of labour-oriented representatives. This was the State's 'heartland' of the Australian Labor Party.

Subsequent governments combined public housing programs with low-interest first-home-owner loans offered by the State-owned bank. Entire new suburbs in the north, west and south were built by private companies, stimulated by the Government manipulation of access to finance and controlled release of land achieved through a Government 'land-banking' strategy. This approach effectively limited rampant real estate speculation for many years. One Labor State premier claimed credit for the proportionately largest effort of any state government in public housing saying that, in his time in office, '. . . the Housing Trust was building 23% of total housing in this state, and a further 13% was provided through funding by the State Bank' (Dunstan, 1998, p. 293).

Services in these new private and public housing suburbs generally lagged behind occupation of the homes, and it was often left to local governments and residents themselves to establish neighbourhood recreation and community education programs. These were not, by and large, areas of poverty or of dependency. They were characterised more by self-reliance, mutual support and a sociopolitical awareness of their place in the city. It was particularly the women in these neighbour-hoods, many of whom worked only part-time or were engaged at home in child rearing, who, while their husbands were at work, estab-lished playgroups and childcare programs, fund-raised for their local schools, and made the streets and shops social places rather than just sites of consumption. In areas where specific groups of immigrants were concentrated, locally developed and culturally relevant infrastruc-tures of shopping, churches and small businesses, as well as health and other social services, grew up over time.

The policy nexus between industry and housing not only helped the State's economy and advantaged young families and newly arrived immigrants, but also had the effect of concentrating both low income and public housing together with the manufacturing base of the State in specific parts of the city. These newer areas were generally close to older similar working-class suburbs and older industries in the west.

While this nexus of residential and industrial location was integral to postwar prosperity, it was also the foundation of future difficulties. In the mid-1980s, the social, political and economic geographies of the city were to take a turn for the worse.

A POST-INDUSTRIAL CITY

Towards the end of the postwar heyday, in the 1970s, the city was dominated by the vehicle industry. Not one, but two multinational car companies had been encouraged to make the city their base, thereby becoming linchpins of the State's economic growth; General Motors first established itself in the west but then extended its plants to the north, and Chrysler, later to become Mitsubishi, settled in the south. In addition, light manufacturing and white goods, textile and footwear manufacturers flourished in the west and northwest. Together with a large shipping and rail industry, these provided most of the city's blue collar jobs.

A snapshot at the end of the twentieth century shows another picture. Nearly all of the textile, footwear and white-goods manufacturers have closed down. General Motors' plants in the west are no longer in operation but the plant in the north has expanded, although its staff car park contains far fewer cars than it once did, thanks to advances in manufacturing technologies. The city's newspaper has carried grim warnings for several years about a possible decision by Mitsubishi to close its operations in the south, and despite a last minute rescue by Daimler-Chrysler in 2000, a progressive jobs shedding program was still in operation for most of that year. At the end of the millennium, the plant owners announced that they were investing in a new plant and they were staying on—perhaps. The rail workshop is largely derelict and the wharves a slight, but efficient, reminder of their former activity.

There is hope that the national government will consolidate defence ship-building in the port, but this will be at the expense of the ship-building industry in two other cities. In reality, prospects are gloomy. The year 2000 ended with newspaper stories (Wade, 2000) that manufacturing sales, investment, profits and employment had reached a new eight-year low with little prospect of rapid improvement. And, despite achieving the highest economic growth rates of any State in 2001, political hopefuls of all persuasions publicly acknowledge that such long-term sustained growth is highly unlikely.

All through the west, the northwest and the north, acres of galvanised iron factories and plant lie slowly rusting, their 'For Sale' signs faded and cracked by the sun and rain. This is the rust belt.

THE RUST BELT AND ITS CONSEQUENCES

This snapshot is evidence of a 30-year manufacturing decline, the dimensions of which were bound to produce significant effects in a city of this modest size. In the few years between 1974 and 1982, for example, over 16 000 manufacturing jobs were lost; 4500 of these were in the western suburbs, caused by the curtailment of operations by just two companies (Philips and General Motors); 2000 manufacturing jobs were lost in the north as a more modern GM car plant was built (Forster, 1986). In the 1990s, these closures continued. John Spoehr, a local student of these changes, comments that:[6]

> There's been a massive shake-out in manufacturing employment in the last decade through increased productivity and deliberate

attempts to improve profitability in industry. We've seen massive reductions in employment in those regions where car manufacturers and their suppliers do provide a significant percentage of local employment. There's not a lot of local leakage into other parts of the State, and maybe 60 to 70 percent of people employed in the passenger motor vehicle industry in the north come from the north. So it's no surprise that when you've got the loss of thousands of jobs in the passenger motor vehicle industry that you're going to have a cycle of unemployment, long-term unemployment and underemployment in that region.

The northwest, which consistently has the highest unemployment in the State, is in that void between the north and the south. It tended to have a fair bit more of the textile, clothing and footwear manufacturers concentrated in that area, which was even harder hit than the manufacturing industry in the north and south. The longer term trends in the north, west and south are testimony to the notion of locational disadvantage, that is the class concentration spatially of disadvantage, and not just in income measure.

It is this combination of a concentration of loss of employment and its long-term effects on particular people that constitutes the rustbelt phenomenon. The global rust belt trails around the United Kingdom, through parts of Europe, Canada and the United States, and through Australia and New Zealand—an indelible blemish on the economic complexion of some of the wealthiest countries in the world. Despite their unique and separate histories and locations, countries and cities with rust belts have much in common. In some senses, the post–industrial city in this story could be anywhere.

The rust belt is not all that matters in these cities, but its presence does more than strip residents of economic capacity and social well-being. The stain of the rust belt penetrates the State and national imaginary and leaves its mark on State and national policy decision-making. Governments search for ways to stop its spread, to make up the GDP by alternative means and contain the effects of social exclusion and worklessness. The rust belt also penetrates individual lives, acting as a powerful incentive for those individuals still in employment to work harder, to focus more on security and refrain from challenging industrial giants still in residence lest they too withdraw (Bauman, 1998b). The rust belt can thus be said to be produced by, but also generate, broader social, political and economic contexts (Appadurai, 1996).

POST-INDUSTRIALISM: THE DE- AND RE-REGULATION OF THE NATION

The phenomenon of post-industrialisation is an outcome of a dynamic, interactive and iterative combination of factors which often go under the catch-all label of 'globalisation'.[7] 'Globalisation' is not a radical *break* with what has gone before. After all, the story of an ever increasing reach of capitalism and concentration of ownership and wealth was one told by Karl Marx in the nineteenth century. 'Globalisation' is the latest 'grand narrative' that is offered in the West as the way to explain everything (Luke & Luke, 2000). It is perhaps best thought of as a *time* when ongoing economic, social, political, cultural and environmental changes *spatially* coalesce in a way they haven't before.

'Globalisation' is not a set of layered spaces of activity that nestle like Babushka dolls, setting the global as the all-powerful opposite of the 'local'. Global and local *processes* and *relations* mutually construct and interconnect, in a complex set of international flows, nodes and networks of institutions, activities, information and images which link together people and the material world. 'Globalisation' effects are differently experienced in different places, and are inequitably distributed. The economic, political, environmental and cultural changes that are occurring at this time are not just abstract forces; they can be seen and felt in cities and neighbourhoods, where they are folded into ongoing local social-material ecologies and life worlds.[8]

THE STATE OF AUSTRALIA

For much of the twentieth century Australia was, compared to many other places, a comparatively egalitarian society. There were no great extremes of wealth and poverty among white residents, no permanent aristocratic class or significant numbers of fabulously wealthy corporate magnates. High degrees of social mobility, both upwards and downwards, worked to prevent the formation of a rigid class structure. This *relative* equality was a complex achievement: isolation, the small size of the economy and the dependence on primary production and natural resources as the major source of personal and national revenue all played a part. But it was not just a product of history and geography; it was also, in part, the deliberate outcome of a particular set of public policies developed over time.

The Australian 'wage earners' welfare state' (Castles, 1985, 1994) was a 'welfare assistance' state, in which government did not provide extensive universal and free benefits. On the contrary, it was primarily through reasonably remunerated, readily available work for the (white) male resident, supported by policies that made it possible for him and his family to be self-sufficient, that the population was to attain a decent standard of living. In the welfare assistance state, government intervention 'helped people to help themselves'. Quality of life depended on tariff protection, mechanisms to arbitrate and fix wage levels, financial regulation, intervention in the market through public expenditure, control of labour supply through immigration, low participation of women in the labour market, unequal wage awards, and the White Australia Policy (Smyth & Cass, 1998). It also relied on a strong government commitment to full employment, the redistributive and targeted social security system of means-tested income transfers, mechanisms to support home ownership, the public provision of education, health and transport, and Keynesian aggregate demand management (Freeland, 1998). These social policy directions served to ameliorate the hardship associated with basic wages. Because of the emphasis on the importance of work and self-sufficiency, Australia could be considered to be '. . . a classic "Poor Law" welfare state . . . [with a] heavy emphasis on self-reliance through the market, with social security provided only through means-tested payments to those who fall below some standard of minimum income' (Travers & Richardson, 1993, p. 204).

Australia was *never* a welfare state, despite some Keynesian strategies undertaken by the nation-building postwar Menzies (Federal) Government, and despite moves made by the subsequent Whitlam (Federal) Government of the 1970s towards free university education, national infrastructure and regional development. And it was not equitable. The welfare assistance state did not treat everybody equally. Aboriginal people, women and immigrants struggled through the twentieth century to be counted as citizens, workers and breadwinners for diverse families; their voices became increasingly louder as the century wore on. Arguments for recognition of these different groups and the 'politics of identity' proved to be one weak point in the state edifice built up to meet the national imaginary of the workingman's paradise.

International economic competition combined with domestic politics (particularly 'identity politics' and escalating long-term unemployment) and decreasing Federal and State revenue caused the 1980s Hawke-Keating (Federal) Government to cast around for policy solutions. International critics of Keynesian and welfare state policies, which were influential with the postwar Western governments, provided the formulation of the policy problem and its answer. They argued that the social and economic 'problems' Australia was facing were *caused* by government interference in the economy and that enhanced competition in a free global market would produce both efficiency and quality. This ready-to-wear policy agenda was enthusiastically picked up by the then Federal Labor Government, even though it entailed the systematic unpicking of most elements of the welfare assistance state. As Hugh Stretton (1980) remarked at the time, Australia got the welfare state backlash before it got the welfare state.

The version of neoliberal policy[9] initiated by the Hawke-Keating Government in the mid-1980s was significantly moderated by its social democratic concerns for equity and justice. But neoliberalism came into its own with the election of the Howard Federal Government in 1996 which, in well under a decade, completed the virtual deconstruction of what has been called 'the Australian way' (Smyth & Cass, 1998), namely guaranteed minimum award wages, full employment and a national standard of living maintained through a generous social wage, consisting of a mix of public services and arbitrated wage-associated benefits such as leave provisions. What is left behind after this social and economic wage base is stripped away is the Poor Law state. Australia had once been a state with some benefits for all of its citizens, but now only the most needy could make claims on the public purse. The meaning and reality of public good had been inexorably altered.

Australia is now a different place. Governments no longer talk of full or full-time employment, simply employment and employability. A raft of measures (including reductions in childcare subsidies and requiring unemployed young people to do voluntary work) have produced what is called the Australian 'productivity miracle' (Nankervis, 1999), in which there is economic growth as well as increasing numbers of jobs that are mostly part-time and poorly paid, and in which vastly improved output is achieved by those who are employed working harder and longer. In the Poor Law State in which money, employment and industry are increasingly deregulated, one in five Australians is now dependent on welfare payments and another one in five requires some level of government income support (Birrell, Maher & Rapson, 1997) to survive as a member of what is now the most 'flexible' workforce in the OECD, according to Michael Pusey (1998). The gap between the rich and poor is growing, with official statistics in 2000 reporting that since 1985, the incomes of those at the bottom of the income scale had fallen by 10 percent as measured against those in the middle of the scale, where there were less people than before. Meanwhile those at the upper end of the income spectrum increased their incomes by 6 percent (Australian Bureau of Statistics, 2000a).

The production of socio-spatial polarisation, in which both rust-belt suburbs and gated wealthy enclaves are isolated from the remainder of the city in which they are located, is structurally inherent to this particular form of neoliberal-inspired economic growth (Allen, Massey & Cochrane, 2000). However, the Australian government response to all criticisms has been that 'Globalisation made me do it' (Kuehn, 1998). As in the United Kingdom,

> The global economy is repeatedly invoked as an external factor which limits the possibility of government intervention in general and its responsibility for economic insecurity in particular . . . The participation of national governments and international institutions in the active construction of a global market . . . is ignored (Levitas, 1998, p. 113).

TALES OF TWO CITIES

'Living decently' (Travers & Richardson, 1993) in a de- and re-regulated post-industrial Australia is getting harder to do. As noted, the gap between richest and poorest has widened.[10] The median income has dropped as a consequence of wage restraint and increasing casualisation and underemployment. Costs have risen. Things that used to be free or cost little because they were part of the social wage—health, housing, transport and education—have all been changed to operate on a more aggressive user-pays basis.

It is not just the poorest among us who have noticed that money doesn't go as far as it used to and that security is a more risky prospect (Fincher & Nieuwenhuysen, 1998). The wealthy increasingly isolate themselves in the most secluded and secure parts of major cities, leaving a shrinking and insecure middle class to plan the best way to avoid further downward moves. Insecurity around career, lifelong employment and a house and mortgage are widespread. Poor families are now living in very hard times, with little hope of ever finding full-time, well-paid and secure employment (Bell, 1997). Intergenerational poverty is now a very serious issue (Pech & McCoull, 1998). It is the same macro- and micro-economic restructuring that makes an unskilled northern suburbs resident of the city redundant and trapped in 'place', a northeastern resident worried about the viability of their employer and the next impending organisational restructure, and an eastern suburbs young adult with university qualifications more desirable, more highly remunerated and more mobile (Fincher & Saunders, 2001b).

There *are* numbers of people living below the policy-ascribed poverty line in the post-industrial city, but they may not all be there forever. Rather than focus on who is 'poor', in receipt of welfare or not at any particular moment in time, it is more useful to talk of the deepening social and economic inequalities in the city (Sen, 1992). But the notion of a city divided sharply and neatly into rich and poor is an oversimplification of material reality. While the vast proportion of people living in the west and the north are *all* economically vulnerable, they are differently positioned in their networks and neighbourhoods. It is what the shared experience of vulnerability *means*—what the *effects* of social, economic, cultural and political resources possessed by, and accessible to, people in different geographical and social spaces are— that is a more important topic than quibbling over measurement (Saunders, 1998) or dual or quartered cities (Marcuse, 1993).

MAPPING THE QUALITY OF LIFE

One egalitarian and pedagogical effect of the globalised print and visual media is to distribute images of 'the good life' into the vast majority of Australian homes, and most city residents now consider a car, computer, TV, video, telephone, ready access to health and dental services, an occasional restaurant meal and an annual holiday as normal components of an average lifestyle.[11] The processes of global economic change and the neoliberal policy responses to it, however, have mapped new patterns of goods and services onto the geographies of distinction. Not everybody enjoys that good life. In the post-industrial city the hallmarks of the Poor Law state are stark.

SERVICING THE POST-INDUSTRIAL CITY

A recent benchmarking study of the city's state neatly captures the overall dimensions of change and its effects:

> Indicators of economic outcome . . . in the most recent years show per head output and earnings to be accelerating but at levels that trail behind Australia as a whole. Employment is growing strongly in property and business services, accommodation, cafes and restaurants; but has declined in total, particularly in agriculture, manufacturing, transport, finance and education. Unemployment rates have fallen since the beginning of the decade, but remain the highest in

mainland Australia ... Some people ... suffer disadvantage. Housing is affordable, even for those living on half the average household income. At the same time, the number of people nearing poverty is increasing (South Australian Business Vision 2010, 2000, p. 6).

However, the efforts of the key policymakers to put a positive spin on alarming trends produces a seemingly paradoxical but also accurate picture of things getting better and worse at the same time.

Residents of the post-industrial city now encounter a vastly different landscape from that of three decades previous. It is a terrain that is globally recognisable. Both the Federal and State Governments have been engaged in:

- *Privatisation*

Both tiers of government have sold or leased formerly publicly owned assets. The State Bank, which fuelled postwar development, was deeply in debt after freewheeling 1980s speculation went sour[12] and has been sold. The city's major sewage treatment plant (referred to as 'the pong' by its northern suburbs neighbours) has been leased to a transnational conglomerate, as has the city's airport in the southwest. The northern city bus line is now run by a transnational whose headquarters are in the United Kingdom. The city's electricity supplier, taken over by the State in the immediate postwar period and a major lever to attract companies to the State via cheap power, has returned to private hands through a lucrative long-term lease arrangement. Each change of hands, from public to private, has been accompanied by contractual arrangements protected from parliamentary and public scrutiny by 'commercial in confidence' procedures, significant public disquiet and polarised media commentary.

- *Downsizing*

There has been substantial shedding of jobs in the public sector. From 1991-97 the State public-sector share of employment dropped from 18 percent to 14 percent of total employment, a loss of some 19 000 jobs (Commissioner for Public Employment, 1997). It was mainly clerical, maintenance and transport staff, residents of the rust belt, who were 'set free' by contractors taking over public utilities. Significant numbers of these State employees left with payouts in return for the long-term security they forfeited—a dubious prospect given the local economy.

- *Reductions in services*

State and Federal cost cutting has led to substantial reductions of beds in public hospitals and the closure of some private hospitals; rerouting and reduction in many public transport routes; delineation of several public housing areas as sites for private enterprise redevelopment, reduction in public housing maintenance programs as well as rent increases; designation of some houses as 'empty' awaiting the approval to demolish; increased costs of childcare and closure of some centres that could not exist without substantial government subsidy; contracting out and reduction in the number of employment and training services; reduction in the provision of free legal advice and legal aid services; increased charges for medical and pharmaceutical goods and services; and increased payments required for technical and vocational education, higher education and schools.[13] Over a ten-year period, the western suburbs in particular have had many school closures, only in part due to the declining and aging population.

- *Tighter targeting of services*
Free and low-cost public dental, community health and mental health services are now only available to those on welfare or minimal wages. Low-cost emergency services at hospitals are increasingly used as a cheap alternative to local GPs and specialists. The safety net approach to public housing has had the effect of concentrating even further together groups of people who are placed in similarly desperate situations.

- *Collapse in community infrastructure*
Many neighbourhoods that had established their own childcare, recreation and sporting facilities have found that they now have fewer users and members who are able to afford even the low fees necessary to pay for maintenance of facilities. Local governments are increasingly being asked to bail out cash-strapped football and bowling clubs and they, like their senior siblings at the State and national level often have other priorities and plans.

The net result is that those who can least afford it, the 'one-third of families' in the State that are 'struggling to meet basic costs' (South Australian Business Vision 2010, 2000, p. 22), now have reduced services, and reduced access to free services, and those services that remain cost much more.

The private sector that most supports everyday neighbourhood activities has changed too. Banks have been dramatically affected by both new technologies and corporate philosophies associated with global economic changes. Across the country there have been branch closures, and a shift from complete branches to agencies, electronic tellers and point-of-sale access. Thousands of bank workers have lost their jobs in this 'downsizing', at the same time as services have been reduced and changed. In particular, those who live in rural areas, those who are illiterate, old, blind, and those newly arrived from other countries with little or no English have been among the most disadvantaged by these changes.

Shopping, too, is changing. Ongoing trends in local government land-use priorities, retailing philosophies and public consumption habits have combined to produce the continued growth of large malls, increased monopolisation of the grocery dollar by transnational companies, continued growth of high-entry-cost franchised food outlets, extended shopping hours and the demise of some department stores. Many small independent petrol stations have closed. In this city, much suburban strip shopping and the corner delicatessens in the western and northern suburbs have closed, together with butchers, florists and small hardware stores. Customers with cars are advantaged over those who are dependent on public transport and what they can carry home. Small retailers work longer hours for less return. The family small business is increasingly fragile, except in the eastern suburbs where those with disposable incomes prefer to have both malls and specialty shops, and spend enough to make both viable.

POST-INDUSTRIAL ECONOMIES

The State Government is understandably obsessed with economic recovery. A fetish for balanced budgets is offset by the necessity to offer incentives to transnational companies to settle, albeit briefly, in the State. Some large foreign-owned high-tech companies have been offered buildings, exemptions from State charges and start-up costs by the State Government, details of which are not public knowledge.

In this particular city, as in many others, the State Government has dubbed some of the rustbelt factory areas 'manufacturing parks'. Some successful niche manufacturers and small businesses inhabit the spacious husks of former industrial giants in the western suburbs, while new warehouses have sprung up in the northwest. The ubiquitous 'technology parks' have been established in the inner north and the inner west, adjacent to and in partnership with university campuses in a hopeful and downmarket simulation of Stanford and Silicon Valley. These new knowledge-work locations house combinations of call centres, defence and boutique sci-tech and software companies, many of which are globally oriented. These new industries, some of which are indeed very successful, employ few people; all of them are highly educated and mostly resident in leafy, green suburbs.

Like latter day Argonauts, senior public-sector officers and politicians travel around the world to find an answer, a new golden rule for economic recovery. They return home speaking effusively of the futurist city in France (the local version spectacularly failed to eventuate after years of Federal and State investment), and the 'economic miracles' in Ireland, New York, Manchester and Singapore that could be replicated if only . . . City planners are inspired by a vision of the city as an Antipodean Geneva, and seek an olive-oil and wine-led future, with local residents and tourists promenading on leafy city boulevards, consuming gourmet meals and the culture industries with equal relish.

Some local government councils in the west have actively encouraged the saving and renovation of 'heritage' buildings for conversion into restaurants and antique shops, as well as supported the inevitable waterfront markets and warehouse-conversion apartment blocks. Numerous other cities around the world facing the same economic desperation adopt the same measures. Increasingly, it is not only the problems of the rust belt that look similar no matter where you are, but also its solutions (Short & Kim, 1999). Perhaps it really *is* the case, as Sharon Zukin (1997, p. 229) puts it, that '[such] cultural strategies suggest the utter absence of new industrial strategies for growth i.e. the lack of local strategies that have any chance of success in attracting traditional productive activity'.

One small business that profits in place of the local corner store is based on mobile personal services. Each morning from the western and northern suburbs the lawn mowers, dog groomers, cleaners, personal trainers and car detailers criss-cross the more affluent areas in an eerie retracing of the movement of nineteenth-century domestic servants to the big houses up the hill.

What has proliferated in the post-industrial city is not bread, but circuses. This State Government, like many others, has gambled for economic security. It has made poker machines legal and it draws substantial revenue from gambling, causing critics to scoff that the government is the biggest 'pokie addict' of all. 'Pokie lounges' are now a feature of most hotels, financially rescuing them from declining public alcohol consumption (produced by police breath testing and steep drink-driving fines). The poker machines are concentrated in a familiar geography. The highest numbers of poker machines and documented cases of gambling addiction, as well as very significant sums of money being inserted into welcoming steel slots, are concentrated in the south, west and north, the very areas of reduced services, fewest jobs and lowest incomes. Government plays down the link.

The global/local neighbourhoods of the post-industrial city form shifting patterns within a complex geography of distinction. While there are differences of population mix, histories and a hierarchy of housing, there are also commonalities. Living in reduced circumstances has been forced on large sections of the city's residents by combinations of economic, cultural and political change. They have been made poor and less secure because of decisions made far away in corporate head offices, by parliamentary committees and economists' think tanks. Mobile companies have moved their operations, leaving their labour force behind in the rust belt. The systematic deconstruction of the welfare assistance state has meant reduced and higher cost services, as well as legitimating more tenuous employment.

It is difficult to be optimistic about a possible future in which many can work less and enjoy the creative use of leisure, a future in which we re-define the meaning of work, when so many in this city would gladly work more if only they could. And yet, image is everything. Economic and social recovery, if possible, depends on projecting an image of confidence rather than decay, of control rather than chaos.

Perhaps this need to avoid the 'ironic geographies of decline' (Allen et al., 2000) contributes to policies for rustbelt neighbourhoods that are geared to plans, targets and results, rather than the everyday realities of life in a '. . . labour market without enough full time jobs for those who want them and characterised by diminished prospects for those whose labour and skills were at one time in demand' (McDonald & Siemen, 2001, p. 217).

Photo essay

3 | Place of trouble/ troubled places

The difference that schools make is within the context of a society riven by inequality, in which the experiences of school students are shaped by the material realities of differential access to wealth, to housing, health care, nutrition . . . (Yandell, 2000, p. 120).

If a filmmaker were to go into any disadvantaged school in the post-industrial city on almost any day, the resulting footage would show scenes of children and young people boisterously playing outside, happily painting, hammering and clattering away in workshops, tapping quietly on keyboards, debating and chattering in groups, sitting and listening to teachers and researching in libraries. However, the rushes would also show many incidents in which relationships between students and between teachers and students are vexed, acrimonious, gut-wrenching and downright sad.

SCHOOL SCENES

A 'look' at some recent footage[1] taken of principals and teachers who either are in, or who have recently been in, disadvantaged schools will serve as an introduction to everyday school life in the rust belt. Think of these glimpses of daily life as partial representations, not the whole truth. Study them first. Afterwards I will consider how these stolen moments from the school world come to be like this.

BEHIND THE SCENES

You are not of course a filmmaker, and there is no film. This script is a writerly device to economically and truthfully present a major issue in, and for, disadvantaged schools.

Disadvantaged schools are often characterised by trouble. They are said to have more troublemakers enrolled. Some parents try not to send their children to disadvantaged schools because they want to avoid them getting into trouble. Teachers say that they would rather not be sent to work in disadvantaged schools because they will have too much trouble coping. Systems and policymakers are troubled by these things and want to find ways to end the troubles.

A further exploration of what all of this trouble means for the teachers and schools involved is useful before examining how this situation comes to be and what might be done.

SCENE ONE

A meeting room with a seated semicircle of seven primary school principals, four female, three male. All of them are in their forties, semi-formally dressed. They hold cups of coffee and one of them fiddles with a cigarette lighter. There is one empty seat. The principals are waiting for the chair of the meeting, their line manager, to arrive and have begun to chat.

PRINCIPAL ONE: 'Eight years ago, I could not have a conversation in my office without kids out there screaming out abuse at me . . . they'd be banging on the door. The school was totally out of control. When I took over, it was a shambles. The kids were so angry. It was awful . . . it was really, really awful. When I won this school somebody in the Department rang me and said, 'Have you got a death wish?'.

They all laugh knowingly.

PRINCIPAL TWO (*chimes in*):   In my first year we did discipline 80 percent of the time. It's eased off now, three years later, in the sense that I think that there's well-established procedures, and kids and parents know that there will be consequences and things will happen, things will be followed up.

PRINCIPAL THREE (*nods agreement*):   Well for me there are weeks when it goes up and weeks when it goes down. I think a realistic figure is 40 percent of our time now is spent on discipline.

PRINCIPAL FOUR (*breaks in*):   In our first year I would say we spent easy 70 percent of the time on discipline. Last year 50 percent. This year 30 percent. It's a relief to know it does go down to a dull roar.

PRINCIPAL FIVE (*shakes his head*):   But it never goes away. As a school we spend heaps of time on behaviour management and it's by far the most prevalent agenda—and all schools like ours are like that. At the camp last week we had to suspend about eight kids. It was one of those ugly 'boys' bullying' numbers, and since then, for myself and the counsellor, following that through has been about 60 percent of our time, doing all the parent talk and checking with each other—where is it all up to, who have we seen, who haven't we seen, what do we do with this child, how do we get the message across—and that sort of stuff is going on all the time. So in a busy time that's a lot of time, and in a normal time, it's probably about 40 percent. We just don't get to do the classroom work that we'd like to do. And that's always a dilemma.

PRINCIPAL SIX (*pauses and then takes a turn, since it is clearly expected*): 'Things are different now for us, too. The place used to be in crisis. I remember there were kids running on the roof, there were brawls on the oval, it was just horrible. I think the changes that we've made are just that we manage it better. Our staffing arrangement has enabled us to bring, rather than having teachers placed here, we have teachers who've applied to come here. Generally younger people. And we've put people in collaborative teams so that they can support each other and that's worked really well. But the problems haven't gone away. They haven't been fixed or anything. We're better at controlling and managing the behaviour, but if we didn't have systems in place, it would be just as it was five years ago. Basically my success is just better control.

PRINCIPAL SEVEN (*leans forward*):   I understand exactly what you mean. In every classroom there are three or four kids that can be huge problems. Every classroom's got them. But because we manage them in certain ways, only one is usually a real problem for me—so you might have only eight in the school that are real pains to deal with. But if you took the counsellor away there'd be 24. A lot of the follow-up that is done by the counsellor and the school admin makes a huge amount of difference. If you can't follow up it gets all wobbly round the edges and frayed, and it all starts to fall apart and the staff confidence starts to erode.

I think it's probably better for the classroom teacher to have the skills to deal with problems at the class level, that's the best option, but it requires a lot of skill to do that. They don't all have it. And the classroom teacher can only take so much of it and the problem has to be moved somewhere else. And so it moves up and down the scale. It helps if the principal or deputy also knows about behaviour management. That's some of the stuff I've heard from other schools where it all goes wrong. A student gets sent to the principal or deputy and then they're back and staff don't feel that anything's happened—no magic's happened . . . So we have to have procedures and we have to be clear about it, and sometimes you get it wrong too!

The door opens and the group falls silent.

SCENE TWO

Interview with a high-school classroom teacher: male, late forties. He has an open-neck shirt and an anxious expression. Close up.

TEACHER: From day one all of my wonderful plans have been undermined by the majority of students in the class. Most of them believe that 'school sux', that 'science sux' and that to show any interest in learning is not cool. This has happened despite the fact that we do run a genuinely innovative program in Year 8, as part of middle school reform. These negative attitudes are not new to me but my considerable efforts to turn them around have not been very successful. What is new this year is the appalling attendance of most of the students. Only eleven students out of the 29 have had reasonable attendance (three or less lessons absent out of nineteen possible lessons), while another nine students have had appalling attendance (seven to sixteen lessons absent). It's not really possible to create a stimulating learning environment in a classroom where the majority are switched off mentally and many can't even be bothered attending. My efforts to establish and maintain basic participation and performance expectations for most of the students have not been successful. I'm talking about basics like writing down notes in a book, listening to the teacher when he or she is talking ('Hello, has anyone got a mirror, I want to check if I still exist!'), doing some homework occasionally, students participating in the lesson to the best of their ability. Most students are not interested in doing these things.

My plan to build class rapport through an excursion early in the year didn't work out as intended. When asked beforehand if they wanted to go on an excursion to the Science Centre everyone present put their hand up in favour. But on the day before the excursion the numbers who had paid were so low that I visited the class and asked why. Some gave lame excuses while others were up front and told me they never intended to go and would take the day off school. After I argued with them, pointing out that they had put their hand up to go, some of them decided to go after all, otherwise the excursion attendance would have been even worse. As it was, only 18 out of 29 attended the excursion.

Only nine students out of 29 have a complete set of book notes even though two 'catch up lessons' in school time were provided (for book and assignment work), in view of poor attendance. The topic we studied in term one was the human body. I've tried to make the work interesting by asking students what their questions are and by setting project work. I've avoided being up the front talking all the time, I've provided lots of choice and tried other new ideas, some of which have been relatively successful. One requirement was to give a short talk to the class on a topic they could choose (anything to do with human body systems, any disease or anything to do with medicine). Lots of research time (at least five hours) was provided beforehand. In the end only nine students out of 29 managed to present a talk to the class.

There are some great kids in this class and all of them have an interesting story to tell. I have some stories to tell about the students in this class, some sad, some bizarre, some tragic and some amusing. I'm still in there, I'm still trying to stay positive and I'm still trying out new ideas and strategies to see what works. I haven't given up. However, I've also decided that the problem is not just mine, that we need to look below superficial slogans like 'achievement for all' to the reality of what is really going down in disadvantaged schools (Kerr, 2000).

SCENE THREE

Interview with a principal in her office. There is student art work on the pin-up board behind her and a glass case of trophies to one side of the desk. She is wearing a smart suit.

PRINCIPAL: I've recently moved into the leafy, green suburbs from a disadvantaged school. There's a sense of tradition and order about the place, so staff and kids know that this is the way we do things here. In disadvantaged schools, it's just non-stop. Regardless of what kind of system you put in place, it's a daily onslaught—the needs of the kids, their personal needs, are just demanding whether they're behaviour or particular social issues or just personal things—it's not like you can forget about it all. In the eastern suburbs, there's not that sense of lurching from one spot to the other, the difference is that the focus can be consistently about learning. Teachers in advantaged schools still spend hours and hours of their own personal time . . . the time's probably equivalent here but what they're doing is significantly different. They get a personal reward out of it, instantaneously, whereas when you work with kids in disadvantaged schools you have to have a sense of the greater good of all. If you're working with a kid, tutoring them, or doing dragonboat racing, it adds up to the same amount of hours but you're getting back a whole lot of things that are personal that keep you wanting to do it and do more of it, whereas you don't get that in a disadvantaged school, you just get exhausted.

I think you do two layers in disadvantaged schools . . . you have a layer about relationships and the community because that's distinctly different from the culture of the school, and then you have another bit that's about learning and the formal curriculum. In leafy, green schools, where I am now, there's much closer congruence between the students, parents and community and the teachers and the school, so you don't have the same discipline and welfare demands.

SCENE FOUR

Interview with primary principal: pan in from corridor where a small boy is seated on a chair outside the office door, snivelling quietly to himself. Move to close up of principal.

PRIMARY PRINCIPAL: It must have been about three weeks ago that I had one of those flashes where I thought, 'What am I doing here?', and I thought about it and I realised that over the past five years I've had the belief that I could make a difference. I could have some influence over the cycle of disadvantage in this community, in the school. I thought that there are students going through the school, that in a few years' time I would be able to say, 'Hey, the school being the only stability in kids' lives and the nature of our activities and programs, I've really contributed to making a difference'. And about three weeks ago, I think it was one afternoon after things were a bit rough, and I suddenly realised that that was not true.

In fact, I felt that I was just an agent of the system that was reinforcing the disadvantage and all the dysfunctional stuff that was happening because we don't have the resources to effectively manage and support students. So what I've ended up doing—I end up suspending kids, excluding kids . . . So the school is just an institution that's continuing and reinforcing all the impact of poverty. I saw myself, 'Here I am, I'm an agent, I'm part of this process that's reinforcing that'. And that revelation . . . It really made me sit up and think, and as a result of that I've made a decision that I'm not going to stay here any more. I think I've had my time. I think it is time I moved. I've been applying for other positions.

As a filmmaker, you can see that you have illustrations of a central feature of disadvantaged schools, the task of keeping order. This clearly takes considerable time in and out of classrooms. But can you present these extracts just as they are?

TOIL AND TROUBLE

There *is* local research demonstrating that there are more incidents of bullying and violence in disadvantaged schools, particularly in the rustbelt north (Bagshaw, 1998; Johnson, 1998). Data on suspensions and exclusions is heavily skewed towards the northern and northwestern suburbs and shows that boys and Aboriginal students are by far the most significant 'offenders' (Thomson, 1999c). 'Doing discipline' is, therefore, spatially distributed: rustbelt schools *are* dealing with keeping (the) social order much more than more privileged schools.

> An experienced principal who moved from one side of town to the other told me that she had suspended two children during all of 1998. The year before in a disadvantaged school she had exceeded that in a single day, on several occasions. A newspaper article on a selective state high school in New South Wales entitled 'Brightest and Best' (Armitage, 1999) quoted a teacher as saying that in eleven years at the school she had never once had to raise her voice (my researcher journal).

THE TIME-ORDER ECONOMY

Schools in the rust belt are by and large well managed. All schools work within a State-wide Student Behaviour Management Policy which details responsibilities and rights of schools, students and parents, and provides standardised prescribed codes and forms of punishment. The disciplinary routines that are established in State schools typically consist of a set of overall school rules, with classroom rules and 'consequences' established by classroom teachers. The overall school policy outlines the procedures for removing 'difficult', students from class or playground and details the various misdemeanours and breaches of rules and procedures that lead to 'time out', suspension and exclusion.

In orderly rustbelt schools, there are additional disciplinary measures: year/level coordinators (in secondary schools); the formation of teacher teams; the introduction of specific student groupings which separate or put together particular individuals (managing the student mix); and ongoing in-service in classroom organisation and teaching methods that promote order. Teachers new to disadvantaged schools often participate in specific induction programs on handling challenges to teacherly authority, and in basic counselling and conflict resolution methods. It is not uncommon for disadvantaged schools to spend much of their staff meeting time on matters that are primarily concerned with order—yard safety, improvements to the withdrawal room, changing the drugs policy and so on. There is a considerable apparatus for, and expenditure of resources on, the development and maintenance of order.

Orderly and disorderly rustbelt schools often serve neighbourhoods in which there are places and times of aggression and violence, and in which a minority of children live in a milieu of anger and despair. The schools can often be havens for children and young people, provided they establish clear routines and procedures, transparent guidelines which everybody knows; are procedurally fair; are not authoritarian or hierarchical; work hard on listening to and connecting with students, families and the wider neighbourhood; and have a range of strategies and responses to discipline and welfare issues. Establishing this regime takes time, as the hypothetical script of everyday school life indicated.

Ann Manicom (1995) argues that having to pay attention to health and welfare matters is an integral part of the social organisation of teachers' work in disadvantaged schools. Children who are hungry, tired or ill have less energy for schoolwork, and working with them on such matters inevitably reduces the time allocated to the curriculum. As Manicom says,

> The constant recurrence of health and welfare problems means that time is continually taken, week after week, year after year. Time taken now does not mean more time available tomorrow: time taken from instructional work now to attend to health does not mean more instructional time tomorrow (p. 39).

What is significant is that the time devoted to welfare and discipline is *not* demanded of all schools. Manicom concludes that 'The cumulative effects of such processes distinguish teaching in [disadvantaged] schools, and are an instance of how schooling practices can be seen as classing practices, that is as *constituent of class relations* and inequitable schooling' (p. 39, my emphasis).

It is also important to note that this discipline and welfare time is not evenly distributed among all of the students in disadvantaged schools. It has to go to those children and young people who are literally crying out, yelling out and walking out. There are generally about four to five children in each class who are ongoing and persistent time consumers, with other children and young people requiring intervention and support more sporadically.

There are many children and young people in rustbelt schools who *do* conform to behavioural expectations, and among them are some students who thrive in the selective curriculum. But, because so much of their teachers' time is taken up with the unavoidable tasks of keeping order and attending to welfare issues, orderly students in disadvantaged schools actually have less teacher attention and time than similar students in more privileged localities. By contrast there, teachers have less trouble to manage. In the rust belt, teachers have no choice but to deal with the most urgent issues.

Knowing and living the time-order economy leads to another common phenomenon in rustbelt schools—teacher guilt and frustration about not being able to do enough for these more orderly students prepared to take on the demands of the prescribed curriculum. The tug of 'How can we spend more time with the "good" kids?' can easily translate into a no-win struggle between teachers, some of whom say, 'We need to get rid of the few who are making it hard for those who do want to work', while others assert, 'We need to work harder to make it better for those who are most at the margins of schooling'.

These emotional and social time-order economies of discipline and welfare are enduring features of schools in working-class localities. They have recently taken a turn for the worse, as neoliberal policies have made life harder for all concerned in the rust belt.

TROUBLED TIMES

There are increasing discipline and welfare demands in disadvantaged schools, according to school principals. They say it is to do with the current social and economic context. Increasing poverty and deepening

social fissures have not stayed in the neighbourhood but have permeated everyday life in schoolyards and classrooms. They are, as many
teachers and principals suggest, 'in your face' everyday. Rustbelt school
principals are unequivocal in their belief that there is an increasing
incidence of 'social order' and welfare problems and significantly
greater alienation of students and parents. This is at a time when the
'discourse of derision' (Kenway, 1990) continually positions schooling
as in crisis and failing. School principals argue, even at the risk of being
accused of excuse-making, that this worsening situation has its origins
in wider social and economic changes.

There is research evidence to support the claim by principals that
things are getting worse in their neighbourhoods. One place to look
for evidence is in school completion data. Studies of school retention
rates Australia-wide suggest that in 1995 some 9 percent of students
(10 percent of boys and 7 percent of girls) left school before Year 11
(Marks & Fleming, 1999). Continued falls in school retention rates,
despite the withdrawal of unemployment income support for 15- to
17-year-olds, hint that this figure may now be much higher. Early
school leaving is concentrated in particular localities and populations:
Aboriginal and Torres Strait Islander students and students in regional
and rural areas are over-represented amongst early school leavers, as
are students in rustbelt metropolitan localities.

Studies of early school leavers suggest that, although work-related
reasons are the most common reason for non-completion of schooling
(Australian Bureau of Statistics, 1999), lack of achievement and dislike
of school are often allied with desire to get a job (e.g. Angwin et al.,
1998; Batten & Russell, 1995; Marks & Fleming, 1999). Principals know
that behind the official retention figures sit long-term patterns of
truancy, non-compliance and lack of achievement, patterns which often
begin in primary school. Malaise with schooling is not just measured in
early school leaving or suspension and exclusion figures. The statistical
blandness and relative small size (less than 10 percent) of the early
school-leaving 'problem' partially obscures what these figures actually
mean in the families, schools and neighbourhoods most affected.

ALIENATION FROM SCHOOL

Principals in disadvantaged schools suggest that there are enough
students who seem to no longer believe that they have a future that
involves work for it to be noticeable as a trend. Most of these
students' families, friends and networks of peers and relations are

either underemployed or unemployed. Deep in the rust belt, schools daily deal with the consequences.

> We have families where nobody knows what it's like to go to regular work. Going to school for some of our kids is like, well it's like going to prison . . . at school there's all these routines and rules. For some of our kids, they're the only person in the whole household who always has to go anywhere during the day and that makes it really difficult—the child who's coming to school sees it would be much nicer to just be home. They want to take days off whenever they feel like it (primary school principal).

The vast majority of these work-poor families have not lost the work ethic (contrary to the policy rhetoric of workfare and tabloid television representations of the dole-bludging family). They still look for work, often participate in the 'black economy', often undertake ambitious home and garden projects, and do take up whatever sporadic casual work opportunities are available within reasonable travelling distance (cf. Newman, 1999; Shirk, Bennett & Aber, 1999). What has changed is their degree of hope and their faith in the government and in schools (though not necessarily in education). 'We have a small percentage of families who say in meetings, "What's he want school for, there's no jobs anyway". They openly say that there is nothing that they can get from schools that will help them' (primary school principal).

Such comments (and they are now commonplace) are perhaps an indication that working-class parent support of the institution of education as the major means of social mobility is waning. While Connell and his colleagues (1982) did not find this in the late 1970s, they did speculate about the possibility, given that the de-industrialisation they identified had already begun to affect their blue collar research subjects.

Students, too, question the purposes of schooling: 'Almost without fail, every kid that's involved in some incident about disrupting the class or not doing their work, or truanting . . . and you say, "Now what is it that you think you might be aiming for?"—and it's blank' (secondary school principal).

This schooled anomie creates difficulties for teachers, who typically tell students that there will be long-term benefits from staying at school and putting up with a less than exciting curriculum—you-need-to-learn-this-in-order-to-get-a-job. Students can and do give everyday neighbourhood evidence against the argument that the better educated you are the more competitive you are in the competitive job market: they dismiss this as a ploy to get a pool of better educated underemployed. It is difficult for schools to continue to advocate a school–work contract and the possibility of 'careers' with those who are convinced otherwise.

Alienated students generally refuse to actively engage with much of the curriculum on offer. Many are physically present and mentally absent, but the more energetically resistant typically attend only those few classes they enjoy, truant and openly challenge some of their teachers. In secondary schools, in particular, these young people construct rituals of refusal with adults in authority: these tendril out from school and home, and through the neighbourhood spaces in between: 'Their parents say, "I wasn't very good at school either", and "I think you should be stricter with my son, he's hopeless at home too, I can't control him, I think you should do something here",' (secondary school principal).

When challenging authority, many of the questions students ask go to the very heart of the tangle of schooling. They query school conventions and the relevance of school knowledge, and want no explanations in reply:

> There are more kids here who the teacher will quite politely and calmly say to them, 'Look, what are you doing, can you get on with your work?'
>
> 'Why? Why would I?'
>
> And, 'Please don't go and stand there in the yard, that's out of bounds.'
>
> 'Why? What's it to you?' (secondary school principal).

These young people assert that school teaches them nothing that will help them get a job, that there are no jobs, that school doesn't teach things useful for work even when it tries, and the evidence is that no one gets a job, so why bother . . .

These learned patterns of alienated behaviour begin in the primary years, and have strong associations with failure, often in literacy and numeracy. Truancy and a range of lesson avoidance techniques are often well established by the upper primary years. But lack of achievement in literacy and numeracy does not simply cause such alienation—nor can addressing failure cure it. Turned off students often do *not* respond favourably to an offer of remedial literacy and/or vocational education courses as the 'solution' to their alienation. More often than is acknowledged in government-commissioned research into work experience and work-based learning, the *most* reluctant students often fail to attend work placements after they have agreed to participate, or walk out when asked to do menial, repetitive and/or difficult tasks. In response, some schools decide that they will not offer work-place learning to any of those that they categorise as likely workplace miscreants, given that such placements are dependent on ongoing good relations between (often hard-pressed) local employers and schools.

It is little wonder that those who spend large amounts of their time simply policing recalcitrant young people find their patience and endurance wearing thin. Being the literal face of authority, engaged in numerous face-offs every day, takes considerable personal energy, and it is hardly surprising that on occasions, teachers decide to take the line of least resistance: 'There are just lots of kids who aren't at school and there's nothing you can do to get them there . . . On some really difficult days you say, 'I'm not even going to ask, just leave it today' (secondary school deputy).

YOUNG PEOPLE 'ON THE LOOSE'

Unemployment and deepening social malaise do not necessarily equate to increasing crime and more substance abuse, as suggested in hysteri-cal law and order campaigns (cf. Miller, 2001). However, they do mean that more young people are visibly hanging around.

Rustbelt schools report a minority of ten to fourteen-year-olds, mainly but not solely boys, absent themselves during school. They often ride their bikes around the streets and are sometimes highly apparent. Some adults are alarmed at the sight of such young people, equating them with gangs, or some kind of trouble in the making. Youth workers and researchers are quick to counter the notion of a 'crisis' (e.g. Bessant & Hil, 1997) and rapidly lose patience with those who believe that such children simply need supervision and control: 'We quite often get phone calls with someone saying, "There's gangs of young people in the park," and you say, "Tell me more about it," and you find out that it's four or five young people sitting on a bench having a chat' (council youth worker).

Many parents feel incompetent in the face of these wilful young people and the disapproving gaze of neighbours, schools—and the state.

There are more parents that can't cope . . . That's a common phrase that you hear when the counsellor rings or when I ring to talk over the problems that they're having in the home. It's 'What can I do? He doesn't listen.' I think there's a feeling of not being empowered with their own children, that they can't handle their own children . . . 'You're not allowed to do this. You're not allowed to do that.' It's as if they think the state's taken away lots of their rights and the children have more rights. That's a lot more common from parents than I've ever heard before (primary school principal).

The school represents (the) social order and is often called upon to rectify neighbourhood discipline if parents cannot: 'There's young children still roaming the streets at eleven o clock. And a neighbour rings to tell us . . . "Well what can I do? I can't get them to come in . . . They won't listen."' (primary school principal). Such involvement is not always, however, without its lighter moments: 'I had a phone call from one mum who suspected that her son was selling drugs at school and I found out later the reason she suspected was because he tried to sell her some . . .' (secondary school deputy).

Rustbelt schools frequently find themselves acting as advocates for the provision of recreation facilities and programs for young people who have little option other than to frequent parks and paths. However, they feel less inclined to act in advocacy roles when older neighbourhood youths come right into the schoolyard to deliberately create trouble.

Most rustbelt schools know only too well the feeling that they are under siege from young people on the loose in the neighbourhood, and they struggle to find ways of responding. All schools report increased problems with 'outsiders'. Sometimes this is as harmless as ex-students and local residents wandering through the yard on the way to somewhere else, sometimes it is simply young people visiting friends during lunch hours. On the other hand, 'outsider' visits also can be related to sorting out disagreements (a possible fight in the making), or continuing sexual liaisons in school time and place. They can less often be concerned with arranging and having physical fights, or conducting commercial transactions of varying degrees of legality.

A few rustbelt schools have endured unwanted front page newspaper coverage arising from incidents between insiders and outsiders on school grounds, disputes that have resulted in serious injury. One school has employed lunchtime security patrols, and nearly all rustbelt high schools now send staff out on yard duty with mobile telephones. Nevertheless, students are still much safer in their school than they are in most other places.

FAMILIES AT THE END OF THEIR TETHER

For most Australians these are now hard times. All schools deal with squabbles and feuds amongst students, gangs, forms of substance abuse, child abuse, depression, other mental illnesses and a range of family issues. However, the effects of poverty and the concentrated housing of low-income earners in particular neighbourhoods exacerbates and intensifies these welfare issues in rustbelt schools. Family breakdown is not confined to any one social group, but the deliberate construction of public housing in particular suburbs together with the designation of a number of places as 'emergency housing' means that rustbelt neighbourhoods have disproportionate numbers of newly created single-parent families. This, in turn, means that schools in these neighbourhoods deal with more children and young people who are grieving for loss of family, taking on more responsibilities at home and coping with a parent who may also be suffering. Rustbelt schools also deal with hunger, malnutrition and health issues, which are strongly connected to family financial difficulties.

But contemporary stress and pressure combine with individual biographies and circumstances in old/new ways that profoundly affect some more than others. According to rustbelt principals, many families seem to have developed a siege mentality as a way of coping.

> What I deal with most in the junior school isn't discipline, even though that's how it's usually presented to me, it's family stuff. What the kids are dealing with on a day-to-day basis is a family and a community that doesn't know how else to cope and the kids are acting it out on a day-to-day basis (secondary school deputy).

Continued pressure to find work, to make mortgage and rent payments, to pay bills and the escalating costs of services (including schooling) take their toll. Principals who know this nevertheless find it difficult to deal with the consequences when they literally appear in school.

> We seem to be dealing with more issues of domestic violence and parents with alcohol problems. Gambling is a new dimension that has hit a number of families. We are getting parents who are drug addicts coming to pick up their kids and you've got to deal with it in the yard. I think they've probably always been there, but it wasn't to the extent that they were openly visible . . . I've had a parent withdrawing from heroin in the passage way. I've never dealt with issues like that before. And family crises and break-ups, we're getting to a stage with long-term poverty that they haven't had one break-up they've had three or four, and there are quite a number of different step-parents entering into children's lives (primary school principal).

When principals talk of 'more', their memory is necessarily partial and limited. They speak of a period covering the last 20 to 30 years, from the boom period of the 1970s to the present day. Some of them, as is the case with the primary principal just quoted, have been principals since the mid-70s, and their view that things are getting worse does have some claim to truth, given their experience.

Many rustbelt schools have increased their welfare services not only to children but also to parents. It is not uncommon for disadvantaged schools to be called on to assist with tasks as diverse as accident litigation, divorce and separation proceedings, filling out benefit forms; advocacy with government agencies, particularly 'the welfare'; grief counselling; health referrals; and ongoing parenting advice. Such extended family-support functions are not recognised or funded, and even as schools try to cut back on this function, knowing it is not their 'core business', they inevitably end up doing quite a lot. Some rustbelt schools routinely provide low-cost or free breakfasts and lunches, one has recently begun a sports equipment home loan scheme to complement the more usual library book, toy and musical equipment loan schemes, and several have a range of free vocational programs available for parents.

Those schools catering for adult re-entry students have noticed a huge increase in welfare issues. The demands for transport assistance, childcare and emergency funds for minor dental and optical expenses and accommodation bonds (all necessary adjuncts to school attendance for young adults) have escalated, as the capacity of local non-government agencies to provide them has declined. One school now provides trailer help with moving, a food cooperative, a second-hand clothing exchange and a daily bus pick-up and drop-off service to and from school. There is little support and few resources available to schools for such activities. School staff are very mindful that money and time spent on neighbourhood issues and family welfare is time and money taken away from learning. They only do as much as they can and they focus on those things that they know to be related to students' wellbeing at school and learning.

While all schools in the city State do some of these things, the sheer increasing volume of neighbourhood and family demands puts rustbelt schools in a no-win situation. The consequences of attending to such issues are more student involvement in school learning, but less time and money to attend to the learning itself.

ESCALATING HOSTILITY IN SCHOOL–PARENT INTERACTIONS

Dealing with concerned, disgruntled and angry parents is a regular occurrence in all schools. The usual scenario is that one or two parents will arrive and demand to see the principal. The problem almost invariably has to do with either some kind of dispute between children or a perceived injustice on the part of a teacher towards their child. Some parents are distraught, some calm, some angry. 'You get the full range of reactions, from "Yeah, we don't know what to do either", to parents who are really, really angry at the school' (secondary school deputy).

School–parent clashes are happening with increasing intensity across the system, to the point where principals' associations and the education union have made approaches to the State Government to introduce firmer rules and some protection for staff involved (Buckby & Woolford, 1998; Lloyd, 1998e). Perhaps it is one of the effects of an increasing 'consumer' rights' discourse at work in schooling and/or increasing litigiousness (Crouch, 1998b) associated with a consumption-oriented risk society (Beck, 1992). The phrase 'loony parent' can be heard with increasing frequency in schools and district offices across the State, as people struggle to understand and deal with what is going on.

Most rustbelt school administrators are careful with their words, weaving together language and theorisations that barely cover their struggle with neighbourhood reality and their own precarious positioning.

> When we say that people have tough lives it's because we respect the community. There's not one parent out there that you couldn't say is doing their best for their kids. There are people who, maybe by our sets of values and circumstances, are not doing the best . . . but from their perspective they're doing what they feel is the best and they work very hard at it (primary school principal).

However, it is in the rustbelt schools that the meeting of parents and administrative staff more often come to flashpoint. One recent case even made the newspapers when a female primary school principal took out an injunction against an unemployed male parent who was threatening her and staff if they did not resolve bullying experienced by his junior primary daughter. Curiously, such incidents are more common in the north than in any other part of town.

It is not easy to deal with ongoing disputes between students that involve whole streets taking sides in incidents of Montagu-Capulet proportions and retain a dispassionate sociological view.

> You can say it is the socioeconomic context, they are out of work, but somewhere along the line there's people sitting there doing this to each other. I dealt with one dispute over six months where I thought that the worst thing was that this group of parents were teaching this group of

kids to hate with a passion and to never forgive. There's something there about being alive—you get angry and you feel alive and powerful, but what you're fighting against is a *blancmange* . . . Everything is really desperate and they are concerned about their kids, they are concerned about their lives, they've got no way of getting out and they just rail against it. And we often get in the way and their kids get in the way and other people. If you can't put that in a context then what you end up with is—it's the pathology that the kids are bad because the family's bad and the parents don't care. I've never come across parents who don't care but I've come across a lot of parents who have no idea how to express their caring or disappointment or their anger so they just either give up or yell and shout and scream at us (secondary school deputy).

There are hints in this commentary about how it is that these phenomena come to be described and understood as belonging to individuals. Social processes appear in schools embodied in particular lives and in people who still have some (albeit restricted) agency. Holding off moral judgements about character and focussing instead on the behaviours and how they are produced is no easy task; it produces a kind of institutional schizophrenia in rustbelt staff. Staff must simultaneously discipline and understand, disapprove and explain, and offer ways forward within constraints and practices they desperately want to change.

Rustbelt schools must set up procedures and routines to try to head off confrontations and at the same time invite criticism and complaints. They send home 'How to make a complaint' brochures translated in multiple languages, knowing that in the majority of cases parents will just arrive and demand to be heard immediately, regardless of what else is happening.

We say to parents, 'We want your feedback, we want you to come and talk about it', and so they do. And that's great and we talk about what are the structures and what are the procedures to follow like—talk about the problem, focus on your child's learning, focus on re-lationships—and we're *constantly* working with parents to get them to do that (primary school principal).

The alternative to an open approach to problem solving is a sullen standoff between school staff, school councils and parents.

When I got here it was the parents versus the staff routine. The parents wanted the school to be theirs, and they wanted to get into it, whereas the staff felt that every time the parents came into it, they [teachers] got hammered. It was verbal abuse or there were letters to the Minister, and what they thought were minor issues became huge ones. When I first got here the school council was fairly weak and didn't really know what it was doing, it was full of depressed people complaining about kids riding their bikes on the weekend without helmets. So we spent quite a lot of time on building community relations (primary school principal).

Dealing with crises and developing productive parent interactions have to start from a position of respect and recognition of the right of parents to have and voice concerns. However, schools also have legislated responsibilities to act as surveillance agents on parents and to report their suspicions of any unacceptable parenting practices. Schools therefore are always at a distance from parents, particularly those who are under duress. Parents are often reluctant to expose themselves to the school for fear of being 'dobbed in'. At least *some* of the hostility between working-class parents and schools has a long history in the practices of 'the welfare', which monitors and controls families to the point of removing children, and to which schools are now tied as outreach watchdogs.

Rustbelt school principals now feel certain that complaints are part of a push and pull of power between parents and the system.

When the [State] Liberal Government first came into power they made it quite clear that the Minister's office was open to any complainant at any time, by phone, in person. The parents have developed some quite unusual networks. Even if they never meet in person they'll ring each other up and egg each other on about complaining and so the word gets round that someone will always listen . . . The way they see it is that it's getting justice from the system, and justice often means the school saying, 'Sorry we were wrong and you were right' . . . It's frequently the case that what the complainants are asking for is neither just nor reasonable, so the argument becomes absolutely stuck (secondary school principal).

The power–saturated processes of parent–school relations irrevocably shape everyday life in rustbelt schools. It has recently become tabloid television fodder. One typical example concerned a school taking legal action against the mother of a truant to force her to get her child to attend school.

We were portrayed as the terrible people who never got her child to school and we didn't teach him properly and we were horrible to her. The television stations were quite prepared to listen to her and give her credence. Nobody rang me and said, 'What do you think about this?' . . . And then of course she came in the next week and said,

'Oh, I didn't mean to upset you, it wasn't my fault', but she was the one who got the media on side, and she got money for it. And there it was on the television, our school, our student report held up . . . and that report was from the teacher who had had most success with the kid . . . The teacher was quite upset (primary school principal).

The actions of this parent who sicked national tabloid television onto a school were far from that of a completely powerless victim, although the end result for her child will most likely be the continuation of the 'destiny effect'. The end result for the rustbelt school is a feeling of being unfairly silenced, and for the system—another portrayal of public schools not meeting public expectations.

DIMINISHING SUPPORT FROM OTHER AGENCIES

Disadvantaged school welfare needs are supported to some extent by the State system. Schools with the greatest percentage of children in need are identified through a formula called an 'index of disadvantage': this takes into account parent income, parent level of education and occupation, transience and numbers of Aboriginal students. Primary schools that are designated by this means as disadvantaged have school counselling time over and above their normal staffing complement. This is not the case in most other Australian States and is, in the post-industrial city, a legacy of a former social democratic policy regime. In recognition of the particular social needs of adolescents, all secondary schools in the city and state have student counsellors as part of their staffing entitlement, but no extra counselling staff are given to disadvantaged high schools.

Systemic effort has gone into developing programs in rustbelt schools to support young people who have run foul of the disciplinary system, to intervene before they get to the point where the school no longer tolerates their presence. One such line of response is programs designed around conflict management, peer mediation and outdoor education to promote team and communication skills. These do have some success. However, school-based programs are often not enough.

Schools look to other government and non-government agencies to support them, and there is a mechanism in place to manage this inter-agency connection. School counsellors are often the main point of connection with support structures outside of the school, but services are accessed in this State through a formal 'inter-agency referral' process, in which 'cases' are prioritised and equity of access to services across the region assured. Schools can directly access system attendance counsellors and educational psychologists who diagnose and support students with disabilities. Schools also establish their own networks with community and church-based agencies.

However, having a system of inter-agency support only works when the inter-agency services are in a position to assist. Rustbelt schools report that there has been a significant deterioration in access to the kinds of support services that make a difference—general and mental health services, welfare services, community policing. This is a direct result of funding cuts to these agencies and of new purchaser-provider organisational models which reduce the response-ability at the local level (Thomson, 1998b). The waiting time for the provision of services grows, and services become more selective about the clients they see as they work to get maximum 'outcome' for their 'input'.

> We've had more than a handful of kids who have been through the service providers that are there, and they no longer want to know them because they are now too old at fourteen or fifteen for their target group, or they're unreliable and they've missed a number of appointments . . . so there isn't anything for them in terms of mental health services. The parents or the care giver or the foster parents do not have the dollars to access anything else. This is what poverty looks like for us. And it tends to be they're fed, they're clothed (and if necessary we can do that here), but we just can't access the health stuff that they need (secondary school principal).

Students who are depressed, suffering eating disorders, involved in substance abuse, living in stressful family settings, embarking on a pattern of offending, engaged in chronic truanting or who have difficulties managing conflict are, according to school principals, much less likely to be rapidly attended to than they would have been five or six years previously. Such delays are difficult for the young people and place considerable strain on their families, friends and teachers. 'Curriculum isn't the answer. Buying them uniforms and giving them breakfast, they're not the answer either. We're looking for much stronger community supports in terms of health and wellbeing and there's nowhere for them to go' (secondary school principal).

The retraction of public social and health services exacerbates some interactions with parents too, as schools become one of the few government agencies open and available. 'Care in the community' often ends up in the neighbourhood school.

There is a significant contraction of mental health services, both in terms of community health outreach services and outpatient services. What it is at the moment is that you can only get to see somebody once a month and in between time you go and create mayhem in your community, and with public agencies like schools, and your neighbours and with people living in the street (secondary school principal).

Rustbelt schools frequently bear the brunt of public frustration with retracting public services. They handle the distress when referrals do not eventuate promptly or at all, when one visit to a service is all that is offered before payment is requested and when services that used to be available are no longer in place. They are also frequently the public face of government and a place where general anger and frustration at public policy directions can be voiced.

As government agencies and services have retracted from contact with the local community and have moved to telephone help lines and central offices, the school's become the only place—perhaps the only place apart from the police station—in the local district where you can go and have a go at somebody who works for the government (secondary school principal).

Such complaints often begin with a minor matter such as lack of pick-up and drop-off parking in the street or a trivial discipline matter and end in a general diatribe about hard times and unsympathetic policy regimes. Rustbelt school staff must maintain a professional detachment in these circumstances despite the fact that it is the students for whom they are responsible who actually feel the policy pinch in diminishing levels of public services.

Given all of these changes for the worse, it is hardly surprising that new school reform projects and system plans for better literacy and numeracy outcomes are greeted with some scepticism in rustbelt schools. School administrators and teachers appreciate the policy sentiments, but are not sure, in the current worsening circumstances, how they can deliver.

TROUBLING STORIES

This social order and welfare trouble, one of the most common and enduring features of rustbelt schools, is also one of the most difficult to discuss. It is the most common reason for teachers attempting to avoid placement in an 'undesirable location' (the euphemism for rustbelt schools in the post-industrial State). It is what earns disadvantaged schools and low-income neighbourhoods their 'reputation'. It is the phenomenon often cited by parents, researchers and policymakers alike to 'show' that disadvantaged schools, their staffs and curriculum are of lesser 'quality' and lower 'standard'. It has been and is used as evidence for a plethora of theories about the deficiencies of children, families and neighbourhoods (Valencia, 1997). It is also the single biggest drain on disadvantaged school resources and staff time. And, more than anything else, it is the texture and the rhythm of everyday life in rustbelt schools.

Discipline and welfare both constitute and are constituted by the continuous connections between school, home and neighbourhood. The everyday practices of (the) social order profoundly shape and are shaped by the relations between parents, children and the school. They inexorably mould and are moulded by the institutional practices that interconnect teachers, learners, pedagogy, the curriculum, assessment, school structures and cultures. They are one key to the production and reproduction of the socio-spatial distribution of cultural capital and life chances. They are inextricably tangled in the production not only of knowledge but also of identities. Understanding the Siamese twins of discipline and welfare goes to the very heart of the mixed educational mandates of schooling—of sorting and selecting, achievement for all, and the making of productive and orderly citizens and workers.

There *are* contemporary policy explanations of the difficulties of maintaining (the) social order in rustbelt schools. In the United Kingdom, one story gaining prominence is that of an excluded underclass with a culture of non-compliance and phobic abhorrence of education (e.g. Johnson, 1999). This story lumps together people who live in particular localities in ways that are both insulting and redolent of older forms of ghettoisation; it posits a culture of poverty without systematic investigation of the veracity of such an idea or reference to the very considerable literatures on the topic (e.g. MacDonald, 1997; Morris, 1994). The underclass story has considerable purchase in the United States where it is irrevocably melded with discussion of race (e.g. Wilson, 1997). In both the United Kingdom and the United States, it is strongly gendered in the systematic representation of 'welfare mothers' (Mink, 1998; Shirk, Bennett & Aber, 1999) and teenage mothers, or 'gymslip mums' (Bullen, Kenway & Hay, 2000). This story has yet to take significant hold in Australia, and available evidence supports a far more heterogeneous view of young people and rustbelt neighbourhoods than that implied in the notion of an underclass.

One of the most common concepts in the United States and in Australia used in relation to discipline and welfare is that of risk. It is worth spending some time looking at risk in particular to see how it is that particular stories have particular effects.

INDIVIDUALS AT RISK

Young people present themselves in classrooms and programs as individuals, and schools have to respond to their particular and unique issues. The ways that policymakers and schools understand and respond to them is usually to just see the young people as specific and isolated cases to be diagnosed and treated, rather than as people in social contexts.

Government policymakers of all persuasions are likely to discuss individuals and their problems, and to see policy 'answers' in terms of individualised interventions and naming (and shaming) those who have 'failed' individuals. Consider how rural youth suicide is most often disconnected in policy talk from general discussions about the decline in the youth labour market and, in particular, the appalling state of un/employment in many rural areas. Rural youth suicide is similarly disconnected from conversations about the construction of sexuality and gender, and from tales of particular classed masculinities in which identities are strongly connected to work, drinking, driving fast cars and generally 'hooning around'. Take work away from this cocktail of behaviours and what remains are pastimes that are potentially problematic—and for some, life threatening. Policies that just deal with suicidal intentions and behaviours potentially miss major interconnecting issues, and it is the disconnected problem-posing and consequent narrow explanations that allow this to happen.

The question of 'risk' is precisely of this order—whether risk is just about student 'cases'—or whether it is also about the social, cultural, economic, political and institutional processes and practices in which these young people are collectively positioned—these are significant analytic choices. When applied to students, the use of 'risk' discourse[2] constructs a kind of black box around particular students so identified. This black box often extends to cover families and their cultures. Everyone inside the box is seen as somehow different from everyone outside.

There are six aspects of the 'risk' black box that need to be noted:

'Risk' as norm

The 'risk' black box establishes through exclusion a norm, a kind of ideal, which constitutes the behaviours, knowledges, beliefs and social practices to which everyone should aspire. Some students are designated as not the norm and they are therefore 'at risk'. When 'risk behaviours' are examined, they expose their alter-ego, the norm. A cursory glance at the norm and its other soon reveals its classed, gendered and raced foundations. Failure to read is now described by policymakers as a 'risk'. However, the children 'at risk' who do not read are also generally poor, from families in which parents have had little success in formal education, mostly male, and very often poorly behaved. How and why this particular constellation of class, gender and institutionalised achievement is produced is hidden if the focus is just on individuals who are ab-norm-al. The fact that the alter ego of 'risk', the norm, is also produced at the same time, by the very same processes that produce the ab-norm-al, is obscured.

Inbuilt 'risk' solutions

The 'risk' label paves the way for descriptions of the consequences of 'risky behaviours', which contain their own in-built solutions. For example, failure to read is, in current economic circumstances, strongly correlated with potential lack of involvement in the labour market and offending behaviours. Looking backwards, it is often assumed that teaching young people to read will prevent them from either unemployment or prison. You must learn to read if you are to get a job and if you don't want to end up being one of those illiterate criminals! Whether universal literacy will just create smarter criminals and more white collar crime is overlooked. The causal assumption between 'problem' and 'solution' is a very thin and reductionist apparent logic. But importantly, if 'risk' is seen as a simple question of literacy, then this sets the terms of the intervention, namely remedial, back-to-basics approaches to literacy in combination with social skills training. It is not that literacy is not important—it clearly is—but this explanation of illiteracy-as-risk takes the focus away from the other policy interventions that might be necessary in order to deal with the number of jobs available to the now literate 'fixed' young person, and the social conditions that also contribute to patterns of unemployment and criminal behaviours.

'Risk' as othering

Importantly, the label of 'student at risk' positions students so designated as separate from other students, suggesting that 'at risk ' students have no common concerns and interests with the norm-al. That a few students have walked out, yelled out or otherwise made themselves visible in class, for example, does not mean that the norm-al are all riveted and working hard. Questions of how relevant and meaningful the curriculum on offer is may involve significantly more than those who have been put in the 'risk' box. The designation of some students as needing 'fixing' in some way serves to hide how the curriculum, pedagogy, assessment and other institutional practices of the school might not be doing as well as possible for very many young people. The logic of isolating some young people is that only 'risky students' require a separate program. The alternative—a holistic policy and programmatic response to the broader group of young people—is left unexamined.

'Risk' as sameness

The notion of 'risk' homogenises all those 'at risk', suggesting that there is something common to all students exhibiting 'risk behaviours'. This lumping together of a variety of issues and needs in one category makes 'risk' amenable to one magic educational solution—such as remedial reading lessons—rather than opening up the many differences that exist between young people who are pushed to the edges of schooling. At the same time as 'risk' reduces the complexities and differences in lives to a few educational factors, there is paradoxically a proliferation of categorisations of specialised individual 'riskiness'. A variety of non-educational 'expert' professional systems from the health, psychology, psychiatry and special education disciplines get to work on 'risky' people. Work on 'risk' thus replaces, rather than accompanies reform work done on the practices of schooling, many of which are heavily implicated in the production of 'risk'.

'Risk' as identity

'Risk' works to become the young person's 'official identity'. Here is a homeless young person, rather than a young person who is temporarily homeless. There is a junkie, rather than a young person who has an addiction. It seems that it is difficult for schools to deal with questions of identities and diversity, both of which are socially constructed and situated. Schools tend to operate with cohorts of norm-al students and 'other' individuals. Allowing for differences that are both individual and social may be an approach that leads schools in some new reform directions. If schools were thought of as a space where a vast range of identities were co-constructed, the simplistic notions of 'risk' identities would be challenged.

'Risk' as damaging

'Risk' significantly misrepresents the lives of those who are propelled to the social margins in ways that can be damaging to the people concerned and produces policies which work counter to their stated intentions. If 'risk' is located within individuals, families and cultures rather than in a set of organised institutional and social processes, then the positive attributes of individuals, families and cultures are sent off stage and out of frame. The policy solution is located in things that must be done to and for individuals, families and cultures, obliterating and working against those things that individuals, families and cultures might do for themselves.

DOUBLE TROUBLE

In addition to isolating those risky students who are seen to 'cause trouble', policy rhetoric often separates curriculum from discipline and welfare. The discipline welfare tangle is often constructed as ensuring discipline and providing welfare, but keeping a 'balance' with the 'core business' of the curriculum. A comment by one head of a government school system is a good example of this thinking.

> An underemphasis on welfare can lead directly to failure in achieving our educational objective for individual students. An overemphasis on welfare to the detriment of learning achievement may deny students the means to reach their full potential through their own efforts and deny them the chance to escape from inhibiting circumstances in their own background (Spring, 1998).

Here the individualisation of background and effort is married to a sacrosanct curriculum and ameliorative welfare system. A binary of curriculum versus welfare is constructed. Welfare is about 'fixing' students so they can do what 'we' have decided is important. It is a necessary task, but one which potentially takes us away from our 'real work'. Discipline is not mentioned. It is taken for granted as an adjunct to the curriculum, whereas welfare is problematic.

What is never examined is that in this construction *both* discipline and welfare are processes that aim to 'fix' students, that *both* discipline and welfare work to isolate 'problem' students (re)producing raced, gendered and classed effects, and the curriculum is not seen as a possible contributor to, or producer of, the discipline problems. In this narrative construction of (the) social order, if schools fail to find the balance, then they might be seen as failing institutions, unable to manage the time-order-economy efficiently and effectively.

Whether they have sufficient resources to do so is another story.

AN ALTERNATIVE NARRATIVE

One of the functions of schooling is the disciplining of bodies and minds. This disciplining is both overt and pastoral. It is of behaviours and knowledges. It occurs through the timetable; through student grouping; through the organisation of rooms; through the designation of specific places and times and ways to play; through the assignation of school subjects to be conquered and moral and conceptual values to be adopted. Learning mathematics occurs at the same time and in the same place using the same pedagogic processes as learning how to behave appropriately, how to take turns, how to share pencils and how to listen and obey. There is no separation of instruction and discipline. They are one and the same. However, the school mandate is also to sort and sift students according to this same disciplinary regime. This inevitably produces disciplinary trouble, either as learning or behavioural failure or as both together.

The selective academic curriculum is by its very construction one that produces success, average achievement and failure (Connell et al., 1982). Those students who are 'the failures' are not all passive and accepting of their educational lot: many 'poorly' behaved students also have significant histories of bruising encounters with school learning. There is evidence to suggest that 'poor behaviour' arises in part from being unable to keep up with the class requirements; being unable to get help, and the kind of help needed for schoolwork; finding that customary ways of being and local knowledges do not 'fit' with the ways of being and knowing in the classroom; and being just plain bored. Most students who are 'underachieving' and 'unmotivated' find little engagement with the learning on offer, they do just enough to get by, passively refuse to play the game to either win or lose and avoid overtly flouting the rules of engagement. Dealing with discipline and welfare as if they are separate from curriculum, and with only those who stand out, speak out and walk out, hides an integrated educational ecology of knowledge and power relations.

In rustbelt schools, the maintenance of the discipline-welfare-academic social order takes a particular turn. The moves that students make in school space are a result of both their life circumstances and the institutional practices of schooling. In turn, their moves shape their life trajectories and educational practices. Having no way to influence the curriculum on offer or even to legitimately explain its inadequacies, students 'switch' to a variety of counter moves, most of which are seen in the school context as discipline issues. Having no desire to appear as grieving, frightened or desperate, some students switch to anger, to huddle in groups with friends, to distracted engagement with the lessons on offer. These appear as resistance to learning. The trouble that occurs in disadvantaged classrooms and schoolyards is a snarled assemblage of:

- individual and family responses to poverty (e.g. Fine & Weis, 1998);
- the struggle for identity by students within the options and spaces made available by the disciplinary and pastoral systems of the school—succeed/fail, conform/rebel, norm/other (e.g. Miron, 1996); and
- the degree to which students decide that there is a point and purpose to 'doing school' (e.g. Willis, 1977).

There is considerable practical knowledge in rustbelt schools with track records in improving 'behaviour' and reducing the sorting and selecting effect by working for 'curricular justice' (Connell, 1993). What is required are *combinations* of curriculum and pedagogical reform, an unwavering commitment to retain those who are at the edges of school, and more coherent, consistent and compassionate welfare and discipline procedures in which students have a chance to tell and record their versions of school life and events.

My experience in an urban, racially-isolated high school in Philadelphia indicates that the more students become engaged in their schooling, the less problematic they become in the classroom. It doesn't do you any good to get the halls clear of wanderers and then subject students to the same tedious teacher-centered work. That's one of the reasons they started wandering in the first place. So you need to help them gain both ownership and responsibility for their learning—you can't have one with out the other. In addition, students need to see how these skills will pay off now as well as down the road (Fecho, 1998).

A more engaging curriculum reduces *but doesn't eliminate* social order demands—these are created out of the positioning of the schools as mediators of unequal social relations.

THE HIGH COST OF ORDER

As life gets harder for many in the post-industrial city, it is important not to simply '. . . publicise the more spectacular forms of cumulative disadvantage, and thus distract attention from the general rise in inequality and unemployment and family dissolution that is affecting all social classes' (Popkewitz & Lindblad, 2000, p. 10). But it is equally important not to hide, as policy most often does, how it is that systematic processes of schooling are ineluctably bound up with social, economic and political contexts.

The time-order economy in rustbelt schools actually means that they have less time available than more privileged schools to focus on curricular, pedagogical and institutional change. They have less time to attend to the life chances of their students who are facing uncertain options, in rapidly changing times, in increasingly vulnerable localities. They have less time to attend to the very things that would switch the time-order economy away from overt disciplining to learning.

It is a mistake however to assume that all rustbelt schools are similarly placed. Some have very particular issues with which they must contend.

4 | Bringing particularity into site

Despite the seduction of endless space (and the allure of serial time) place is beginning to escape from its entombment in the cultural and philosophical underworld of the modern West. Not yet wholly above ground, it is there to be glimpsed, in this locale or that, here and there, now and then, whatever, somewhere (Casey, 1998, p. 339).

Any visitor to rustbelt schools will not be told a straightforward and common tale. A morass of particularity and specificity will reveal the patterning that can be variously described as class, poverty or disadvantage. There will be congruence in the stories of inadequate funding, escalating welfare and disciplinary demands and an unsympathetic policy milieu. But there will also be stories of events and issues that are particular to the neighbourhood and/or school. The ways in which particular social relations and practices, localities, systemic policies and constellations of individuals and histories coalesce in the institution of the school will be deemed by the local narrators to be as important as the commonalities. There is something at odds here with the ways schools talk of themselves and the ways they are described in policy.

The work of rustbelt schools has been positioned for well over two decades by State and national policies that categorise them by the socioeconomic status of their enrolments and neighbourhoods. The lexical marriage of SES and education has most enduringly been called 'disadvantaged schools'. This categorisation of 'disadvantaged' has been a policy mechanism for directing some additional resources and providing particular programs deemed necessary to address the needs of this set of schools. What is in focus in this naming and framing are the common issues that disadvantaged schools face. What is constructed by the term 'disadvantaged school' is a presumed set of social problems. The name becomes a reification that can be studied and manipulated, and interventions can be made in its forms and functions. The ways in which the very term itself works to produce the common characteristics of the category are rarely, if ever, discussed.

The category 'disadvantaged schools' sends to the margins, and very often offstage altogether, the significant differences between schools. So a further move is required, one which gets beneath the assumptions of sameness amongst the schools to reveal something of their particularities. This move is one that focusses on the production of important intra-category differences; it is also one that involves listening carefully to what people in disadvantaged schools are saying.

THISNESS

Rustbelt school administrators, teachers, parents and students routinely begin their sentences saying 'This school … These kids … This community …'. What is this 'thisness' that is being discussed?

Listen to one northern suburbs primary principal telling the story of thisness.

> We're the only ones with falling enrolments in the cluster. Our particular area is actually aging, just the immediate streets around our school. The people have all been in their Housing Trust homes for a long time. I don't know if they've taken up the option of buying, but they've been there, and their kids have all been through the school and they're all looking after their grandkids or they're on the old age pension. If you go up the road, less than a kilometre, or down the main road to the high school, there's been a new Housing Trust influx, so it's interesting, you actually have to look at the hundred [the smallest census category], to get it down to that level.
>
> My other schools have been one in the country and then several in the western suburbs. This student profile is very much Anglo, and lots of families in generational poverty. The west is really multicultural. We had a big influx of kids from Vietnamese and Cambodian background where I reckon [there is] one of the big differences—for some

groups education is still seen as an avenue for social mobility. Whereas I reckon for large numbers of parents at our school they no longer entirely believe that. They want better lives for their kids, for their kids to have an easier life with more options than they've had, but I don't know that they are really confident that the school system is going to deliver that.

And so I reckon the hostility . . . it's also a very violent community—I was really shocked when I first came out here and all my teaching had been in disadvantaged schools and I thought I knew them . . . so I reckon that's one difference, the cultural mix and generational thing . . . even compared to my last school which would have a similar number of kids in poverty, but there you've still got the cultural mix and you've still got more families where this is their first generation on the pension. Not like this.

Here is a claim for particularity of population and difficult school–parent relations that play out through children in classrooms and schoolyards. Here is a recognition of a threat to school viability arising from enrolment decline and an expression of isolation from other nearby schools.

NEIGHBOURHOOD CONTEXTS

In order to understand thisness, it is necessary to think of the school as a particular material place. Each school 'place' is a distinctive blend of people, happenings, resources, issues, narratives, truths, knowledges and networks, in and through which the combined effects of power-saturated geographies and histories are made manifest (Allen & Hamnett, 1995; Massey, 1994; McDowell, 1999; Rose, 1995; Soja, 2000). The school place is porous and permeable, a site in which 'flows' (Appadurai, 1996), practices, conflicts and settlements that operate across varying scales of influence come together (Swyngedouw, 1997).

The school as a place is embedded in context and cannot be detached from it. It is simultaneously 'context derived' and 'context generative', so that:

The very capability [of neighbourhoods] to produce contexts (within which their localising activities acquire meanings and historical potential) and to produce local subjects are profoundly affected by the locality-producing capabilities of larger scale formations (nation-states . . .) to determine the general shape of all the neighbourhoods within reach of their powers (Appadurai, 1996, p. 186).

Because neighbourhood places 'both constitute and require contexts' (p. 186), the capacity of a neighbourhood school to make a difference (to generate context) is completely imbricated with context-dependent factors, mediated by the actions of local subjects. So, while the school and the neighbourhood may be patterned by class, gender and race relations on a larger scale, at the local level, a veritable kaleidoscope of variations and capacities to act are to be expected.

The capacity of 'disadvantaged schools' to make a positive difference in students' learning is specifically and generally context dependent, and aspects of how this happens can be glimpsed by considering thisness. There are three major categories of neighbourhood contexts (the local workings out of larger global, national and State processes) which constrain and position what it is that school staffs can do. They are significant components of local thisness. These are the school mix, neighbourhood resources and neighbourhood issues.

SCHOOL MIX

Each school population is different. In rustbelt schools, students and their families are variously affected by social, economic, cultural and political trends and events, which in turn have particular effects in the schools. It is not that these effects are unknown in other schools. But in the rust belt, these events are concentrated and they can become major motifs and issues to which schools must devote considerable time and energy. These localised effects require, and sometimes receive, particular kinds of educational and whole-of-government responses and support.

Individual school populations are variously affected by the following.

Changes in the labour market

Family unemployment/underemployment/tenuous employment (the local working out of macro- and micro-economic reform) varies throughout the rust belt. It plays out in particular schools in a range of ways. Here are just three:

- Many students have no money for educational expenses. A few schools in areas of very high unemployment find that the majority of their students cannot afford to pay for activities such as swimming, a visit to the theatre, the bus fare to work experience or for art materials to do their homework projects. In order not to single out those children, or to deny them these activities, these schools find themselves in the position where they have to provide everything at only a token cost or completely free. This skews school budgets and programs. These rustbelt schools spend more money, of which they often have less, on things that do not appear in the ledgers of schools in other locations and they thus have little money for the things (such as computers) to which leafy, green schools devote large sums, and their colleague rustbelt schools spend some.

And sometimes students just miss out.

We can't do Saturday morning sport because we can't get the parent support because they don't have third-party-property insurance on their cars so they can't take the kids to other schools, or they don't have a car at all, or they just don't have the petrol money. We do have a basketball team on Thursday afternoons but it's $2 a week to get into the stadium. Often we have players who don't turn up and they'll say, 'I didn't come because I didn't have the $2', and I say, 'Don't worry about that, we'll cover it', and we provide the uniform, but it just gets down to $2 being really hard to find (primary school principal).

The cost to children of not wanting to own up to not having a paltry sum like two dollars is hard to measure.

- Truancy and/or lateness and/or undone homework are often associated with the everyday routines in households that have erratic casual work. Teachers must work on educational ways to make school the best place to be during the day. Encouraging students to attend on time and maintaining the continuity of their learning, even though the class has moved on in their absence, are tasks that require both understanding and patience, not to mention much additional work for school staff. This is not a pedagogical requirement in schools where large numbers of children are dropped and picked up at the school gate by working parents, and where the working days of school and parent employment are contiguous. In areas where there is high parental unemployment and large numbers of parents and teenagers working casual hours and shift work, maintaining routines around school becomes a major issue.
- The assumed nexus between work and school credentials, the linkage between cultural and symbolic capitals, is undermined by the everyday experiences of chronic underemployment. (See

Chapter 3.) Secondary schools in the areas of highest youth unemployment report a range of different responses from young people. One group of students are unrealistically confident that they will easily slip into a chosen career. Another group takes up part-time work as soon as they can. Principals know that their wages are often a necessary addition to the family income no matter how much changing hours and days as required by employers conflicts with school. Another group takes up vocational courses as 'the solution' on offer, avoiding or giving up school subjects that have no immediate utility. These days the ultimately self-defeating resistance to schooling (documented three decades ago by Willis, 1977, as the means by which working-class lads got working-class jobs) has been transformed by the changing labour market to the situation where getting a working-class job is a prize available only to a few. This situation places particular schools in a cleft stick: holding out false hope or little hope are equally unpalatable.

Changes in families and families under pressure

While all schools in and out of the rust belt report an increase in the number of families suffering from poverty and its associated effects, some schools in particular know that their neighbourhood is harder hit by changed economic circumstances than others. One principal newly transferred to the northwest in 2001 from the northern suburbs was shocked by the degree of hardship that is now commonplace.

> I worked here fifteen years ago and the people didn't have much, but I could visit them at home. Now they won't even let you in the door. They have absolutely nothing and they are really ashamed of their poverty. We're providing breakfast and lunch for kids at school—it's just so much worse than the disadvantaged school where I was last year (primary school principal).

Schools in the areas of highest unemployment are also in the areas where there is emergency public housing.

> It's a self-perpetuating cycle. When somebody in crisis comes to the housing people they say, 'We've got some houses here', and if they can afford to people will go elsewhere, but if they're really desperate, a real emergency, they'll accept it and they'll come here. And so you get a whole street full of people in crisis (primary school principal).

These schools have unusually high concentrations of families living very hard lives. They deal daily with children and parents literally teetering on the edge. 'The angry abusive parents . . . we get them all the time . . . I mean I'm the principal of the school and I'm suspending their child . . . they're coming in and protecting the very little they've got and it's their way of surviving. And that's all the result of poverty' (primary school principal).

Whereas in the postwar period it was mostly the elderly who were impoverished, poverty is now concentrated amongst families with children (Harding & Szukalska, 1999). Many rustbelt families are utterly dependent on welfare payments, and have no reserves to draw on and few supports. Rustbelt schools in high welfare areas report that significant numbers of children appear to be dealing with the pressures of living in domestic situations that are not only unstable but also strained to breaking point from financial worries and their inability to access support services.

Demographics in the city are changing. There are increasing numbers of separated, blended and re-blended and extended families (Hugo, 1999). All schools in the city have different combinations of families that make specific, time-consuming and often unrecognised demands on staff, curriculum and time. In the rust belt, however, some of these demographic effects are manifest in very specific ways.

A couple of schools are located next to women's shelters and a continually changing stream of traumatised children come and go. The additional demands on staff in dealing with grieving and often angry children are rarely recognised. One school has many children with sick and dying parents—it serves a public housing estate next to a public hospital. Children from this estate not only have to take on additional domestic responsibilities but they also face the daily fear and distress of living with a parent whose wellbeing is uncertain.

> Last week there was this kid who just went off and swore at the teacher and was sent to the office to cool down, but he just ran off and climbed off on the roof. So we had to get the fire brigade and the police . . . And it turned out he's living with his grandmother, his real mother is in hospital, and we didn't know any of that, and he was just at the end of his tether. This is a nine-year-old. It's just the nature of poverty here and how it impacts on us . . . (primary school principal).

Some families find keeping a roof over their heads a complicated and difficult matter. Teachers report regular incidents of 'midnight flits', 'staying with grandma' and children moving between family members. Many schools report that families now face escalating waiting periods for referral services, particularly for depressed and substance-abusing adolescents.

> There are some very serious issues here . . . you know, we've had kids who've . . . threatened their parents with a kitchen knife and whilst they haven't brought the knife to school, their behaviour's fairly berserk, and then you're sitting round and hearing, 'Well, the earliest time we can get them in to see a psychiatrist is a month's time'. What are we supposed to do in the school in the meantime? (secondary school principal).

Schools point to the de-funding of local employment and family counselling services and mounting demands on local charities which the charities cannot meet. This adds further to family pressures.

> The crisis care and respite care is down to zilch. There's almost nowhere you go just for a break from your kids if they're going nuts, and most of the kids who have behaviour issues at school have them at home . . . There's whole parts of the community that are actually in crisis themselves just dealing with the stuff that they have to deal with and what to do about it—they feel so powerless (secondary school principal).

Dealing with children and young people exhibiting evidence of considerable insecurity and anxiety requires regular time away from instruction, and involves classroom teachers and administrators alike. The time-order economy of schools in neighbourhoods where this becomes a dominant feature is inevitably distorted, becoming over-whelmingly about the daily management of welfare issues. It is important to understand that this small minority of schools gets only a little extra support in recognition of these very particular issues, and in a few of the schools it is often as much as they can do to 'keep a lid on' the situation. The time they have for reform is negligible.

Changes in migration and diaspora

Schools are also subject to changing patterns of migration and diaspora which show up as specific curriculum and counselling needs. Not surprisingly, new arrivals (migrants and refugees) have to find low-cost or public housing and most of this is located in the rust belt. Several rustbelt schools are located in neighbourhoods in which there are hostels for refugees fleeing intolerable political situations. Others serve more established populations of immigrants. All report significant short-falls in the community services available to children and families, and, as a result, increased pressure on the school to step in. Cuts in interpreter and translation services are matched by reductions in the provision of adult migrant English classes; both of these inevitably require children to act as family translators. Schools in which there are significant Aboriginal populations do receive some support, but all comment bitterly on the lack of fit between the available resources and community need.

Each school, nevertheless, attempts to provide an inclusive curriculum, language and learning support, dedicated rooms, and services for parents suitable for the particular cultural composition of the school population. This gives each school a very particular character, much of which is very enriching if it can be taken up as a curriculum resource.

> We've trained and set up parent literacy workers ... we've got parents running physical coordination programs ... we do four languages for mother tongue ... but just the management and organisation—getting adequate office space—you spend a whole bucket of time doing all that and being creative with funds ... (primary school principal).

Many of these programs are now only maintained by virtue of the good will, creative energy and commitment of the staff, because government resources are entirely inadequate for the task.

Transience

In a few schools many of these factors come together. In public housing areas in which emergency housing predominates and there is high unemployment, there is an intensity and an intensification of issues and pressures. One of the most 'countable' measures is school transience—children moving in and out of the district. A small number of schools have more than 40 percent of their school population who come and go during the year. In a school of 200 this amounts to 80 children moving in and out of the school.

> This morning I did four enrolments, two of those are living with friends, they've just moved here from somewhere else. Sometimes they've been kicked out of their house, I don't ask, and others just live with friends until the friends get sick of them and then they move to the next set ... Some kids have had seven or eight schools and they're only in Year 4 or 5 ... the kids are never in a place long enough for anyone to work out what their learning needs are (primary school principal).

These schools also often have to completely reorganise classes more than once during one year just to accommodate the changing population. This effectively puts paid to the idea of close teacher–student relationships which are at the heart of good pedagogies. In one year teachers will work with classes that go from overcrowded to small and back again. Much of their time will be devoted to helping children settle in and trying to find out the extent of their formal learning.

Schools affected by high transience spend funds supplying books and equipment for more children than they are funded for. Global budgets that allocate on the basis of average enrolments are grim jokes in these schools, where staff argue that recognising their material reality is a simple matter of justice.

NEIGHBOURHOOD RESOURCES

Students and their families are directly affected by the local neighbourhood and its changing labour market, family composition and patterns of migration. Schools have to deal with these. However, the effects of neighbourhood context also affect institutional capabilities. Appearances to the contrary, schools are not compounds which provide everything within their fenced perimeters. They depend on having access to particular kinds of services and resources available in the immediate neighbourhood and local region. The cultural, social and economic capital of the locality is important to the local schools. The capacity of each school to run mandated, not to mention desirable, co-curricular programs and provide equally and equitably for students is tied to neighbourhood resources.

Consider the following.

Community infrastructure

Schools rely on not only local health and welfare services, youth services, public transport and migrant-support programs, but also on public libraries, neighbourhood houses, local recreation facilities, sporting and arts organisations, local government, service clubs and churches. These are some of the neighbourhood 'assets' (McKnight, 1995) that support learning in and out of school and contribute to general wellbeing. In rustbelt neighbourhoods, many of these services are routinely underfunded, and in recent hard times many have been rationalised, retracted and regionalised. In addition, fewer people have the disposable income necessary to meet the low fees charged to cover the running costs of locally established and managed organisations. It is not uncommon for neighbourhood-based sporting clubs in low-income locations to struggle, and many depend on low-cost access to school ovals and changing rooms.

Amenities and services available in poor neighbourhoods vary according to location. Geographical features count. Being sandwiched by main roads or located on a peninsula and connected to the local service centre by a bridge, for example, means that access to the full complement of community infrastructure and services is limited. Newly established suburbs on the edges of the city are by far the worst off. One rustbelt school had to have its school canteen function as the local shop for the newly built neighbourhood before the local shopping centre was established. Nappies, milk, tea, sugar and soap powder sold to parents after school hours were as important to the local families as the sandwiches and pasties sold to the children at lunchtime.

The rust belt is characterised not just by the signs of passive welfare dependence, youth alienation (graffiti, vandalised buildings, queues at job centres) and overwhelming needs. Rather, these sit together with the tangible signs of community organisation and a multitude of self-help groups and far reaching networks. In the north, working-men's clubs are popular meeting places. In the west, a multitude of ethnic and religious organisations have meeting rooms and clubs. In some places, local football and netball clubs still survive and some thrive, and a busy and productive arts community is visible in the west. However, the degree to which schools are connected with these regional organisations varies. Some schools are just too far away to benefit from them. Others do not see community connections as a high priority. The most pressured simply do not have the time to make contact and they remain apart, disconnected from local assets that, with closer contact could provide mutual benefit.

Employment and employment networks

Schools depend on numbers of small, medium and large businesses to provide not only jobs for parents and school leavers, but also work placements and mentoring for students.

Sometimes this is a success story. Localities that boast a concentration of globally oriented companies are often able to combine businesses in ways that benefit the whole community, including its schools (Kenway, Kelly & Willis, 2001). An internationally recognised wine-growing area in the state has large numbers of international and national visitors. One local secondary school has been able to devise a successful senior secondary oenology program drawing on the very considerable local winemaking expertise, a horse-training program with a real race horse on loan from the local international-prizewinning stud, and hospitality and tourism programs which place students on work experience in award-winning restaurants, five-star accommodation establishments, modest hotels and bed and breakfasts.

Schools in the rust belt are the antithesis of such well positioned and enterprising places. In the rust belt, the continued existence of car manufacturing plants and some of the flow-on industries, together with the proliferation of call centres, defence-related industries and niche manufacturing, provide some opportunities for educationally based interaction. However, opportunities are limited even in these 'economic successes' and some schools have been better able to take them up than others. In particular, specialist vocational schools have been generally more successful in obtaining work placements and organising course articulation. These leave other rustbelt schools that also have work experience programs and some vocational courses with fewer options. In addition, the decline of strip shopping in the rust belt, the automation of banks and service stations and the slim profit margins available to most small businesses (which have also recently had to cope with a new time-consuming taxation regime) have further reduced the opportunities for vocational and work education.

The decline of manufacturing has also reduced civic leadership in the rust belt. A school wishing to establish mentoring programs for young people will find it is in competition with neighbouring schools for the small amount of time available from businesspeople. Rustbelt schools increasingly look to benefiting from proximity to public and quasi-public sector bodies, such as regional university campuses and technical colleges, for vocational opportunities for students. But they often fail to see opportunities too.

> We have 450 staff . . . We are a big employer, people have no idea how big we are or how comprehensive. They think of us as just a welfare agency . . . Schools are running round training people for technology, but you've got these big strong boys with nothing to do and we'd love to have them lifting old ladies in our nursing homes, and we could particularly help them engage with the more compassionate side of their lives . . . so instead of them thinking, 'Oh my God, there's no more jobs on the roads', maybe they can work for us . . . and we could give them a first aid certificate and instruction in safe lifting, and we could really do with them . . . (chief executive of welfare agency).

So, while the degree and kind of employment and industry available to local schools varies, and some schools and some students are more clearly advantaged by proximity to either technical colleges and/or successful industries (cf. Jensen & Seltzer, 2000), it is also the case that opportunities are missed.

A particular discourse of what constitutes vocational education delimits how it is that schools take up the local employment opportunities available to them. Nowhere is this clearer than in the outer northern suburbs where schools adjacent to the extensive market gardens producing most of the city's fresh vegetables have largely failed to make connections with the very considerable expertise, knowledge and employment networks of what is locally known as the 'salad bowl'. How much this is due to the fact that most of these agri-businesses are owned and operated by extended families of predominantly Italian, Greek and Vietnamese Australians is a moot point.[1]

Availability of voluntary labour

Schools depend on the capacity of parents to donate time to their children's schooling. Parents are expected to have the time and space to help children with homework and projects, to attend parent meetings and come to the school when summoned to discuss a child's concerns. A minority of parents are also called to transport children to and from sporting and extra curricular events. And some parents are required to do more: school councils have a number of legal responsibilities, such as management of school funds and maintenance of school grounds, and in this State they require eleven parents to attend at least one, and often more, meetings per month.

Other voluntary labour is also expected: school canteens often rely on shifts of willing (usually) mothers; parents act as tutors for small groups of students in literacy, speech pathology, physical coordination and remedial tuition; parents are engaged in significant fundraising activities, and in working bees. The contribution of this unpaid voluntary labour can make significant differences to school programs.

This labour, however, is not evenly distributed. In the parts of the rust belt where there are high percentages of family members engaged in shift and casual work, schools find it almost impossible to engage parents in the range of possible school activities. However there are also parts of the rust belt where parents who have been made redundant choose to take up voluntary activities in their children's school and the presence of their willing hands, albeit often unskilled, can markedly benefit groups of children. Indeed, some rustbelt schools have found small amounts of money to both train and pay parents to act as assistants to teaching staff.

> We had the big cuts in 1996 and we lost 3 percent of our school assistants, but then we got literacy grants and early intervention money and we all converted it to school assistant hours and there was no one left around to employ but we found them in the end . . . we're recruiting and training parents, and they go into Year 3–4 classrooms half an hour every day. And each week they focus on a different skill, whether its decoding or predicting or fiction or reading a contents page. Then everybody reads for half and hour and this group of parents—they're hearing kids read every second day, and that's just making so much difference . . . but with the trend to cash grants rather than supplying staffing, it has the effect of casualising employment (primary school principal).

The desire to make differences for children via literacy tuition and remedial intervention, the most common ways in which parents can be employed and deployed under the supervision of a teacher, thus inadvertently creates the same kind of casualised and temporary employment as other rustbelt jobs. By contrast, in more middle-class localities, many schools have well-educated mothers available during the day to act as unpaid classroom helpers.

Age of locality and school facilities

Schools are generally built as part of the development of suburbs. It is not at all uncommon these days to see more up-market real estate developments advertising the mix of State and non-government schools as part of the local 'amenities'. There are, in the post-industrial city, a number of examples of developers putting pressure on for, and even in one case funding, the establishment of a government primary school as part of the suburb's establishment.

Yesterday's populous manufacturing labour-force suburbs have become today's rust belt. Forty and fifty years on in these localities, there are now a number of schools aging less than gracefully and in desperate need of renovation. The State Government *has* tried to keep up with the deterioration. The political will to upgrade is hampered by lack of funds. The State budget is still recovering from the fiscal damage caused during the 1980s, when many financial and Government institutions invested heavily in speculative ventures and were caught in the first aftershocks of financial deregulation, movement of global capital and the manufacturing plant exodus. As already noted, the conservative policy response included the sale of the State bank, commercial leasing of State utilities and services and considerable reductions in State expenditure. One of the casualties was the education capital works budget. In the post-industrial city, there is now a lengthy schedule of school rebuilding programs, only a few of which can be afforded each year. To their credit, both the previous long-term State Labor Government and its Liberal successor distributed capital works funds across all quarters of the city and country, and gave additional, albeit rapidly dwindling, support to localities where low-income parents, through their school councils, were unable to raise funds for minor improvements. However, as the State economy worsened throughout the 1990s, the Government has relied increasingly on a finite supply of money raised from school closures and the subsequent (fire) sale of real estate, together with the disposal of 'surplus' school ovals, to bankroll school renovations.

Today, schools in the rust belt, typically in safe seats held by the political Labor opposition, are less able to mount campaigns for better facilities than those in blue ribbon Liberal locations (Thomson, 1999). Rustbelt schools generally still do not have the same kinds of built learning environments as those in more wealthy localities, and they are unable to compete with leafy, green school parent fundraising and school council 'clout'.

We actually don't have much room for kids here now. We've got kids everywhere. We've got transportable buildings here and there . . . the capital works stuff is just a disaster. It's increasingly being cut back all the time and two years ago we wrote about a major upgrade and a review and we haven't even had a reply. I had the big blokes in the department out here six months ago to tell me what they were going to do about it and so far I've heard nothing so I just don't know what to do to even get an answer to the question . . . (secondary school principal).

While rustbelt schools are usually less able to accumulate funds to pay for relatively small renovations and minor upgrading of facilities than their leafy green counterparts, the capacity to raise funds locally is also variously distributed around the rustbelt schools. Some schools have been fortunate to have had additional oval space that they have sold for housing blocks, with funds going to the State as a contribution towards the overall cost of upgrading. Some schools have had catastrophic fires, the consequences of which have been short-term pain but long-term gain in the form of new facilities, furniture and equipment. A handful of rustbelt schools are located fortuitously adjacent to major sporting facilities and are able to raise funds by charging sports goers to park in the schoolyard during events.

In a few locations, the rustbelt school plant is hopelessly outdated: one school slated for closure in a few years' time could not operate its small bank of computers at the same time as the air-conditioning, for fear of complete power failure. Contrast this with the concerns in one particular leafy, green school recently upgraded:

> A teacher came to talk to me yesterday from the computing room upstairs in the senior school—we have outstanding facilities there by the way—and he said, 'You got a minute? It's pretty hot up there in computing', and I said, 'Well find a spare room that's cool and move your class in there', and he said, 'Oh, no, I mean we'll have to upgrade' . . . I kept thinking—if he says anything more about the air-conditioning . . . (secondary principal, formerly from the rust belt).

Rustbelt schools that have been renovated, generally due to their own as well as departmental efforts, note that students enjoy better facilities and learn better in more pleasant environments. Teachers who have carpet rather than noisy linoleum, curtains that allow audio visual equipment to be used to advantage and proper cooling and heating dread having to go to a school that still does not have such 'luxuries'.

In secondary schools, there are urgent policy-generated require-ments for upgraded workshop facilities so that industry-approved vocational courses (hospitality, metal and wood trades, electronics and auto repair) can be taught. Not by chance, the schools in which there is the greatest demand for these vocational courses are in the rust belt. There is also now the added policy pressure for the provision of computer stations and pods in rewired and air-conditioned rooms. Rustbelt schools face a nasty conjunction of policy imperative, greater need, lack of local funds and political clout and scarcity of government funds. On top of this is a political agenda biased towards provision for the most acute, the most likely to gain media attention and opportuni-ties required by conservative politicians with an eye on their re-election prospects. Some are better able to deal with all of this than others.

Neighbourhood narratives

There are local stocks of stories and images that circulate about partic-ular schools and neighbourhoods. This local lore can act as a resource for renewal as well as a considerable barrier.

A few secondary schools have been able to reinvent themselves as more modern versions of technical schools, mobilising memories of times when such schools provided almost foolproof paths to employment. One such school has worked to link itself to stories of a particular community identity in concert with other local efforts to promote tourism and regional festivals, markets and attractions. It has also adopted a school uniform in the colours of the local football team, thus simultaneously associating itself with place, tradition and contemporary public success. Very few schools have either the opportunities or the savoir faire to re-narrativise themselves so specifically, in part because they do not have access to these kinds of positive local stories and images.

However, the widely held (but not universal) antipathy of principals towards overt competition with other State schools also plays some part in the reluctance to explicitly investigate the neighbourhood anthology of current and residual tales for what might be plucked and exploited. More often than not, and despite their ambivalence, schools are nevertheless surrounded by neighbourhood narratives. Local legends and myths about particular schools abound, and have long lives.

This school was known as a 'nice' school in the seventies and eighties: it had religious events and an orchestra, in the days of the Australian working-class generational thing, when that was what a 'good school' was . . . There's always been a 'thing' between this school and that school and some people send their kids there and not here and vice versa. People position themselves culturally and class wise (primary school principal).

Oral 'grapevines' proliferate with yarns about what happened to the child two doors away, with retold conversations of people 'in the know', with recounts of the deeds and doings of particular students and/or staff. These everyday 'factual' oral tendrils work to hold individual schools in their place in the regional hierarchy. They produce long-term patterns of enrolment and expectations that are hard to disrupt.

We're not really on the nose in the area at the moment, but you can go on the nose in two weeks for good reason or no reason at all . . . I think that generally we're seen as doing quite a good job but there's some rough kids that go there . . . we're tainted by association, and we used to be that high school and people don't want their kids going to that high school, and it doesn't seem to matter how good a job you do, we're being residualised not because of what we do but because of what we used to do . . . (secondary school principal).

Only very concerted and expensive public relations and image management can make inroads into the local 'grapevine', and many schools are not willing to devote time and energy to what often seems a mysterious and impenetrable local process when they could spend precious and scarce time and energy on more substantive learning issues.

NEIGHBOURHOOD ISSUES

In addition to the variously configured effects of social, economic and cultural change on children and their families (school mix) and the various neighbourhood resources and networks available to rustbelt schools, there are also idiosyncratic local events that impact on specific sites.

These are not small incidents that pass quickly, having made a temporary impression in the rhythms of everyday life. They can be single dramatic occurrences from which there are ongoing and long-term repercussions preoccupying and irrevocably altering the trajectory of the school involved. They can be a series or pattern of happenings that act to redirect the time and energies of the school and those concerned with it. Schools are not without some support in dealing with these idiosyncratic things, but often external assistance is immediate and short lived and there is little recognition of the longterm impact on school capabilities and resources.

The key to identifying such events is to see whether and how the school's energy and time is consumed for considerable periods, making it very difficult to concentrate first and foremost on instruction. Some of these events are noted below.

Neighbourhoods under review

Increasing or declining enrolment in schools is a direct consequence of the age of a neighbourhood and its declining birth rate. In recent years, often clumsy and contentious systemic policies to determine school 'viability' have led to the closure of several neighbourhood primary and secondary schools, compelling the remaining students to travel long distances or drop out of school altogether. Being a school in a declining neighbourhood means taking part in endless discussions about possible options, all the while feeling that there is little purpose in making long-term plans given that the future of the school itself is dangling.

> This school is small and likely to amalgamate. The uncertainty's gone on for a few years now. It started towards the end of 1995 and we lost about 50 students straight away and then we went downhill rather rapidly. This year we are actually maintaining the status quo. I under-

stand that there's a letter coming to us from the government telling us that we have permission to look at moving to another site down the road together with another school, and when that comes I imagine that we'll lose kids quite dramatically. Down the track, when we're on the new site, they'll come back (primary school principal).

In the rust belt the long decline of a school under constant systemic review plays out in a politics of 'voice and exit', which profoundly embitters teachers and families.

This place has undergone two reviews in under five years, shall we close or shall we not? The first one was really ugly, and then there was another one which ended up with the amalgamation of two other schools. The uncertainty affected not just Year 8 enrolments but also the senior school. And so really until it's settled down—we have five years of stability—then the retention and enrolment is not going to be that flash (secondary school principal).

Neighbourhoods are profoundly affected by the demise of schools. Families have reason to worry about school closures.

When the secondary school closed, bus routes went, bus stops went, it was bit by bit. You see some of our parents pushing a trolley down the street. They live near the school, and they push the trolley to the mall, do the shopping and push it back, because there's no bus now. It's a long way to walk pushing a trolley (primary school principal).

Changes in demographics, external review and possible closure all create anxiety and uncertainty which not only affect enrolments but also the capacity and willingness of the school to plan ahead. A small number of schools are located in public housing estates slated for closure and it is not just the school that is uncertain about its future.

They're going to knock houses down and rebuild. We don't know what kind of population will be there when that happens. The people here are really worried about it. They're quite anxious about getting chucked out of their home and getting shifted off somewhere else where they don't want to be (primary school principal).

While some teachers have managed to turn this difficulty into a curriculum opportunity (Comber, Thomson & Wells, 2001), this is the exception rather than the rule. More often than not, children and staff are de-moralised and de-motivated by the likely demise of their family and educational homes. The possible and feared future scenarios become the lived present of the school, a colonisation of the present by the future that infuses the micro-transactions and patterns of everyday life.

Neighbourhood factions, feuds and tragedies

In neighbourhoods where there are significant concentrations of families with the anxieties and stresses of living uncertain lives, there are often eruptions that spill over into schools. In the last few years, particular rustbelt schools have endured some of the following.

- Gang-like fighting, in which ongoing territorial disputes between young people of post-school and school-going age have extended from weekend pub and club collisions into school time and school space. Weapons have been used and physical harm to one or more individuals has resulted. Inevitably the media has become involved.

> We now employ a guard who works on the premises and that works for the staff and we haven't had any more trouble. But it was written up on the front page [of the newspaper] and it was just awful . . . reality is in the eye of the beholder and it has done enormous damage to us. We lost about a class of students straight away and a couple of teachers because of the drop in numbers. But it has fed a set of stereotypes and racist attitudes because of who happened to be involved in the fights (secondary school principal).

It is both the results of sensational representations as well as the fears of staff and students who no longer feel safe in the school that become the major preoccupation and part of the 'identity' of the school concerned.

- Racist harassment, in which organisations dedicated to right-wing racial politics target schools with high populations of students of Vietnamese and Cambodian origin. After systematic recruitment of some Anglo students, there is a period of intense surveillance of everyday school life until an incident triggers allegations of unfair treatment of white students. The school principals are targeted and named via website, local leaflets and posters. On two occasions, there were pickets and marches on the school grounds, which were duly recorded on national television.

    Principals who have had to take security measures at home and at work have simultaneously also had to deal with worried parents, frightened children and anxious staff, not to mention central office requests for reports about the incidents. Past harassing campaigns against particular people and schools went on for months and affected not only daily morale and the sense of safety of all who worked at the site, but also deterred potential students from considering the school as a possible choice. The harassed schools are each known in their local areas as 'the one that was on television' and in which 'children are not safe'.

- Spates of vandalism, in which whole blocks of classrooms have been taken out of operation, destroying years of teacher resources as well as the year's accumulation of students' work. While small acts of vandalism can be repaired almost immediately, significant damage can take one to two years to restore, and dealing with the parade of architects, contractors and on-site builders is added to the task of running school programs with reduced facilities. Living with the presence of burnt-out buildings for long periods of time is very difficult administratively, but also emotionally. Long-term planning is disrupted because many conversations are entwined with uncertainties about when the buildings will be usable.

- Neighbourhood tragedies, in which the school becomes part of a wider net of grief, fear and media representations. While schools deal in the short term with the shock of the tragedy, there are also long-term consequences. A small number of suicides among young people, for example, can produce an immediate crisis requiring concerted counselling intervention, but for some considerable time afterwards, the school is caught up with the possible as well as that which occurred. The school must act differently with its students, for 'any of them might be next'.

  Schools in localities where grisly and well-publicised murders have occurred are often named in media reports about victims and/or accused. They become part of the background reportage of events. Not only must they deal with the immediate disbelief, horror and fear of staff and families, they must also try to shrug off their reputation by association. Energy swings into trying to devise programs that will show the school, the students and the neighbourhoods in another and more positive light. However, they are forever narratively linked with events.

THISNESS, LIKENESS AND POLICY

Neighbourhood issues come together in specific schools in specific ways. No disadvantaged school is identical to another. Even if, according to routine official poverty calculations, or according to statistical aggregations of parent income and qualification level, schools can be grouped together as categories of 'like schools', the 'like' must be understood both for its commonality and significant differences. 'Like' is a broad terrain.

There are infinite numbers of permutations. Imagine a school with a substantive transient student population, in an area slated for redevelopment, with a low standing on the local grapevine, that then experiences a significant fire. Imagine another school in an area of high chronic unemployment, with a significant and politically active indigenous population, aging buildings and rapidly diminishing sets of public agencies and infrastructure around it. Imagine a school with a poor but stable population, in an area recently redeveloped, close to the city. Imagine a school with high numbers of recent refugee families, enduring ongoing organised racist harassment and then dealing with a gang-related fight that attracts national media attention.

There are two points to be noted about externally related and produced school thisness. Firstly, thisness is not the same for everybody within the institution. Different staff and students will be affected differently by school mix, neighbourhood resources and neighbourhood issues. However, the unique combinations of mix, resources and issues do form the everyday of the school, that is, they shape the school as a life world. The school as thisness is a continually shifting site in which staff and students formulate, develop and realise their desires, knowledges, powers and potentialities diversely positioned by specific local circumstances (cf. LeFebvre, 1971). Secondly, the specific combination of mix, resources and issues shape school life. They demand a particular time-order-and-resource economy. When there is a crisis, time must be devoted to it. If there are students and families with particular needs, then time and often money must be devoted to them. If there is a possible threat to enrolment, then time and money must be devoted to trying to redress the adverse effects. If several buildings are out of action, then the school timetable may have to be adjusted, curriculum options may have to be altered, and patterns of learning disrupted. Thisness is a powerful influence on the distribution of all of the short- and long-term resources of the school.

Thisness creates specific sets of demands on schools. And the differences that sit behind the notion of 'like' schools also suggest a more differentiated policy response. What can be done and what needs to be done are very different in each school's set of circumstances. Rustbelt schools need different combinations of different kinds of support.

Much thisness is not beyond the reach of public policy and public action. Combinations of labour market, health, housing, social welfare and transport policies could make quite a dent in a number of neighbourhood effects, and consequently change things for the better in the rust belt. They could make significant changes for the better in those schools that are hardest pressed. In areas with high numbers of families under pressure, the provision of well-staffed health and welfare services amenable to integrated work with schools would free up school staff and their time, as well as better providing for the particular families and persons concerned. More sensitive and less sensational media treatment of singular events at particular schools and more time devoted to alternative and more complex representations of the rust belt would pay off for those schools currently adversely and unfairly characterised. Adequate funding for school renovation would make significant differences to the working days of students and teachers.

Furthermore, an appreciation of the complexity of disadvantage(s) is the precursor to an overall public policy shift away from one which insists on homogenising and normalising those schools and neighbourhoods that are characterised as disadvantaged (or as zoned priorities for action). Such differentiation is difficult for central bureaucracies to manage and coordinate, and it is perhaps in new combinations of the local and central that ways to sensitively respond to thisness might be found. Without changed policy intervention, the capacity of the rustbelt schools, with their various thisnesses, to make a difference in students' learning is weakened.

However, it is not the case that even in the current straitened circumstances, rustbelt schools cannot make important contributions to the wellbeing of the children and young people in their care. Their capacity to do so is inevitably dependent on the decisions of specifically *education* policymakers. The time-order economy of disadvantaged schools and some of the particular aspects of thisness mean that disadvantaged schools have less time to spend on the greater demands for curriculum, pedagogical and institutional change. They have to do more and depend on educational policymakers for additional resources and support to do so.

5 | Rhetoric and resources

People have every reason to ask what social justice means when their lives are still ruled by constraint and when the places they live in are still badly off compared to the suburbs of the well-to-do. If the same people keep winning, and the same people keep losing, then social justice is further away than ever (Peel, 1995b, p. 64).

In early October 2000, newspapers in the post-industrial city carried two stories about social and educational disadvantage and privilege.

STORY ONE

The first story, the north 'tagged "most vulnerable"' (*Advertiser*, 9 Oct., p. 1), told a tale of a rustbelt suburb struggling to make ends meet. Researchers investigating the geographies of economic vulnerability and opportunity generated a league table of the nation's suburbs. This northern suburbs area topped the list, because it generated only 40c of tax revenue for every $1 in welfare benefits received. This was in stark contrast to a Sydney suburb where $10 of income tax was generated for every $1 in welfare benefits.

In response to this report, an article entitled 'Our riches not counted in cash' appeared the next day (*Advertiser*, 10 Oct., p. 19). The opening sentence set the tone. 'Interstate academics may call us "most vulnerable". But Adelaide's once-upon-a-time satellite city does not see itself that way.' Thereafter followed a series of claims about the benefits of living on the edge of the city (community cohesion, football premierships, schools and space) and the various State Government and local government efforts made to improve services, opportunities and jobs. 'Things are looking up', 'I am optimistic', 'The place will take off', various spokespersons asserted, while politicians of different persuasions acknowledged the need for coordinated action in the face of the effects of micro- and macro-economic change.

Had the various local residents and advocates had the opportunity to read the researchers' press release (University of Queensland News and Views, 2000) on which the first media report was (loosely and selectively) based, they might have seen that the researchers' recommendations—for locally controlled labour market training, public housing that recognised the right of people to choose where they wanted to live, and a program of industrial renewal—closely accorded with their own recommendations for intervention.

STORY TWO

An adjustment to the process of funding for private schools had been sporadically reported on in the *Australian* newspaper for much of 2000. In October it was again in the news. After reports that attacked the Federal Government for favouring wealthy and elite schools, the newspaper published a league table of the funds to be received by the 'oases of privilege'.

The headlines were characterised by emotive appeal—'School for scandal: A windfall for education's elite' (*Weekend Australian*, 9–10 Sept., p. 53). In response, the Federal Education Minister lashed back, 'Lift your game or lose students' (*Australian*, 9 Oct., p. 3). Arguing that his funding index showed that independent schools enrolled significant numbers of low income families just as the State system did, the Federal Minister suggested that State schools needed to 'increase their appeal to average Australians or continue to lose students to the private school systems'. The Federal Opposition argued that government schools would receive on average only an additional $4000 under the new approach while the elite private schools would get an average of $900 000.

According to the Ministerial website http://www.detya.gov.au (DETYA 2000), arguing against the new formula would disadvantage the 70 percent of non-government schools that served low-income communities and imply a return to the previous formula which was complex, able to be manipulated by schools, acted as a disincentive to private effort by penalising schools who raised funds from parents and the community, and ultimately prevented schools from competing fairly in the marketplace. The website text suggested that funding private schools is cheaper for the taxpayer than funding public schools, since only a percentage of the total cost is covered. Further, the most wealthy schools had not had any increase in funds since 1993 and were thus disadvantaged in the market.

These stories and their trajectories from press releases and websites to headlines exemplify some of the difficulties of talking about equity, poverty and resources in these times. There are two important aspects to consider when analysing the different stories.

UNDERSTANDING THE FUNDING LANDSCAPE

Funding for State schooling is a State responsibility. Constitutionally the Federal Government has no role to play. However, the Federal Government does have responsibility for Aboriginal people, immigration, the national economy and the wellbeing of citizens. Federal intervention in State schooling has been justified on the grounds that the Constitution supported actions that would ensure the benefits of Australian citizenship were equally shared. And because most taxation goes to the Commonwealth, States actually do rely on Federal support for State services, including education. In the 1960s the Federal Government specifically funded school libraries and science laboratories to assist State Governments which could not keep up with the postwar building demands, and in the 1970s comprehensive Federal funding for school equity programs began.

Federal funding for private schools also began in the 1960s and was finally consolidated in the early 1980s by a 'needs based' formula that gave all private schools access to Commonwealth funds, but gave the lion's share to the poorest. In the mid-1990s the Federal Liberal Government devised the Enrolment Benchmark Adjustment (EBA) through which funds were directed from public to private schools. Rather than fund on the basis of raw enrolment numbers, the EBA worked on the basis of percentage of 'market share' increase. Federal funding did not follow increased numbers in any sector but the shifts in the ratio of students enrolled in each sector. However, in 2000 the Federal Government adjusted the funding formula for all private schools by developing a new formula also called 'needs based'. After considerable public outcry, additional funds were directed towards public education, but the formula was not changed, thus satisfying the advocates of private school funding.

Federal funding of both State and private schools was, in this incident, narratively connected with processes of nation building, fiscal equalisation and with rhetorics of redistribution and fairness. Histories of public debate about the funding issue, which had always been acrimonious and divisive, were summoned up and deep-seated beliefs about religion, the State and 'freedoms' were called on. At the same time, very few people had access to the actual formulas used to determine funding allocations and had to rely on the media and politicians for their interpretation of policy.

TAKING NOTE OF THE PROCESSES OF MEDIA-TION

The media is an important media-tor of images, impressions and meanings. The search for the angle, the quotable quote, the strong narrative with few subplots and a central conflictual situation plays out in paradoxical ways. Multilayered analyses are not the stuff of the popular press or television. While rustbelt residents want to see stories about their neighbourhoods that reflect their multiple realities and the diversity of their situations, not a single snapshot, this is unlikely to occur unless in response to an alleged misrepresentation. As Bourdieu (1984, p. 253) says, '. . . the reality of the social world is in fact partly determined by the struggles between agents over the representation of their positions in the social world, and consequently, of that world'. That struggle often occurs in and through the media.

Those who live in places described as disadvantaged heartily resent the frequent portrayals of them, their families and neighbours as needy, welfare dependent, poor, unemployed and as objects for academic perusal, policy intervention and public sympathy. However, these residents and the researchers and activists who speak on their behalf can get little political attention, policy action and desperately needed resource flows if they are silent and invisible. Stories that emphasise the capacity of the disadvantaged to organise and do things for themselves bring no extra government support or services and often work to reinforce the view that nothing is amiss. The only way to get the attention of the media or policymakers is to have 'a story' to tell, most commonly one of need and desperation. This is a representation tangle that bedevils much equity advocacy and grass-roots political activism.

The media also renders politicians vulnerable to representations of themselves and their policies as self-serving, greedy, unjust and elitist. In order to remain elect-able politicians must be in the public eye and this means performing and providing reportable and watchable copy. A political attack and counterthrust are almost inevitably the way to maintain political profile. But there is little political control over how the media deals with political debates, and the public gaze can just as easily be negative as affirming. Having ready answers, batteries of figures and apparent logic are the only defences against the autonomous interpretations of journalists and editors. As often as not, this leads to convolutions of logic and euphemism which counterproductively reduce even further the public standing of government decisionmakers.

But while the media can be seen as constitutive of politics, culture and social relations, and politics as the exercise of cultural power, the media should not be mistaken for the source of political divides (Street, 1997).

RHETORICS OF 'DISADVANTAGE'

When debates about equity are media-ted, some bizarre rhetoric results. In the two stories outlined at the beginning of this chapter, there are significant twists: who is asserting the right to be seen as disadvantaged? And who is arguing that they have the future at their feet?

In the course of the debates following the new funding formula, advocates for increased government funding of private schooling laid claim to particular educational rights—the right to choose to attend a non-government school and the right to receive government support for the costs of that schooling. The rationale for these rights, as represented in newspapers, was/is that the ability to choose schooling is a fundamental freedom in a democratic society and that any restriction of that freedom would be an infringement of liberty. If these rights were/are hindered in any way then the individuals affected will be disadvantaged compared to those who have unrestricted choice. What is more, the argument goes, those who choose to go to private schools were/are disadvantaged if their entitlement to government funding is lesser than others. They will be penalised for exercising their right to choose. It is on the basis of this logic, which works to suggest that everyone operates on a level playing field, in which everyone has equal rights and needs, that those who attend and support high-fee elite private schools claim that they are disadvantaged if they do not receive the government funds to which they are entitled, and to which they are indeed only laying a partial claim, since they are still prepared to make private contributions to the costs of education.

The discourse of privilege thus takes to itself notions of disadvantage, discrimination, equity and need. For good measure, in this particular example, the Minister also added into the discourse of 'privileged disadvantage' two syllogisms: (1) 'if you don't like this funding formula then it means you want what we had before'—as if there were only two options possible; and (2) 'arguing against the wealthy 30 percent of private schools getting government funds means the more needy 70 percent of private schools won't get any either'— as if there was no other option than to fund all non-government schools, rather than perhaps just some.

This appropriation of the discourse of disadvantage by the privileged and their advocates contrasts sharply with the reported concerns of the northern suburbs residents. The north is a locality which, on stable and credible measures of hardship, emerges as the most disadvantaged in the nation, but whose spokespeople wanted to avoid all mention of the word disadvantage and assert instead their assets and advantages. It is hardly surprising that this is the case. The popular and public demonisation of particular localities is a phenomenon not confined to this post-industrial city, but is symptomatic of the way in which geographical regions come to be a generic label for social 'problems'. Various oppositions—good/bad, neglect/concern, crude/refined, brutality/finesse, ugliness/beauty—underpin such categorisations in which 'the people become the problem, rather than social structures, policies or power relations' (Powell, 1993, p. 7). It was the labelling of a whole city and its people to which the northern suburbs residents responded, knowing from experience that words do matter.

What is at stake here in the taking up of a 'discourse of disadvantage' is the effect of the words: these are different for different people in different places and spaces. For high-fee private schools and their peak bodies, the 'discourse of disadvantage' potentially brought significant benefits in the form of additional funds with which to extend facilities, technology provisions, co-curricular activities and more and better qualified teachers. For the residents of the northern suburbs the 'discourse of disadvantage' brought unwanted consequences as well as policy attention. Being a 'disadvantaged' or 'vulnerable' area means: fewer companies prepared to invest in the area and fewer jobs; static housing markets; teachers and other public-sector workers choosing to work in more comfortable locations; assumptions made by employers about job applicants' capacities based on their postcode or school attended; and satirisation on television programs as the home of all things uncultured and kitsch. The stigmatisation of classed localities leaves little room for manoeuvre, and it is understandable that, rather than try to persuade the media-tors of an alternative and complex reality, the spokespeople for the area chose, in this instance as in many others, to simply reject and deny the representation.

Ironically, their rejection also obscured the local landscape and the material reality of everyday life in the rust belt.

Rust-belt schools are not on a level playing field with those in more privileged and leafy locales. There *are* stark differences between schools that serve the very poorest in the country, those that occupy a funding middle ground, and those that provide for the wealthy. This is the story that supporters of blanket increases in private school funding sought to silence, and it is the story that rustbelt residents and their teachers struggle to say in words that do not harm them further.

A RESOURCE HIERARCHY

Australian State schools, like those in many other countries, have never been equal. Despite their commonality as belonging to 'the public education system', there have always been schools that have been disadvantaged relative to others.

In the late 1960s and early 1970s there were many Australian State schools in working-class neighbourhoods in which classes were taught in corridors, in which rooms were overcrowded and in which facilities were few (Roper, 1970). Over time, the combined efforts of State and Federal Governments eliminated the very worst facilities and equipment deficits in State schools, and there are now none that match the desperate state of US urban ghetto schools (e.g. Devine, 1996; Kozol, 1991, 1996). Many Australian schools in poorer neighbourhoods have been upgraded and enjoy new teaching areas, gymnasiums, pleasant if not elaborately landscaped surrounds and sufficient rooms to comfortably house all students. A handful even have architecturally noteworthy new buildings that push at the boundaries of what is expected in and of pedagogical spaces. Yet others do still have inadequate grounds, substandard laboratories, insufficient teaching spaces and portable buildings held together by running repairs and layers of paint.

In the 1990s, the burden of raising funds for upgrading increasingly fell to schools themselves. School councils across the state shouldered responsibility for everything from window cleaning to the purchase of new carpets and air-conditioning, right through to the building of substantial sports and performing arts facilities. The story with equipment was the same. Government funds supplied to individual schools failed to keep pace with inflation and the escalating demands for new technologies, better and bigger library collections, up-to-date science equipment and modern teaching aids. Even basics such as paper and pencils cost more. Pressure on school budgets was passed on to parents, who were increasingly asked to make up for shortfalls in funds as well as paying to meet the rise in their expectations of what constituted a quality education.

Such private contributions are congruent with the Australian welfare assistance state which asks everybody to make a contribution to public services. But public schooling was an integral part of the social wage, and historically such individual contributions were kept to a minimum. Contemporary neoliberal policymakers reject the social wage and emphasise self-insurance; their credo is that people should look after themselves, that the state cannot afford to have an unbalanced budget and must rein in expenditure by expecting those who can to contribute for things which they may formerly have paid next to nothing for (see Chapter 3). According to this ideology, public education is a private benefit, not a welfare service. Federal Government policy promotion of private schooling simply emphasises the notion of schooling as an individual 'positional good' (Marginson, 1997b).

This escalating reliance of all State schools on parent contributions occurs at the same time as the shift away from the policy recognition of social context and economic and social disadvantage. Focussing on the choices of parents hides the fact that the relations of distinction are being exacerbated in the new harsh resource regime. Old privileges are being strengthened and deeper divisions carved out.

SCHOOL FUNDING: THE BIASES

Within the State school budget, funds are divided between centralised functions and schools, with schools receiving the largest proportion, allocated on a per capita basis. The school allocation (most of which is for staffing) has some habitual, 'taken for granted' inbuilt biases:

- Big schools get more than small ones, even though there has recently been an adjustment in the State for size and rurality;
- Secondary schools get more than primary schools. This is a historical rather than a costs-based calculation. When these allocations were decided there were set textbooks and little equipment required for the very general primary curriculum

and it was perhaps less unreasonable. Today all students require considerable equipment and expertise.

- The generally bigger size of secondary schools means that they have a double advantage over small primary schools.
- Some students attract more per capita funding—in particular, Aboriginal students and those requiring special education.

Different resource capacities, both in staffing and in finance, are built into the general allocations at the outset. These interact with the shifts brought about by increased emphasis on parent contributions.

PAYING FOR EDUCATION

Since the 1970s, State schools have typically set a 'school fee', the exact amount determined by the parent-dominated school council, to cover loan of textbooks, excursions, copying, library books, sports equipment and the like. This was not legally enforceable and schools were, in theory at least, unable to penalise students whose parents refused to voluntarily pay.

In the late 1990s, some State Governments moved to make the voluntary charge legally compulsory. In the post-industrial city, the attempt to legislate for State school fees caused considerable public debate, media attention and contention amongst state school principals. Headlines such as 'School fee boycott' (*Sunday Mail*, 1 Nov. 1998, pp. 1, 2), 'Teachers oppose fee push' (*Advertiser*, 9 June 1998, p. 14), and 'Fight over school debts' (*Sunday Mail*, 25 Jan. 1998, p. 7) indicate the level of heat generated by the move. Some State schools began to use debt collection agencies and small claims courts to recover the 'school fee', and many State schools asked for more than the government-recommended limit. This again produced headlines—'School sues family over unpaid fees' (*Advertiser*, 28 Mar. 1998, p. 1). Government attempts to make fees compulsory were at first narrowly defeated by the parliamentary opposition. Eventually, the voluntary 'goods and services' charge schools asked at the beginning of the school year was enshrined in administrative guidelines to schools and then passed through the legislative process at the end of 2000.

This State Government was the first in Australia to formally decide that public education is not free. Both State and private schools now officially have fees, and the day-to-day running costs in State schools are now covered by an income derived from government grants (the global budget), parent contributions and fundraising.

Ready comparisons between State and private schools, now that fees are expected in both sectors, are regularly reported in newspapers. Some use figures that are eye-poppingly large to make their case. A typical report, 'School costs soar' (*Sunday Mail*, 23 Jan. 1999), went this way:

> This year, parents can expect to pay an average of $7000 in extras—such as textbooks, uniforms, travel and sport—no matter which school system they choose. But the gap between private and public education appears to be widening with private school education costing 16 times more than the government scheme. Australian Scholarship Group spokesman Terry O'Connell notes: 'An average family with two children can expect to pay nearly $340 000 in two years for private education or over $56 000 for government schooling.'

Importantly, the differentials in parent contribution are not confined to those between the public and private system. Within the private system there are high- and low-fee schools. These also appear in the State system, where they map onto the existing geographies of distinction.

STATE SCHOOL FEES

Because many Australian parents cannot afford to pay any school fees (Australian Government, 1997), there is some assistance available for particularly poor families in this State. Children whose parents cannot pay are entitled to a line of credit at the school to cover basic school expenses.[1] But like free lunches in the United Kingdom and the United States, this 'line of credit' still serves to label the students who receive such assistance and, no matter how carefully handled by the school, to humiliate parents. Importantly, the scheme does provide a guaranteed income for the schools.

Rustbelt schools typically set their school fees at the level of the credit given to its students, which means that they set fees below those asked in leafy green locations, where schools have been raising their fees at quite a fast rate. Here is a snapshot as reported in the local newspaper in the late 1990s:

> Eastern secondary school A: annual fees rose from $330 in 1997, to $380 in 1998, to $420 in 1999.
> Eastern secondary school B: annual fees rose from $320 in 1997, to $380 in 1998, to $400 in 1999.
> Northern secondary school A: annual fees rose from $190 in 1997, to $200 in 1998, to $205 in 1999.

Northern secondary school: annual fees are just below average for secondary schools and below that of Eastern primary C, which charged $195 in 1997 and increased its fees to $220 in 1998 (taken from *Advertiser*, 22 Jan. 1998, pp. 1 & 2 and 16 Nov. 1998, p. 6).

By 2000, several of the better off State secondary schools were asking parents to contribute around $500 per child. Rustbelt secondary school fees lagged behind at around the $200 mark. In 2001 the occasional leafy, green secondary school had upped the ante to closer to $1000 per child inclusive of camps, 'voluntary contributions' special levies, year books and the like. Thus, despite the safety net of the line of credit for approved poor students in all schools, and some redress in global budgets for disadvantaged schools, differential parent contributions exacerbate the gap between these schools and their privileged counterparts. The different capacities of schools to raise funds over and on top of fees, through activities such as sponsorship, fundraising and the like, only adds further distance between the comfortable and the vulnerable.

This increasing gulf between schools in wealthy and poorer areas has prompted principals to call for an increase in the welfare subsidy for poor families (Lloyd, 1998a). It has also caused Opposition politicians to demand increases in levels of State funding for state schools, and welfare groups to warn that the very poorest can now barely afford to keep their children in school (Brotherhood of St Lawrence, 1998; Gibson, 1998; The Smith Family, 1998).

MINDING THE GAP

When principals meet in professional or collegial groups, school resources are almost always an item of discussion. What appear to be small amounts of money translate into tangible differences between schools.

> I look at colleagues' budgets and I can't believe the amount of leeway they've got. Here we get down to the last cent. And if the budget's out you have to go back and rework it. It's not a matter of saying, 'Yes, we've got $5000 to get somebody trained in this new literacy program', it's an absolutely major decision. You don't have this lovely amount of money that just sits in the bank growing (primary school principal).

Rustbelt principals are often silenced in the face of tales of need and disadvantage emanating from other parts of town. But principals who have transferred from rustbelt schools to leafy, green areas can become powerful advocates for their colleagues: 'It's money and resources here like to blow your mind . . . I keep thinking if a teacher dares to come and say, "We haven't got this" or "We haven't got that"— I just want to say, "Don't open your mouth"' (secondary school principal). They discuss the real differences between schools with the voice of authority and experience: 'When I moved to this school I opened the freezer door in the Home Economics Centre and it was full of chicken fillets. At my old [rustbelt] school we used to use mince, mince and mince—*when* we actually cooked' (secondary school deputy).

But understanding and acceptance of the actual differences between State schools is not universal. Because all State schools have less funds than they want, the pleas of rustbelt schools become minority voices among the many crying for a bigger share of State resources.

Lack of funds in rustbelt schools means less money for computers, copiers, projectors, tape recorders, televisions. It means less money for art materials and basic classroom materials, such as paper and pencils. It means less funds for copying, internet access, visits by performers, excursions and professional development programs for staff. Rustbelt school staffs acutely feel the deficiencies in their capacity to provide as well for children as they know they might.

> It's about the students not having access to as many resources in their homes—technology is an obvious issue—we try to ameliorate that by having a bank of laptops that the kids can borrow and they're heavily used. But at the moment we can only afford to have eight of those in a school of 850 [students] (secondary school principal).

Rustbelt principals despair of *ever* being able keep up with the kinds of access to information technology they feel their students have a right to. They query a Government policy that sets a standard for the provision of information technology, a ratio of five students to every computer in each school, but then fails to ensure that all schools are in a position to provide it.

> We've got one computer room and we've maintained that for a while. About a year ago we replaced [the computers]. The old computers have gone into classrooms, so we've got one computer per classroom, plus the room of fifteen plus a few other odd ones scattered around. If you're looking at the State policy of one computer for every five students, well we're nowhere near that. We're at the limit of our budget. We're putting a huge amount of money into computers each year. It's hard to see how we can extend that unless we just keep hold

of very old computers and hope they don't break down . . . I don't think we can afford the one-to-five ratio of the latest and up-to-date. I don't think we could ever manage that (primary school principal).

The disparity in income, equipment and plant is repeated across rustbelt schools and their more wealthy counterparts with multiple variations—a shifting differential of numbers of novels, footballs, laboratory chemicals, cleaning equipment, play equipment and numbers and age of tables and chairs.

A spatial economy is manifested in bank balances, buildings, equipment and consumables and it all too neatly maps onto other maps of privilege and disadvantage.

GETTING BY

Rustbelt schools rely not only on government funds; they also depend on getting the school fees from the minority of parents ineligible for government support. But many of these parents are only marginally over the poverty line and are financially stretched to the point where school fees are often last on a long list of annual expenses. Some parents refuse to pay school fees. There are some who fervently believe that public education should be free and that there should be no fees at all. They take their concerns to the local member of parliament and the newspaper making the question of disadvantage visible again, in another ambiguous iteration.

For rustbelt schools, there is the vexed matter of how to deal with those who don't pay. Each principal has to deal with a variety of staff and parent opinions about what is locally referred to as the school 'debt'. And those parents who pay their fees often feel that they are subsidising those who do not.

It causes tension particularly on school council; those parents who pay school fees, they can't understand why these people can't forgo a couple of packets of cigarettes to pay it . . . One teacher here was at a wealthier school last year and he said they didn't have a problem there. People paid up because that's what they felt morally that they were meant to do. Here it's a huge joke—'We're not going to pay it', especially since there's precious little you can do (primary school principal).

Some rustbelt schools do institute policies of withdrawing school supplies and activities for children whose parents are in 'debt'. 'I'm quite tight on not letting them run up bills for excursions and things like that. I hate to see kids miss out but we've got to make a stand somewhere. The school can't keep covering all of those things' (primary school principal).

Others find debt collection or withdrawal of privileges unacceptable because it punishes children for parents' decisions, implicitly endorses the notion that fees in public education are acceptable, and is not only counterproductive but time wasting. 'Why in the hell should you have to hound people about $2 for the excursion when you could spend your time far better elsewhere?' (primary school principal).

Regardless of what decision is made, the lack of funds and the lack of payment of fees in rustbelt schools causes tensions and ongoing debates about poverty and public education that more wealthy schools do not have to face. These debates go directly to the values of all of those involved in the school site.

> I've got secretarial staff who are in the front line in the office who believe that if you are efficient and get the money in from people then you're doing your job well. And so even yesterday I got a swag of letters of demand to go out to parents about why they haven't paid their fees and half of them are the Aboriginal parents in the school and I just refused to sign them. What I've got to do now is work out how I have this conversation in ways that don't make me look like I'm favouring the Aboriginal parents (secondary school principal).

Each school population has heterogeneous views about poverty:

- The poor are wilful and could help themselves if they only wanted to and are bludging on the rest.
- Everybody should be treated equally regardless of their social and economic circumstances and to treat anybody differently is to be discriminatory.
- Governments have a responsibility to look after those most in need and State schools should embody this commitment.

The imperative to reach resolution on these big political questions is right inside rustbelt schools, fracturing and fragmenting interpersonal networks and alliances in ways that were less apparent when school budgets went further and there was less pressure to find money. The politics of disadvantage pit parent against parent, school staff members against each other, and staff members against parent. What is at stake is the capacity of each rustbelt school to come to some consensus about how to manage ethically when there isn't enough to go around.

GETTING MORE

Rustbelt schools have a limited range of strategies they can employ to obtain more funds. They can work to:

- Attract more students through better promotion. Precious dollars are spent on brochures, newspaper and radio advertisements, new foyers and making cosmetic changes to public areas of the school.
- Attract more students by tailoring the curriculum to meet niche markets, for example, with vocational specialisations for parents worried about unemployment; gifted and talented programs for parents concerned that State schooling is unchallenging and a lesser option than high-fee private schools; or catering specifically for students who are most heavily funded in global budgets, namely Aboriginal and special education students.
- Obtain sponsorship, if they are fortunate enough to be in a locality where a sponsor with ready cash is available. One school's sponsorship gain however is often others' loss, and many interschool relationships are crushed in the sponsorship rush.
- Chase grants, thus skewing school priorities and programs towards those which are readily fundable. Grant getting thus engages with policy steering at a distance, via financial incentive/coercion.
- Work harder at fundraising. This is usually unsuccessful since the rustbelt neighbourhoods generally have even less disposable income than the school. And fundraising can be both unsuccessful and dispiriting, no matter how much goodwill it generates.

> I heard on the weekend of a private school fete that raised $60,000 in one day, and our total fundraising—we'd be lucky to raise a couple of thousand. And we'd have to work very hard for it. We busted our little boilers last year and the committee got themselves organised and it took nine months and we got $3000 and we got curtains for two rooms (primary school principal).

Senior State school education bureaucrats are not sympathetic to complaints about the inequalities of fundraising. One school system chief executive commented:

> The . . . criticism is that schools rely more heavily on local fundraising then ever before. The fact is that school fundraising accounts for about 4 to 5 percent of total school disposable income. I have to say

that to ignore teacher salaries as part of school operating funds, as some critics do, is a pretty shaky way to approach things. Teachers account for about 87 percent of a schools' resources (Spring, 1997).

From the top of the pyramid, a difference of $100 or $200 per student head must indeed look tiny, compared to the overall education budget. However, at the bottom, in the classroom, the everyday effects loom large. 'You know we're down to four practicals instead of ten in home economics in a semester of twenty weeks, just because of the cost of the ingredients' (secondary school principal).

Arguing for more money in public is difficult. Any appeals to colleagues, bureaucrats and politicians depend on being able to produce detailed information about the size and consequences of 'debt'. This amounts to a statement about how it is that students in the rust belt are not getting as good an education as they might. In volatile political climates in which criticism of the public education system is an everyday occurrence, in the face of potential media beat-ups, in the light of a school market in which exit is encouraged by the rhetoric of right of choice, this is a risky strategy. Furthermore, many principals hesitate to tell their students and parents that they could enjoy better facilities, equipment and more varied programs in other wealthier localities.

The effects of taking up the discourse of disadvantage are as un-attractive as the known effects of saying nothing.

SUMMING UP

The rustbelt schools are part of a Federal funding system which has created resource differences between public and private schools. They are also part of a State education system in which inadequate funding levels combine with the policy of encouraging parent contributions to schools to produce systemic and systematic difference. This simultane-ously increases the gap between rustbelt schools and others, and makes it increasingly difficult for these schools to argue on the basis of need, since broadly based definitions of need are no longer recognised as a legitimate policy matter. The fissure between what rustbelt schools can do and what their students both need and deserve is rapidly widening.

What exists as State and Federal funding practice is not a resources distribution technology for reducing dis/advantage and distinction. It is not more resources for doing more. Rather it is a technology that both consolidates and enhances the differing capacities of schools to provide all children with equal life chances.

6 | Staffing matters

> *Teachers' work is defined by the social and political policies of the particular time, it is never a question of defining technical skills alone (Lawn, 1986, p. 153).*

Salaries for teachers and support staff are the largest component of the total State education budget. They are the biggest single budget item for central office, district services and schools. Not only the policies of the progressive 1960s and 1970s but also those of the managerial 1980s and 1990s relied on the teacher as the most important resource in the system and the classroom as the basic 'unit' of reform. What varied over time and policy regime were the degrees of autonomy and professionalism afforded to teachers in their work.

It is no surprise that in the rust belt, teachers and support staff are seen as the key to 'doing justice' in the schools. If schools are to deal with increasingly diverse families, many of whom are struggling to cope with escalating costs and diminishing supports and services, at the same time as they are to change their curricula and pedagogies and become more 'effective', then staffing is the key.

SYSTEM RESPONSE-ABILITY

States have given various degrees of autonomy to schools to decide on the composition and mix of staffing and to select their teachers and support staff, and none has made the move to hire and fire at the local level. One of the major reasons for the retention of centralised systems of recruitment, placement and transfer is geographical. In Australia, the vast and thinly populated rural areas contain many small, isolated schools and a few larger regional ones. By far the most efficient way to ensure that they all have teachers is via a central system. In each State, an elaborate code of industrially negotiated incentives works imperfectly to provide largely young and inexperienced teachers and administrators to the very many 'hard to staff' country and rustbelt postings.

The centralised staffing system in the post-industrial city's State is bedevilled by its own ongoing problems. These include the following.

- *Historical biases that are difficult to industrially renegotiate*
  State primary schools get fewer teachers than State secondary schools. Primary schools are generally smaller and are organised into home classes in which children remain most of the time, whereas secondary schools are organised around subject specialisations. Senior secondary students get more generous staffing than junior secondary because the post-compulsory curriculum is thought to demand more expertise and personal attention.

- *Short and longer term supply and demand problems*
  There is a shortage of teachers in the country and a surplus in the city; a shortage of secondary teachers in particular disciplines; an aging teaching labour force with overall shortages predicted to begin within the next five years; a reducing number of applicants for principal positions; and an oversupply of young teaching graduates in the city who rapidly get tired of short-term contracts and find other work at home or abroad.

  Tinkering with the centralised central staffing system began in the 1970s, with the first merit-based selection for positions as administrators of large and complex schools. Over time, a system of locally advertised merit-based promotion and teaching positions has been created, with the majority of schools now able to advertise and locally select nearly all of their administrative and middle management positions. However, some schools— those in the country and in the rust belt—find it difficult to attract applicants and must rely heavily on the central system.

  Rustbelt schools find that there are few applicants for the positions they advertise and the advantages of the local selection system work less well for them than other schools. They have a number of young teachers on contracts of various lengths and experienced teachers on temporary placements.[1] These schools were not always like this. When they were newly built and served the children of the workers in newly established manufacturing industries, rustbelt schools were not seen as undesirable postings.

> There were a fair number of people for whom this was their first school and they bought houses in the area and they lived in the area and they were part of the community and they saw the changes as they went on . . . they had an understanding of the school and what the cultures were (secondary school deputy principal).

Within the memory of teachers still in the system, the rust belt was once somewhere they too might choose to live, as well as work. In stark contrast to this more settled past, there are now two overriding concerns for the rustbelt schools—achieving staff stability and attracting the right staff.

STAFFING STABILITY

Many rustbelt schools experience considerable staffing turbulence. The magnitude of 'turnover' in disadvantaged schools is considerable. One secondary school which, through combinations of leave, promotion and transfer, had seven different principals in the last ten years and over 30 people in three deputy principal positions is a typical case. Staffing *churn* is no simple problem to resolve, since the needs of teachers as well as children and the schools must be balanced.

> A number of teachers are coming up towards their seventh, eighth year and they said to me, 'I'm putting in a transfer, it's not because I'm not happy here at the school, it's the travel. But it is tiring in our classrooms and it is really draining.' They said, 'I want to take some control, I'm putting in a transfer form'. Well just about everybody who put in a transfer form has got their first preference. So we've got five new staff and some of those are temporary and that's partly bad luck and it's partly because we've got falling enrolment, so you keep that flexibility up so that you're not facing having to get rid of people. And last year we had—we are a small school—270 kids, we had a staff of fifteen full-time equivalent, and we said farewell to eleven teachers. That's hard to do, year after year. And the junior primary's the same. The last two years they've had 50 percent turnover of staff (primary school principal).

Such movement in and out of the school makes it difficult for children to establish relationships with their teachers.

> The kids would be saying to their teachers at the end of last term, 'Are you going to be here next year?' And it's like they don't trust you until you're there, until they know that a teacher's going to be there and want to be there and stay there . . . one little kid said to me the other day, 'Are you going to stay here forever with us?', and it was just that business of knowing the people and knowing you are going to be here . . . (primary school principal).

Staffing turbulence also makes it extremely difficult to establish trust between the school and its parent communities. This trust and familiarity is a very important aspect of managing everyday discipline and welfare demands.

> This is my fourth year and I have to say that this year is a lot better. I think I've developed a lot of credibility. I've basically had the school rebuilt and it looks good and parents are proud about the look of the school. I know all of the parents now and I've had something to do with most of them so there's a kind of relationship there. But I've been screamed and shouted at and I've felt quite intimidated by the parents' anger and hostility and aggressiveness. In my first year and a bit I was really surprised by the level of aggression. So I think that the development of the relationships are absolutely critical for teachers and parents and for deputy and principal. And it takes time, you have to be there for a while, you have to have developed some credibility, you have to demonstrate you're fair and that you will listen and follow things up, so it's less of a problem now, touch wood (primary school principal).

Most teachers do not live in the rust belt. Local parents see their children's teachers come in and out of their neighbourhood every day like the tide. They see the overall movement of staff from term to term and year to year. They see teachers who are reluctant to build connections, to engage with them and the school from which the teachers know they will sooner or later move. They see those teachers who stay in their children's school struggle to support the waves of newly appointed. Why is it that our school can't keep teachers, they often ask. It is little wonder that working-class parents question how much the State school system has their children's best interests at heart.

Staffing churn undermines ongoing reform projects based in common understandings, since the sharing of beliefs and dreams necessary for collaborative work is always beginning again. Teachers who stay in the rust belt for more than a couple of years get tired of supporting and assisting people new to their schools and then fare-welling them after only a matter of months.

They become inevitably frustrated when the necessary focus on induction for new teachers means that school plans for reform are put on hold. School change is more a pattern of stop start, stop start from year to year.

THE RIGHT STAFF

Rustbelt school principals become quite obsessed with ensuring that students have teachers who are both keen and well equipped, intellectually and professionally, for the pedagogical challenges of working with their particular school mix. Establishing relationships, dealing with disciplinary and welfare demands as well as actively generating necessary ideas for improvement and working cooperatively with colleagues in a demanding setting, all require both personal and professional dispositions which it seems are not universal among teachers. Current systems[2] to ensure that rustbelt schools get the right staff are less than successful.

These schools compete for teachers with schools in less challenging locations close to teachers' homes. They routinely get only one or two applications for positions which in a middle-class location would receive 30 to 40. School administrators have different experiences of local selection and their attitudes range from luke warm to dismissive.

> Local selection has assisted us to some degree, but it could be a lot better . . . we get one person a year. I think for any position in schools like this we should be having a say and people should be coming to us if they want to. There are people in middle-class schools who want to transfer into these schools and I quite frankly don't know if I'd want to keep anyone who didn't want to be here . . . I prefer the [centrally managed] temporary placement scheme . . . it's like, 'Come into the school, have a taste of it, let us have a taste of you, excellent, thanks very much we'll keep you' . . . (primary school principal).

By and large rustbelt schools still get many staff from the central placement system. Some reluctant conscripts are happy with their placement after some initial complaints.

> We have teachers who come from other schools who are put here, who believe they shouldn't be in the school because what right does the Department have to put me in this school—that's the attitude we

work with. We have people who come to us and say, 'I didn't apply
to be here so . . .'. The whole issue of how you work on a yearly cycle
and continue to develop that morale and continually show to them
that you're a good school . . . you work to enable that to happen and
some of them in a term say, 'Yeah, it's a great place to work', and then
they just don't want to leave (secondary school principal).

Others put up with the school, reluctant to engage with the 'place'
where they work, staying on year after year, alienated and unhappy.

The very simplest example is people not even knowing the
geographical location. You talk to teachers who have been teaching
at the school for six years and they'll say, 'Where's the train
station?'—which is five minutes away, and especially when the
station is a focal point for youth mobility, that's where they go when
they go out. So there's that geography, lots of people just don't know
it (secondary school deputy principal).

A proportion of the rustbelt conscripts, however, are hostile and
unprepared to change. Most of them focus on students' behaviour as
the major problem and as the major cause of all difficulties.

There's a blame the kid sort of syndrome and an almost total unwill-
ingness to look at any other reasons for lack of achievement, and it
just seems to have got worse this year—and it's 'Why aren't they
behaving in class?', and if they don't, 'It's their fault' (secondary
school principal).

One common result is a stand-off between teachers and students,
but teacher responses to what they see as kids' inherent bad behaviour
vary. Some lower their expectations.

We have quite a lot of teachers saying, 'We have to excuse kids from
doing any homework because it's not part of their culture', and we
say, 'But how's it going to be? How are we ever going to make any
changes?'—that stuff of patronising poverty, we don't have to have
expectations . . . that's the thing we fight all the time (primary school
principal).

Some see that the only way out for them is for the students to
either change or go. 'We've got more people saying, "Hang on, I'm
climbing the wall here, I'm trying really hard, I've got a life too, get rid
of these kids and I could really teach"' (secondary school principal).

A handful eventually just lash out. Many administrators believe that
the current right–wing political and policy climate has created a culture

that is anti-equity and this filters into schools as permission to refuse to see others' points of view.

> That culture of, oh, it's politically correct and therefore it's wrong. It's having an impact because people are backing kids into corners more, being less tolerant of behaviour that is not appropriate I'll give you that, but let's try to find some semblance of working with a sense of humour and some understanding. The hard-nosed disciplinarian is coming back. That's not what works with difficult kids. They don't need that stuff, they get beaten up enough. There's certainly a different understanding of equity, of justice. Even in the last three years, it's quite different (secondary school principal).

Reluctant teachers take up considerable amounts of their peers' time, administration time and stretch the schools' relationship with parents and students close to breaking point. School councils in rustbelt schools are understandably angry at the system's inability to provide well-qualified and motivated teachers for their children.

But not all rustbelt schools have the same difficulties. Schools in the northern suburbs find it much more difficult to get staff than those in other parts of the city. The major hills-to-sea highway functions like a Maginot line, north of which only a few are prepared to venture. This reluctance is compounded in non-metropolitan locations. Just to put the north of the city into perspective, it is worth mentioning how one regional disadvantaged school principal gets the right staff.

> I spend a lot of time entertaining prospective employees, getting them to come to the town, look around, sending them away, making phone calls all around Australia. The recruiting process has become very big for me and occupies a lot of time. I don't wish to get rid of that because the principal being involved, I believe, is the successful mode. However, it costs a hell of a lot of time. To me, it's just so critical; if you don't have teachers recruited for specific purposes and specific environments, then the kids—and we're not talking about the curriculum and the outcomes and so on because poor teachers can't deliver a good or bad curriculum—that's why it's so important to us. And it has to work. And it costs a lot. And the system is supporting us slightly in that they have told me that they will refund the airfares and accommodation costs of any of those people that I've been getting to come, as long as they take the contract. So that's positive, but it's also a downer because I'm risking the school resources. They should be central resources. But it's been a successful strategy so far. I've only had one person out

of about ten who've come to the school to see say no (secondary school principal).

This is time that the majority of principals do not have to spend, time and money taken away from educational issues.

The experiences of rustbelt schools suggest that simply decentralising employment to the level of the school is not necessarily the best means of getting the right staff, since disadvantaged schools will always attract fewer people than their middle-class counterparts. At the same time, the central system which supplies reluctant teachers in a continuing churn is a major problem.

Principals do want some involvement in the appointment process. However, they also want the system to ensure that they don't miss out, compared to their more affluent colleagues. Many rustbelt principals suggest that some kind of incentive-based scheme, which inevitably categorises and stigmatises the neighbourhood and the school, is so far the best proposed solution on offer. They would live with the label, which they feel they wear anyway, in order to get the right staff.

SIZE MATTERS

Overwhelmingly, and not surprisingly, the issue of the total number of teachers is named as *the* single most important policy issue by rustbelt principals and staffs. When they talk of numbers they do not mean the teacher–student ratio, which most often figures in official counts but which also routinely includes administrative and support staff. What rustbelt school principals mean is the actual average class size in which children and young people find themselves in schools. In order to do more, they say, they must simply have more teaching staff.

The notion of class size is, of course, predicated on the one-teacher, one-class arrangement. It is this age–grade arrangement so integral to the grammar of schooling which is so resistant to change (Tyack & Cuban, 1995). Despite the urgings of school reformers, the occasional move to lectures and tutorials for senior secondary students, and the more common team teaching approach in primary and a few middle schools, one-teacher, one-class is still the norm.

CLASS SIZE

There is no official national data collection of class sizes and not all states routinely find out how many students are in each class. Teacher union and principal association estimates strongly suggest that class size has increased over the last decade. One primary principal reflects:

> I don't think a lot of people realise but we've now got the largest class sizes that we've had throughout my career. When I was in the country it was 25, when I was in the northwest it was down to eighteen. Then, when I went to my last school, it was 26 . . . because we used our negotiable equity staffing—you remember negotiable staffing?—and all the disadvantaged schools used it to reduce class sizes. Now it's up around 30 (primary school principal).

Large class sizes equate, in the minds of the teachers, with a classroom in which the 'best' and 'worst' students get their attention and many students struggle on unhelped.

> Reducing the number of kids per teacher would make a whole lot of things work better, one of which may be academic achievement . . . It would be a courageous political and professional thing to say our schools would just work better with smaller classes, better for the vast majority of kids who go to school most days of the week, who work reasonably hard, who want to get on, their parents want them to get on, their parents support the school, they're the kids whose needs are sometimes not the priority when a class of Year 6s and 7s goes to 29, 30, 31, 32 . . . there are at least fifteen kids who don't get as good a trot as they would if there were 22 or 23 in the class (secondary school principal).

That there are students in the class to whom inadequate attention has been paid because others demanded it more is another aspect of the time-order economy of rustbelt schools. In addition to the effect on students is residual teacher guilt at not having done the very best that they might have for all of their students, as discussed in Chapter 5.

Rustbelt administrators acknowledge that class size is not all that matters and that merely reducing class size will not in itself automatically change things. 'There are some teachers who are more effective with 30 kids than other teachers with 20. I know that. But the effectiveness of *that* teacher when they've got 20 to 25 compared to when they've got 30 . . . or 32—is huge' (primary school principal).

Rustbelt principals deal daily with staff, parents and students who want and need smaller classes.

> I reckon if we were offered the opportunity the staff at the school would very clearly opt for smaller class sizes. Whenever there's any special funding and priorities have to be set around issues, class

size is always discussed . . . What is the reasonableness of putting so many young people together in a crowded environment with a teacher who cannot be reasonably expected to be as on top of the curriculum student-by-student as they might, and hence will resort more to social control than to learning, just out of pure necessity . . . I mean whose needs are being served? Certainly not the kids' (secondary school principal).

People who work in rustbelt schools understand that any reduction in class size is a big budgetary item, and they agree that such reduction must begin in the early years.

The degree to which larger classes *in our sort of school* start to create a whole gamut of problems out of proportion to the actual size . . . that occurs from preschool to somewhere near Year 9 or 10. I suspect that having a formula of having smaller classes at Year 11 and 12 is putting the cart before the horse in some ways, the die is not entirely cast—but it's relatively cast by the time kids get into Year 11 (secondary school principal).

Class size has been a major issue for the teacher union for many years and the focus of many campaigns. To date this agitation has had little or no impact on policy decisionmaking, despite polices having impact on actual numbers of students and teachers. 'Take the issues around overcrowding in classrooms. None of our classrooms are even built big enough for the kids that are in them now, let alone the wheel-chairs!' (secondary school principal).

RESEARCH ON CLASS SIZE

Some scholarly investigations of class size were undertaken in the 1970s and early 1980s. This research 'showed' that it was not until class sizes were reduced to fifteen students that significant gains in student achievement occurred. Subsequent re-readings of this corpus of work reveal that it was based largely on pupil–teacher ratios, not actual class size (Achilles, 1999). Nevertheless, the evidence and the magic number of fifteen has been widely used in Australia by school systems and government ministers as the prime rebuttal to demands by teachers and parents for lower class sizes.

The use of research as a rhetorical club with which to beat teachers and their representatives is often difficult for practising professionals to counter. On the one hand it deepens their scepticism of research—how can findings be so much in conflict with their experience and professional knowledge? On the other hand, they are deeply suspicious of the ways in which the research has been read and understood by policymakers. They also bring other research findings—such as that of Sizer (1985), whose seminal Horace was literally overwhelmed by his typical high school teaching 'load' of some 160 students distributed into six different subject classes—to bear on the question of class size.

I suspect the academic research which is always used to debunk the class size argument is a little too narrowly focussed, and it ignores a whole lot of social learning . . . I think one of the more obvious analyses is to look at how many individual learning programs is it possible for an individual teacher to take overall and close responsibility for, day in day out, week in week out, year in year out . . . there's a degree of human possibility that's attached to it. Certainly for secondary teachers as the number of kids they come in contact with goes from 150 to closer to 200, there's got be a quality drop and I defy anyone to suggest that that wouldn't be the case (secondary school principal).

Policymakers do not seem to have yet caught up with the changing findings around class size. Better data collection and more sophisticated statistical processes are now complemented by smaller scale research projects that get into classrooms and talk with teachers. Contemporary research evidence suggests that class size is a 'contextual variable' which does not directly cause students to learn better and teachers to teach better. Small classes *afford teachers the opportunity* to teach better and students to learn better and are thus necessary, but not sufficient, to effect changes in learning outcomes (see US Department of Education, 2000).

In the United States, many States have now opted for ideal class sizes of under twenty in the early years, and ongoing research suggests that there are likely to be significant gains for students as a result—particularly for students from disadvantaged schools (see Achilles, 1999). Despite 'tracking' problems because of student transience, widely varying teacher qualifications and skills, and difficulties in working with non-equivalent achievement data bases (Class Size Reduction Research Consortium, 2000), the available and emerging evidence seems now to support the teachers in asserting the importance of class size. Furthermore, new and more finely grained research points to student achievement gains because teachers are able to spend more time with students requiring particular assistance and less time on discipline (Nye, Hedges & Konstantanopolous, 1999; Stasz & Stecher, 2000). United States researchers also suggest that the benefits of small class size in the early years can now be seen in high schools and college (Pate-Bain, Fulton & Boyd-Zaharias, 1999).

In the United Kingdom, Galton, Hargreaves and Pell (1996) observed a number of teachers at work in rural schools in classes which varied in size from nine students to 33. They say in words that now resonate strongly with those of rustbelt teachers:

> In smaller classes there is more time spent on task; more sustained interactions; more higher order questioning of pupils; more feedback on work; less time spent on routine supervision; less time spent exercising classroom control; and less time given over to housekeeping (sorting out papers, handing out books, etc.) (Chapter 6).

Pedder (1999), also in the United Kingdom, proposes that in large classes teachers have less scope to choose from their repertoires of teaching strategies in order to maximise academic learning time, because more time is required for both organisational and disciplinary matters. Furthermore, the pedagogical processes which are deployed as class sizes grow become increasingly oriented towards control. Likewise, the ongoing study by Blatchford, Mortimore and Edmonds (2000) suggests that students in smaller classes report fewer social and behavioural difficulties, better peer relations and greater capacity to concentrate in class than those in larger classes. This resonates with one of the more robust and enduring research findings about the (re) production of inequitable learning outcomes in which the need to keep social order is linked with pedagogy. Teachers in disadvantaged schools often have to use teaching methods that combine instruction with the task of establishing and maintaining discipline, but a steady diet of whole group, worksheet, copy and memorise activities has the effect of slowing down the rate of students learning, as well as alienating them (e.g. Anyon, 1980; Freebody, Ludwig and Gunn, 1995; Hill et al., 1998; Sharp & Green, 1975). Achilles and Finn (2000) summarise the findings of the class-size research as significant to improvements in learning, instruction, classroom environment, social order, inclusion, increased parent involvement and more motivated and accountable teachers.

One of the most important findings from US studies is that the relationship between class size and academic, behavioural, social and civic learning is linear—that is, every student less makes a difference to the learning of the whole class (Achilles, 1999). This is very important since the dominant opposition from policymakers to addressing class size has been the budgetary impossibilities of reduction to the magic number fifteen. This finding, in particular, supports a more gradual and phased in policy approach, starting with the first four years of school and the most disadvantaged localities. Some of Australia's State Labor Governments have already begun to move on reducing class size in affordable increments.

The finding of class size research suggests that even though the sorting and selecting practices of schooling advantage some students more than others, the time-order economy of disadvantaged school classrooms may be changed for the better by reducing the number of students to which each teacher may attend. This will allow more opportunities and time for teachers to work on changes to their professional practice(s). However, while these issues should be addressed as soon as possible the quality of teaching and curriculum continue to matter a great deal as well.

STAFFING POLICY

Whether research is supportive or not of their claims for increased staff, rustbelt school administrators are firmly committed to the notion of differential staffing, a redistributive system, in which disadvantaged schools get a meaningfully larger proportion of the available salary budget.

> I'm not a subscriber to the reduced class sizes idea as general principle because why should wealthy primary schools have a reduction in class sizes? I mean it has to be differential. Why should every school in the State have a reduction in class size when some of the funds the wealthy suburbs don't really need could be used here? The millions of dollars that would be needed just to reduce one or two students every class . . . I ask myself why should every school get reduced when that money could make a lot of difference in the schools that really need it (primary school principal).

They also argue that schools should be able to decide how best to utilise that staffing. For some this would mean a simple reduction in class size. For others, it would mean first of all tackling some of the issues that most distract teachers from teaching.

> We need a differential staffing, if it means more counselling time, those kind of supports. I see the school counsellor's role not there to manage the crises, it's more providing students with the social skills and running class meetings to maximise participation and management of their own learning. I'd like to see us have more support in that way (primary school principal).

Rustbelt school principals understand that decisions about funding are linked to questions of State and Federal budgets and to wider questions about political priorities. This knowledge just adds to their frustration as they, like many other citizens, feel relatively powerless to influence the economic directions of governments.

> I'm not aware of anything that is around at the moment that would give me confidence in policy support or policy directions to address what it's like in schools. And I don't want to sound like they don't know anything about us in there in central office, because I don't think that's true. I've worked in those jobs and they take it very seriously, and people in central positions do know a lot about what goes on in schools but they've just got different tugs at them . . . and one of the tugs at the bureaucracy is the political climate and while that's how it is, I don't see that they've [central office] got much room to move (primary school principal).

Senior system officers and government ministers and their advisers in the post-industrial city do not appear to agree that class size is a policy lever to address disadvantage. To date they have been deaf to the pleas and arguments that rustbelt schools need more to do more, and are currently doing more with less. They have firm and affordable ideas of their own about what will make a difference. They have swung away from broad notions of reform towards more tightly focussed structural and instructional projects.

7 | The policy terrain

A society that condones excesses of poverty in the midst of wealth, or arbitrarily rewards one skill with one hundred times the wages of another, is not recognising its citizens as of equal human worth (Phillips, 1999, p. 131).

Like many nations, Australia has struggled to adapt to the changing kaleidoscope of seamless communication networks, digital divides, unstable borders, emerging world trading blocs and shifting strategic alliances. Like those in the United States and United Kingdom, Australian policymakers have seen education as an increasingly important national issue, one integrally related to continued economic, political and cultural wellbeing. The move of education to the centre stage of national policy began more than a decade ago and was signalled by the publication of *Australia Reconstructed* (ACTU/TD, 1985). *Australia Reconstructed* was the result of a joint government and trade union visit to Germany. The Australian visitors were highly impressed with the ways in which German education and training was integrated through an apparently seamless movement through schools, training providers and universities. An enviable position in the global marketplace was apparently due to the innovation and productivity made possible through this integrated and national education and training system.

The Australian version was conceived by the Federal Labor Government and its associates, and driven through a series of national agreements between States, business and trade unions. Throughout the 1980s and 1990s, education and training increasingly came to be a principal policy lever for the national micro-economic reform deemed necessary for international economic competitiveness.

TRAINING (THE) SCHOOLS

The Federal Hawke-Keating Labor Government embarked on an ambitious project to modernise the education and training systems to bring them closer to its imaginary of an educational engine driving the machinery of globally competitive industries. The metaphor of disparate pieces welded into a seamless whole was dominant in a welter of policymaking documents and speeches.

The State-based education and training systems were seen as too subject to local vagaries and whims, analogous to the narrow and wide gauge railway lines adopted by different States which were later detached from their parochially focussed State owners and forged into one national system. The testy Commonwealth and State negotiations about schools and technical and further education were not so easily resolved as railways. The new unified national solution came into effect through the development of national ministerial councils, policies, agreements and working parties. A 'new era' of Federal–States relations was attempted.

No educational sector was left untouched by the new 'globalised nation-alism'. A 'unified' university system was established, obliterating the hierarchical two-tier system in a move reminiscent of the comprehensivisation of secondary schools (see Chapter 2). The old colleges of advanced education specialising in education and nursing became the new universities, and all universities were vigorously encouraged to amalgamate and create efficiencies of size, scale and scope. The Higher Education Contribution Scheme (HECS—a form of fees) was introduced, undoing the concept of free tertiary education which had been the source of such pride to the previous welfare-state oriented Whitlam Labor Government. HECS was, however, still in line with a welfare assistance philosophy of part payment for public services. A national qualifications framework, similar to ones developed in New Zealand, Scotland and England, created the massive architecture for a new system of education and training which articulated courses and awards between schools, training and universities. It allowed private training providers to enter the training market and offered the mechanisms for their accreditation and registration. At the heart of this new agenda was a commitment to new relationships between industry and education resulting in new forms of workplace learning and accredited training in schools and further education, and a focus on applied learning and research in universities.

Policy attention swung resolutely to 'producing the goods', and being seen to do so. National goals for schooling were written and agreed to by the State education ministers who were constitutionally responsible for schools but were by then largely dependent on the Federal Government for considerable funding through block grants to States as well as specific educational budgetary allocations. A national curriculum, consisting of curriculum statements and 'profiles' (anticipated outcomes), was painstakingly written and variously adopted by States. In the training sector, assessment focussed increasingly on what people could do, their 'competencies'. In schooling, new forms of outcomes-based and competency-based courses were developed. The resulting grids of outcomes became a curriculum technology through which student results could be measured and reported to parents, systems and potentially the public. The distribution of learning outcomes among the population were to become the measure of equity. Thus, equity and justice agendas were framed by and within the economic imperatives and corporatist agendas of government and competition state practices.[1]

In 1996, the newly elected Federal Liberal Government headed by John Howard, running on a platform of 'freedom from' government interference through 'social engineering', and 'freedom of choice', ended a number of equity school projects but maintained the policy focus on schooling and outcomes.

(NEO)LIBERAL POLICY DIRECTIONS

The Federal Liberal Government made a number of adjustments to the educational policy regime of the former Labor Government. Policy reform decisions, which had already shifted under the Labor regime from the public bureaucracies to government, took place only at the ministerial level with working groups of officials largely bound to confidentiality. Decisions were made well away from teacher and parent organisations, which were dubbed self-serving and unrepresentative of 'mainstream' teachers and parents. Equity advocates were also *verboten*. Federal Liberal policymakers, in another example of global policy borrowing, adopted the charge of 'political correctness' and the 'multi-cultural/aboriginal/equity/parent industry' used by the US and UK right[2] to remove peak organisations from the policy stage. The Liberal Government was, of course, still partisan: it just had an alternative set of favourite consultants, including principals' associations, the mining industry and farmers. The 'closed shop' of decisionmaking and increased use of the media to make policy announcements in order to get political advantage meant that many parents, teachers and school principals felt powerless and removed from positions where they could understand and influence both national and State education policy (Thomson, 1998a).

Institutional reform in school education initiated by this Federal Government included the following initiatives.

Expansion of the private schooling sector

From 1992–93 to 1997–98, the Federal Government contribution to schooling actually increased marginally. However, the apparent increase masked a more significant redistribution of funding away from public schools to the private sector (see also Chapter 7). In line with its ideological commitment to choice and reduction in public service provision, a major shift in funding was effected by 2000, with significant increases for some of the most elite schools. Cynics muttered quietly that this was in reality the national government's preferred means of producing the top rung of the 'symbolic analysts' (Reich, 1991) required for the knowledge economy. There have been dire predictions about the effects of this swing in resources. One politician opposing such policy directions suggested that:

> . . . the budget funding changes to private schools will encourage many schools to expand, use scholarships to cream off the best State school students, and set up campuses in new areas where they will attract more funding . . . the results for public education will be catastrophic (Australian Democrat education spokesperson, Senator Lynn Allison, in Tattam, 1999, p. 14).

One could be excused from thinking that this is precisely what is intended. The (neo)Liberal response to (what it describes as) globalisation entails a commitment to privatised services rather than public, a shift in funding to the consumer, improvement in the performance of the public sector by means of competition with private organisations, and the retention of public services (in this case schools) only for those who cannot afford other options. A variety of policy actors (Angus, 1996; Caldwell & Hayward, 1997; Pascoe, 1996) have suggested that there is now no difference between public and private school 'providers' and what is consequently required is full government funding and contracting out of all schools provision, regardless of governance. One senior academic even went so far as to hint that there was an obligation on those who could afford a private option to stop 'bludging' on the taxpayer (see Coorey, 1998).

Narrowing of Federal curriculum priorities

The Howard Liberal Government introduced new and coercive measures to steer schools towards utilitarian and short-term goals. It simplified the schools policy agenda to one of 'old basics'—literacy and numeracy—and this provided a ready source of panic about the alleged failures of schools and teachers to do well by all Australian children (Comber et al., 1998). Perhaps it was accidental that continued specu-lation about the 'loss of trust' in government,[3] attributed by numerous commentators of various political persuasions to the differential and pervasive effects of social and economic global change, coincided with a renewed Federal focus on civics education. The Federal Government did, however, directly address popular fears about the nation's future by demanding that schools become major players in providing accredited courses to train school students for current (not future) jobs. This policy push coincided with a much reduced capacity and willingness of industry (in particular the 'globalised' and shrinking manufacturing industry) to train apprentices.

The Federal Minister's stated conviction that knowledge about Australian government, work experience, spelling and reading com-prehension constitute the keys required to unlock economic and life success sat perversely alongside the (often mentioned) information age and a 'foundation for life-long learning' (another lexical policy favourite). As one commentator in the post-industrial city put it,

> Schooling is being asked to play a more important role in vocational skill formation and to prepare job-ready, flexible and multi-skilled workers, but at a time when . . . it would have been more appropriate to be concentrating on . . . developing more competent learners and active citizens (Hattam, 1999, p. 250).

The debate about schooling and work became sharply polarised during the time of the Howard Government. Those who favoured 'vocationalist education',[4] where the focus in *all* subjects is towards immediate usefulness and work applications, were in control of the agenda. Those disposed to a more 'generalist approach'—advocating broadly based and futurist learnings in all school subjects, including those focussed on work education—often found themselves labelled as stuck-in-the-seventies, airy-headed elitists[5] rather than as advocates of a more nuanced and democratic approach to the plight of working-class youth. This was a bizarre incarnation of the 'modernist-progressive versus the traditionalist' rhetoric favoured by contemporary government. The argument, rather than being about how best to educate for the global economy as *part* of an overall education for changing times, became reduced to one of education for jobs or not.

Development of a new performance framework

Through the national council of education ministers, the Federal Government promoted the introduction of national benchmarks, drawing on international literatures and trends in outcomes-based education and the development of 'standards' against which all students' progress could be measured (individually, by school and by system). Revised national goals for schooling (Ministerial Council on Education, 1999) gave expression to the beliefs behind this move: the States agreed to aim for: 'Increasing public confidence in school education through explicit and defensible standards that guide improvement in students' levels of educational achievement and through which the effectiveness, efficiency and equity of schooling can be measured and evaluated.'

The phrasing of this goal reveals that the primary aim is to do with *being seen* to perform. The primary action involved is measurement and revelation of data. In another time, the primary aim might be a common curriculum, an entitlement for all Australian school students. With such a goal, measurement would still be involved, but a less technical and more reciprocal and iterative process in both developing and assessing the standards would be articulated.

The Federal Government was unequivocal about such matters: States would have comparative performance tables and they threatened the withdrawal of funds for non compliance—and then also for poor performance. 'Everybody knows' that public revelation of 'results' worked to increase the pressure on schools to perform. Talk of outcomes, choice, accountability and competition, and the selective use of selective information in public, became the stuff of Federal–State relations. Through the development of national benchmarks and testing procedures, the Federal Government did what it could to develop a highly centralised and regulatory system of curriculum taught by schools competing on what was claimed to be a 'level playing field'.

Diminished concerns for equity

Despite scrapping the Special Purpose Programmes, such as the Disadvantaged Schools Programme, which funded schools, development and research, the Howard Liberal Government retained Labor's National Equity Strategy, a framework for monitoring the performance of 'targeted' groups. The NES enabled the plotting, over time, of the aggregate performance of specific groups against the benchmarks and other indicators such as apparent retention. From the 'equity of outcomes' approach of the previous Labor Government in which there was a policy mix of input resourcing, research and output measurement, emerged a slight project, one largely stripped of substance. 'Equity of outcomes' meant no more than regular monitoring and reporting of the distribution of the cake and funding for literacy, vocational education and citizenship—the goods which 'counted'. This 'distributive curriculum' (Thomson, 1999b) was a far cry from acknowledging that the processes of schooling actually produce inequities in complex ways, and a giant step away from any discussion of need, social context and the ambiguous workings of power and control. It was an equity policy that '. . . re-centre[d] the school as the focus of causation in explanations of students' performance and variations in levels of achievement: displacing or rendering silent other explanations related to the embeddedness of education in social and economic contexts' (Ball, 1998b, p. 74).

Federal Government policy privileged education as a commodity subject to the rules of market choice, as well as the solution to global worries—rather than as an equivocal institution that blends together public good, individual benefit, social mobility and economic, cultural and civic concerns. Educational choice was rhetorically represented as an inalienable right, regardless of circumstances and a fundamental value of conservative self-managing individualism. As the Prime Minister (Howard, 1999) remarked in a recent address: '. . . we've tackled the most fundamental challenges facing Australia today by drawing on their own strengths and values—individualism, a willingness to take on responsibility, the desire for choice and opportunity'.

State governments were prepared to argue against parent choice when it came to the placement of children with disabilities. They expected and got backing from the Federal Government for their argument that it would not be possible to provide appropriate staffing and infrastructure in every school and that district provision was the best policy. But this policy is under duress, as a recent news report ('Give us choice, say parents of disabled children', 1999) says, 'Parents of disabled students—and lobby groups—are fighting for the *right to choose* which school their children attend' [emphasis added]. Equity concerns that can be taken to be matters about individuals do thus find a place in the policy regime.

The Howard Government's policy platform and transmutated equity agenda were taken up differently by individual States. Some embarked on ambitious policy projects of their own, within the frame provided by national agreements and Federal emphases.

DECENTRALISATION

All States in Australia have become more decentralised in their operations. This is in tune with international devolution policy trends. However, the post-industrial city has a particular history of localism which has helped to shape the ways that new agendas have been taken up. A little more history is therefore in order.

EDUCATIONAL DE-REGULATION

At the same time that the 'comprehensivisation' of schools was initiated in this State in the 1970s, there was a general loosening up of school system controls. This was in line with international trends towards progressivism.[6] The inspectoral systems of supervision of staff and schools and central budgeting and supply were weakened. The locus of many decisions was placed at the school level through the introduction of legally incorporated school councils responsible for school funds, and expanded school principal roles. The tightly regimented, textbook driven approach to curriculum was substantially shaken, the more extreme forms of student tracking and setting were abolished, and there were experiments with school organisation—structures such as sub-schools, open-space classrooms, alternative schools and annexes were centrally encouraged and supported.

There was still tight control over student enrolments through neighbourhood zoning mechanisms; these also exercised some restraint on demands for buildings and equipment and supported the emphasis on the 'local community' nature and obligations of schools. There was also tight central regulation of teacher and principal appointments, transfers and promotions. A bevy of advisers and an energetic young teaching force moved to take up the new local curriculum and decisionmaking spaces that became available. With the long vision of history, this period of relative de-regulation is more clearly seen as something of an aberration, although it was the formative experience for many teachers and administrators still in the education system.

There has been a gradual, not seismic, change in this State over the last fifteen years. The 1970s de-regulatory localist model was expensive and failed to deliver on its promises. A mixture of arguments for re-centralisation and different forms of de-centralisation grew:

- While the period of de-regulation did support increased student retention, the degree of difference in performance of the various categories of disadvantaged students was unacceptable to many, who vociferously agitated for further reform. There was pressure to 'raise the floor', produce a centrally determined 'curriculum guarantee' for all students, to 'reduce the unacceptable levels of difference between students'.
- School-based curriculum development and change were patchy, and teachers attempting to free up the curriculum had to contend with the continued grip of the post-compulsory curriculum exercised through the public examinations system. A comprehensive central overhaul of the post-compulsory curriculum was the demand from many opposed to the continued domination of schooling by narrow university entrance requirements.
- School staffs and principals argued that in order to reform locally they needed to select their own staff. School councils wanted to select principals to match the needs of particular schools, 'equity advocacy' groups argued that merit must replace seniority, and new centrally determined procedural rules were required to manage equitable school-based selection. Parents also argued they wanted to enrol their children in schools of their choice which required different kinds of central management procedures.

This package of measures is usually referred to as devolution or site-based management. This is about changed relations between local sites and centres in which some former local functions are taken into the centre, and former central functions are moved to local sites. The response to these national pressures was enacted differently in different States over the period of the 1980s and 1990s, but what was common across the country was the trend to *reverse* the previous reforms—to tighten up curriculum provision through the development of national frameworks, and in some cases State syllabus requirements; to loosen up institutional infrastructures such as staffing, budgets and buildings; and to reduce restrictions on student enrolment. More responsibility at the school level produced increased accountability measures. The role of central office changed to one of policy development, monitoring and accountability.

COMPETITION AND DEVOLUTION

Devolution, or site based management, is an international policy idea that has been taken up in the post-industrial city in concert with local progressive visions of parent partnerships, community schools, and a democratically determined local curriculum. However, its most recent realisation coincided with the adoption of neoliberal policies by government. The older democratic stories of local control morphed almost imperceptibly through the technologies of rational planning into a new form of localism that emphasised parent control of school management and local development of programs to meet the specific needs of local markets within explicit learning and quality assurance frameworks.

The 1990s version of localism has maintained much of the rhetoric of local 'community' involvement in decisionmaking, parent and student participation, and school curriculum development, but framed it within the bigger picture of school competition and parent choice. It has also included new forms of performance-based public management, accountability-focussed curriculum frameworks and formula-driven global budgets. The new version of localism is perhaps best called 'semi-competition' devolution to distinguish it from other forms of local decisionmaking and management, because one intention and effect is *some* increase in competition between all schools as the means to produce outcomes. Semi-competition devolution is distinguished from other versions of devolution by processes in which:

- individual schools (providers) are covertly measured and compared with each other, but there are no public league tables;
- the emphasis is on what 'value' individual sites can 'add' to students, rather than also looking at how 'glocalised' (Robertson, 1995) social contexts might influence outcomes and/or the limits to what school sites can realistically do;
- schools must compete for students and produce the curriculum and image that attracts a viable enrolment (cf. Gerwitz, Ball & Bowe, 1995) but within a regime of regulation of parent choice and rules about maximum school size;
- a 'quasi-market' supports a schooling hierarchy based more on old histories, grapevines and appearances than actual school realities (cf. Ball, 1997; Ball & Vincent, 1998).

Some of the characteristics often attributed in the international literature to devolution were obvious in the post-industrial city in the 1980s and early 1990s, well before the introduction of formal devolution policy in the late 1990s. Declining education budgets were the direct result of the post-industrial state adopting, holistically and fervently, the 'globalisation made me do it' policy agenda to reduce public expenditure. Federal and State support for public-choice policies in the mid-1990s produced an increase in 'shopping around' for schools, while continuing school closures and amalgamations (which began in earnest in the 1980s) were effected to save money. It was neoliberal cost-cutting, not devolution, that caused schools in the post-industrial city, concerned for much of the 1990s with their inadequate funding base, to be variously engaged in the entrepreneurial quest for funds and to be demanding escalating contributions from parents to cover the costs of schooling.

The effects of devolution are marked out in the international literatures. While there does seem to be emerging evidence to support policymakers' claims to improved student learning through the 'indirect' effects of devolution (Caldwell & Spinks, 1998), there is also considerable international documentation (see Whitty, Power & Halpin, 1997) and local recognition (Caldwell, 1999) of increased inequities among students and schools. Policies of choice, reducing State education budgets and escalating costs combine with devolved management of funds and staffing that are driven by formulas in which justice and need are inadequately weighted. The result, more often than not, is a vicious cycle of marginalisation of the very poorest schools in the poorest neighbourhoods. Research also suggests that for most principals, despite needing, using and valuing the increased autonomy and flexibility at their disposal, the focus of their activity has shifted too far away from curriculum and pedagogy (e.g. Dempster, 2000; Dimmock, 1999; Southworth, 1999). Principals in competitively devolved schools must try to balance central requirements and local needs and interests, must run schools like multinational corporations but offer a family-like experience to students, and must answer the often uncoordinated and ever increasing flow of faxes, letters, forms and emails, at the same time as 'manage by walking around'. Diminishing resources, rapidly intensifying workloads and escalating policy churn (the rapid replacement of one policy after another) is a moving stairway on which principals often struggle to maintain balance.

Teachers, parents and staff in the post-industrial city read the international research. Few rustbelt school principals, staffs and school councils have embraced the local devolution scheme without also fretting about the consequences. They comfort themselves with those pieces of the literature that suggest that many schools and principals still find ways to innovate and continue to work for improved learning for the full range of students (e.g. Hall, 1996; Riseborough, 1993; Strachan, 1999).

LOCAL IMPLEMENTATION OF NATIONAL POLICY

Appadurai (1996, p. 189) suggests that the task of making positive differences at the local level is 'increasingly a struggle'. He says, echoing Foucault, that 'the models of localisation most congenial to the nation-state have a disciplinary quality about them', and these create 'severe constraints, even direct obstacles to the survival of locality as context generative rather than a context driven process' (p. 190).

Appadurai's notion of the increasingly invasive and disciplinary state and the increasing fragility and puzzling quality of the local, in this case the rustbelt school, is one analytical construct around which to tell the story of the particularities of the policy reform agendas of this State. It is both true, and yet not true at the same time, as we shall see.

8 | Principal acts/acts of principle

The goals of school reform—to provide every child with an experience that will nourish and challenge development, extend capacity, encourage growth, and offer the tools and dispositions necessary for full participation in the human community—are simple to state but excruciatingly difficult to enact (Ayers, 2000, p. 64).

What policy says and what happens in schools are not necessarily the same thing (Ball, 1993). Different aspects of policy take hold in different ways in different locations: and policies are always taken up in particular places. They intersect with ongoing histories, truths, staff capacities and interests, 'thisness' and resources. Agendas are picked up, bent and twisted, paid scant attention to, adopted with little modification, adapted to particular circumstances, rejected out of hand, covertly resisted. School change is always a process of 'vernacular change' (Thomson, 1999d). Despite policymakers' assumptions that schools will simply implement policy and use the monitoring tools (line management, performance management, annual reports, satisfaction surveys) intended to ensure that they do, there is considerable agency exercised at the local level. In particular, school principals act as important mediators of government policy. Their responses translate into tangible leadership practices that make policies happen on the ground—or not.

The story of what rustbelt principals do in relation to policy is just one lens with which to look at local implementation. Principals cannot do things by themselves, and they understand this very well. Rustbelt principals' concerns about getting the 'right staff' include ensuring there is a collective of school staff who will engage with the hard intellectual, physical and emotional work of improving learning for children and young people pushed to the margins—a concentration of staff who are also educational leaders. A focus on the actions of rustbelt school principals is therefore necessarily a view that foregrounds some things and a few people, and not others. Once again, it is a very partial story, but one that is still worth telling. What rustbelt school principals and their formal leadership teams do, does matter.

PRINCIPALS AS POLICY MEDIATORS

It would be simplest to conceptualise the actions of principals dealing with policy as either resistant or compliant, that is, actively working to undermine the government agenda or passively accepting it. This is not the most helpful way to read the stories of school administrators. There are three ideas that are useful in explaining the actions of policy uptake and rustbelt principal mediation.

(1) Principals are active agents not passive dupes.
Tomasz Szkudlarek (1993), a Polish postcolonial scholar, argues (after Bhaba [1984]) that there are *at least* three broad kinds of positive agency:

- emulation—taking action to meet expectations;
- mimicry or simulation—taking action to appear to be meeting expectations;
- resistance—taking action to overturn expectations.

Szkudlarek claims that acts of resistance may result in greater local repression, whereas practices that consist of combinations of mimicry and emulation open up the possibility of space for change (p. 59). Szkudlarek's argument allows a consideration of the implementation of policy as something other than a matter of adherence or rejection, something much more complex and concerned with the immediate as well as long-term survival and health of the institution and the people in it.

(2) What principals do is dynamic and tactical.
Principals' actions are highly responsive to changes in the overall context. De Certeau (1988) calls these everyday resistances. He proposes

that we think of society as a space in which power and its embodiments—institutions, political, scientific and economic rationality, dominant discourses, temporal regimes, enterprises—come to occupy specific places. These are 'strategies' and they serve as the basis for generating social relations. The practices of everyday resistances occupy no permanent place; they are 'tactics', everyday moves that opportunistically wait for times and events that can be turned to advantage.

Many rustbelt principals clearly articulate their role as tactical mediators of policy.

> See, my personal view is that there aren't many policies that get in the way for me because I say, this is where we are, if there are policies that will help me get a teacher to have another talk about what they're teaching and how they're doing it, then we'll work out how to do it—if it doesn't then I just don't do it really . . . What I try and do is work out who can I get to think about working and talking differently, how will this change what they are doing in the classroom, how will it make it more relevant, more contemporary, how will the kids be more excited by this, how can I use this to get kids to finish school . . . So it's how can I use all this to get those things going, to get that outcome, because that's my job in my view (secondary school principal).

The two ideas of tactics and agency make it possible to consider the actions of school principals as active choices made from a range of possibilities that are highly contextual and localised, choices that vary from issue to issue.

(3) Principals' actions constitute a practice.

The final idea that is helpful to bring to the reading of school administrators' actions is the theorisation of 'habitus'. Bourdieu (1984, 1990, 1991, 1998; Bourdieu & Wacquant 1992) suggests that habitus operates as a 'feel for the game', a practical sense of what is possible, given the particular situation at issue. This practical sense is not fixed and the same habitus can lead to very different stances and practices depending on the particular context. Habitus is endlessly transformed and can be practically changed within defined boundaries through the reflexive actions of people involved. Bourdieu suggests that actions are always influenced by the interests and dispositions of the 'player' but not in a determinist, mechanical fashion. He says, 'There will be as many senses of the game, as many practical understandings of interest as there are games' (Bourdieu, 1990, p. 110).

This notion of the 'practical logic' of active agents—a practical logic that is changing, responsive to particular circumstances, locations, constellations of people, histories, narratives and knowledges; a feel for the game that is limited by the social context; that is influenced not only by dominant discursive formations, but also by reflection and new ideas—positions the stories of these rustbelt school principals mediating policy.

These stories are of a particular moment, and will undoubtedly change over time not only as circumstances change, but as the administrators themselves continue to work with them.

VERNACULAR POLICY CHANGE

In the rustbelt, current policies both segue easily and intrude harshly and abruptly into the older patterns of hierarchy within and among schools. Semi-competition devolution and the effects of increased private school funding can be seen on the ground. There is little doubt that there are now in the rustbelt increased tensions arising from the competition for neighbourhood resources, staffing, students and reputation, as well as decreased cooperation among local schools.

INCREASED LOCAL COMPETITIVE TENSIONS

In the western rustbelt, where pockets of low-income housing rub up against pockets of comparative comfort and relative affluence, there is a declining population base, over a decade of government school closures and the expansion of existing private schools and establishment of new ones. Here the question of competition and viability is at the forefront of many principals' minds.

> I think we're starting to see a bit of white flight from here. A long-established family in the neighbourhood has moved house so they could get into another district so they could guarantee they'd get into — High . . . It doesn't matter how good a job we do, we're going to be residualised . . . We're fucked really . . . What do we do—respectable-ise even more? The danger is we get too small. We have about 600 kids. Three or four kids left today. This year we think we'll have about 127 Year 8s for next year, this year we had 155 . . . (secondary school principal).

This school has no choice but to deal with those issues. The approach the principal has taken is to develop one strong curriculum focus; work cooperatively with local primary schools in programs which involve sharing teachers and moving students onto each others' sites; develop a literacy standard so as to ensure that not only do students learn what is necessary for them to move through the school, but reassure parents that the school is covering the basics; and work with local service clubs on a community service program. Each of these things is educationally creative, resourced and enthusiastically directed to the interests of the students, the bulk of whom are working-class young people from fairly low-income home-owning families. At the same time, however, there is a viability edge to each of these strategies, a way in which the principal seeks to denote the singularity of the school and to connect with neighbourhood information flows and networks which bring potential school choosers into closer contact with the school programs.

Some school administrators have their eyes on the most immediate competitor which serves as a reference point for decisions they make. The principal of an old and respected secondary school has fixed on the competition as, not another State school, but a prospective private school.

> [The principal's job] ... is being a strategist and looking at what's happening with public–private schooling, and what would happen if a private school opened just down the road ... We've got the church that's just been built just across from the school and in a few years time, I have no doubt in my mind, that there will be a school on that property or nearby because it's a huge property ... it will be a community gathering place and I know how that community thinks, and there won't be just their kids going there—initially, yes, but if you take a longer term view, it'll be everybody (secondary school principal).

This principal is working to maintain the image and practice of the school as one which enables significant numbers of young people to acquire the valued symbolic capital of university entrance, at the same time as increasing the school's responsiveness to more marginalised individuals and groups, without 'appearing' to be a haven for students seen as needing welfare and remediation. For this principal, the uniform is a highly visible symbol of this process, as is being able to display students' performances across the curriculum in the foyer and in public arenas, to indicate that 'excellence' and the school are synonymous.

For both of these principals quoted, the struggle is how to maintain the viability of their schools, cater for all the students in them (at a time when particular classed and raced students are read by some parents as meaning the bottom of the social field), and do this ethically. Neither of them wishes to engage in overt competition and aggressive glossy image production, but each is positioned in ways that are irresolvable—they must compete or face the prospect of their school being residualised—possibly closed in the first instance, lessened in stature in the other. They feel this acutely. The first principal feels trapped. 'Stratification has always been there but you can see it progressing, taking the next step. I feel quite powerless, what can you do? I guess you have to go into more PR than we have been' (secondary school principal).

It is often the current students' performance around which overt competition between secondary schools takes place. Another rustbelt principal recounts:

> Last week I went to a primary school parent meeting about choosing high schools. I had to follow another school. That was difficult. They do flaunt their statistics all the time and those of us who only have a few statistics to flaunt were a bit more quiet about them. It's not really what the culture of our school is about. It's especially hard to take when it's the kids. The teacher did the statistics stuff, it was the kids who went on rather too much about what a quality place it is, how quality people attend and achieve and what Year 12 results look like, and we just sat there tapping our feet to try and subdue the anger a bit. It's hard to take because our kids do achieve and achieve well, however, within the context of their lives (secondary school principal).

This principal's school also gets students enrolling from the outer suburbs, travelling long distances by bus every day and the principal knows that. The school is not at the bottom of the hierarchy, but somewhere in the middle. Even though this school does not engage in ostentatious displays of embodied symbolic and cultural capital, the same dynamics of competition exist. What this principal feels towards the more prestigious hills schools, other principals further out of town feel towards this school's position, located closer to the city.

Such dilemmas are widespread in rustbelt schools. A secondary school principal from the southern rust belt perhaps best exemplifies the mix of frustration, pride in the school and students, and isolation from colleagues.

> In the south, you've got poverty very much isolated into a particular pocket. We are surrounded by schools that aren't like us, that are very middle class in the way they operate. And one of the issues therefore we are facing all the time is the dilemmas about those sorts of icons that define middle-class schools—issues like school uniform—it takes on a whole new significance when you're located in

a school like ours and you know that you have got kids that cannot afford a school uniform during the week and another set of clothes they wear on the weekend. I get great joy out of our kids because they're the ones who I see being successful and it's a great occasion when they're successful but nobody else appreciates it. My colleague principals round me don't appreciate it, and they'll dump on us and they'll dump in ways that are really hurtful. For example, if I want to get a kid transferred out of our school to go to one of theirs, we have to fight bloody tooth and nail to enable that to happen because they don't want them just because they come from our school . . . (secondary school principal).

The situation of rustbelt primary schools and their principals is also based on classed semi-competition.

Since — primary school has closed there's a little bit more movement across the main road. But that road is definitely a barrier, there's a nice side and a not nice side and the nice ones go elsewhere. We'll get some that cross over from here that go to that school. Some families I've suggested that might be a good idea because, you know how people position themselves culturally and class wise, and if they can't do it here, they can't do it . . . and I say, 'Well it's more stable there', that's the word I use because I think that one of the indicators of disadvantaged children or kids who are poor, whatever you want to call it, is just their freneticism—they're just emotionally and psychologically frenetic and the indicators of that are all this behaviour stuff and if you go to a middle-class school the first thing you'll notice is that the kids are calmer (primary school principal).

This principal has accepted that the rustbelt school is not going to be everybody's choice. Passionately committed to community development and to working in innovative ways with new technologies, the principal has worked with staff for a curriculum that is 'culturally responsive' (Ladson-Billings, 1994), teaching with, in and through 'multi-literacies' (The New London Group, 1966). The principal wants parents to choose the school because of the care it exercises for students, and considerable space is made for them to participate in the life of the school. The staff and principal seek to create a school that refuses to be residualised, despite the fact that it is not first choice for many. This is one of the very few primary schools in the State that does not now have a school uniform. The fact that the school services a discrete geographical area, is still seen as being a 'good' rather than a 'bad' school by parents, and is not in immediate danger of closing (since another nearby school closed quite recently) positions this principal such that this is a viable option.

Competition with the private sector is also an issue for disadvantaged primary schools, and like secondary schools, it is sometimes around a politics of angry exit from the public system.

> We need to connect to the community somehow so we're not hammered like government schools [typically] are—to be a good parent you have to send your kid to a private school. It's rubbish but it's certainly out there. So the profile of government schools needs to be raised. We get the private school stuff from some. We sometimes get it in funny ways, if a kid is getting in too much trouble, then we'll just take him off to a 'proper school'—and then he'd be back, things were so hard in the private school . . . But there are sprinklings of— 'If I had enough money I'd be sending him off to a decent school'. There is that mixed with the 'This is the best school, this is our school, this is the best'. There's a lot of contradictions in all of that, but it's there (primary school principal).

In some areas, the public–private politics turn on issues well out of the reach of the local rushbelt principal. Urban re-development policies that attempt to create a new social mix of middle-class and public housing play out into schools. The tensions are about children attending the school who are seen as undesirable potential peers by some parents.

> We've had huge problems with the new housing estate because initially they thought there was going to be a new State school built there and then that changed because we can take another couple of hundred here. That caused quite a lot of flak. They were promised a school when they bought their house there by the land agents and so of course when our Department said, 'Well the land agent doesn't actually make the decisions about where schools go', that's created a bit of a problem. Then the private school was built there. Mind you when it first opened we only lost five or six kids so we didn't lose a huge number but it was just that group of kids where the parents wanted them to be out of here and couldn't afford anywhere else. They try not to come here because they see this as not the kind of school they would like their children to go to (primary school principal).

Not everything about competition and school promotion is seen as bad. Some administrators argue that the generally negative attitude towards disadvantaged schools is a good reason for focussing on image and public relations. They suggest that the engagement by students in the process can be a positive learning experience, as well as being an 'indicator' that the school is being successful.

> We've got a group of kids who now love the school, who genuinely like being here, who think it is a good school, who approach it with real joy and pleasure—they go out and talk all over the place about the school and talk with real pride about it, and it's a major, major shift from where it was when I first got here (secondary school principal).

However, this particular principal also has other reasons for taking school marketing seriously. This school is not a neighbourhood school, per se. It attracts students from a wide geographical area, over 30 primary schools in fact. In order to maintain the school as a viable institution there is little choice but to engage in some kind of marketing activity.

School principals, who inevitably must lead or support any push for improved public relations in their schools, are placed in ambivalent positions. In a competitive environment they have little choice but to respond, to act in ways that serve the interests of the particular school in which they are situated, to act in ways that are congruent with the schools' history and neighbourhood, and to act in ways with which they can live. However, there are consequences that arise from such activities which work to undermine collegial and cooperative agendas.

> We are being forced into higher levels of competition and if we as principals' associations don't deal with it, then it will be real sink or swim . . . But I'm very happy myself to break the [collegial] rules if it's in the interests of these kids and this school . . . And *everyone* will do the same thing . . . it's a fragile association we have . . . (secondary school principal).

CLUSTERING AND COOPERATIVE ACTIVITY BREAKDOWN

Rustbelt schools have a comparatively long history of cooperative and cluster activity. They have largely worked with the view that their job was to provide the best possible education for a large neighbourhood, rather than achieve glory for a single school. They have been assisted in this thinking by the sheer size and concentration of public and low income housing tracts and a history of experience in local government activities that encouraged local service providers to work together. Despite their shared beliefs and focus, clustering was always a difficult process, although the combined resources, energies and ideas did result in projects which had real benefits for students.

The purpose of school clusters was to extend curriculum options for students; extend student service; provide curriculum leadership not readily found within one school staff; facilitate the transition of students from primary to secondary school; provide professional development and share good practices; work together to advocate for the neighbourhood; and promote educational issues in the local community. Some clusters developed strong community development agendas and saw themselves actively engaged in a sociopolitical process of contesting, in partnership with local networks, the social production of inequalities. These clusters took on strong advocacy roles, supported local arts, self-help and job creation projects, and had a strong commitment to providing educational opportunities for adults in the neighbourhood as well as children and young people. Adult education was part of more comprehensive parent involvement programs in which parents participated in a wide range of school activities—from classroom assistance to drop-in centres and decision-making committees.

> I started working last year with the cluster, it was the first time I'd actually joined it last year, and we were developing a bit of a hypothesis. We thought if we actually took some of the most difficult primary classes and did a big promotion, bringing them over to our high school, doing various fun things, getting the parents interested in the program and enrolling some in high school, then watching what happened to the kids over a period of time, we reckoned that it would make a difference. We had incidental reports from parents who were already enrolled that when they'd sit down with their kids to do their homework their kids thought it was terrific . . . we reckoned it might make a change in the longer term to those kids' future . . . so we were trying to do a bit of social engineering, in a small way . . . it's probably not going to change the world but it might make some small differences . . . (secondary school principal).

A neighbouring primary principal in the cluster saw the process from a different angle, but supports the view that such combined interschool cooperative intervention can have significant impact.

> One of our parents went through the high school as a student and was suspended and excluded and left at 15, and now her oldest child has also been excluded last year and she said to me in the office one day, 'The same thing's happening to her as happened to me'. And after a lot of persuasion we persuaded her to go on this

computer course at the high school, and last week she said, 'Oh this is fantastic, I'm learning all these things,' and it's just brought a whole new attitude to us, to the school, to her kids already and this is two weeks into the program, she's had a whole new lease of life (primary school principal).

These experiences suggest to rustbelt schools that working co-operatively might provide them with new opportunities to break cycles of poverty. A focus on continuing parent education could unite primary and high schools in new and beneficial equity projects. But not all the cluster activity is supported so unreservedly. Clusters tended to develop bureaucratic processes around their activities; they failed to adequately discuss issues related to autonomy and commonality and often got into conflict; they did not share resources equally amongst their members; they competed with each other; they paid out huge sums of money to consultants; and they undercut system-wide industrial agreements (Thomson, 1994).

The level of competition amongst the school clusters, identified some years ago as a problem, has now escalated to such a degree that clusters are changing focus and some are imploding. One important factor in the decline of cooperation is the degree to which schools act for themselves as opposed to acting for the cluster.

You take one individual school in a cluster that says, 'No, we're going to do it this way', and how do you stop the resulting competition? . . . the community is still going to react to different schools, the community's still going to say . . . 'This school's like this . . . and that school's like that' . . . so how do you get the balance between [working] as a comprehensive neighbourhood school and working as a coalition? (secondary school principal).

The breakdown of cooperation is variously sheeted home to a particular person/school, or explained as part of a broader social phenomenon and change.

While we're living in a political environment where individual competitiveness and aggregated individual school outcomes/results are considered to be the be all and end all, there's little capacity other than essentially good will between principals, principal-to-principal initially and then grow that across staffs. I suspect they're the only ways that clustering can happen . . . The other issue which affects that is the degree to which schools have become free (and it's a good job too, this is not an argument against that) to make a whole range of decisions for themselves and wear the consequences too—then cooperative, collaborative efforts across schools create the most labrynthine decisionmaking apparatuses (secondary school principal).

And other systemic processes are also at work in cluster atrophy.

A few people have been appointed principals recently who are not union members and [are] actively against unions. They don't have the same perspectives, coming from a different point of view . . . their focus is *all* on quality assurance and literacy outcomes, and that's where they want to put all their energy. And they're getting lots of kudos from the government for what they're doing. But they have a very restricted vision and so the cluster is not the force it used to be. There's different values creeping in and we're not a cohesive group that's fighting for social justice any more. You can't say the words, and that's hard. As your colleagues you've got to accept where they're coming from, you can argue with them but you can't force them to change their perspective (primary school principal).

As noted earlier, support for neighbourhood activity from other government departments, on which some clusters drew, has dwindled. Community health services have been regionalised, welfare services reduced at the same time as demand has escalated, and local government community centres, which got most of their funding from adult and community education grants and labour market programs, are now struggling. The importance of a supportive policy environment across government areas can be seen in local neighbourhoods. When policy agendas change, and when they change so that they are in conflict with local directions, a number of difficulties are raised for local schools and the families they serve.

In this community you need a coordinated look at the whole problem. It needs education, heath, housing, all those people need to look. When I came in that's what made the difference . . . and the belief was 'Yeah, this social justice policy was happening on the macro level and I'm the principal of a school within this context and yes, we can do something if we do it together'. But over the last five years that's all disappeared (primary school principal).

What is left of the clusters now operates more firmly in line with government agendas. 'Our cluster was going somewhere and it was about educational leadership, and if you take that out . . . then it's just an administrative network' (secondary school principal).

NEW DISCIPLINARY REGIMES

In the last two State organisational 'realignments', the district, which normally contains three or more clusters, has become the base of a line manager, the district superintendent, and a unit for centrally driven policy work. Districts have two loosely coupled functions: educational reform and administration. The tale of vocational funding reveals some of the complexities of using the local district as a site for school change programs.

Firstly, there is the vexed process of decisionmaking—whether the district or the individual site is the level of executive agreement. District decisionmaking can erode democration school decisionmaking processes and privilege principals' voices over teachers and parents.

> We have been given some money for cluster vocational education programs and we all have to put some of our own funds in too. But it appears that there are too many stratas for making decisions . . . to a certain extent principals do have to make an executive decision on whether to be part of the program or not and say 'Yes we're in' and then just deal with the forest fires that are in your school. But that doesn't seem to be the case in every participating school. So the cluster has to wait while one school decides what it's going to do. You get hiccups and in our case, all the schools were in and we planned accordingly and then suddenly three of them pulled out which has had big funding effects (secondary school principal).

Then there are the politics of disadvantage with which to contend.

> There was an awful lot of politicking amongst the principals about who were winners, who were losers. Those things are pretty hard to call with your colleagues when you know that next week you're going to be back in the same room, the same group of people, working on another project . . . which involves resources going to the neediest kids. I think most of the principals' group are committed to that, not all, but most (secondary school principal).

The kinds of guidelines established by the system are important and can either create or resolve local problems.

> Sometimes it would be expeditious to have a set of initial operational parameters presented to you so you opt in or you opt out rather than having to develop the operational parameters on a district basis, which certainly with the vocational money I reckon wasted nine months plus (secondary school principal).

Finally, there is the problem of finding the balance between co-ordination and program delivery.

> The huge amounts of money absorbed in endless meetings and release [time from teaching] worries me because, it's not so much the time, obviously people have to be released, but you wish they were being released to be involved in program delivery or program development rather than parameter development (secondary school principal).

The administrative functions of districts are hardly less problematic. District meetings become the place where central information is circulated and discussed, reconstructed and interpreted before it is taken back by each principal into their school. The agendas of testing and accountability are driven by professional development through the districts, and school principals are encouraged by superintendents or by their peers to engage in discussions about data and quality assurance. The degree to which this becomes punitive and coercive varies according to the propensity of the local superintendent. The district as an administrative unit ensures that principals are increasingly constructed as each other's monitors, with the district meeting the site where the gaze of peers brings the recalcitrant principals into line with accepted norms and departmental policy. 'You get principals in principals' meetings talking about how to—not how to do the curriculum better—but how to do the measurement or how to do the graphing better' (primary school principal).

But it also must be said that there is considerable difference of opinion amongst principals about various elements of the policy agenda, even if this rarely surfaces as debate in district meetings.

THE EFFECTIVE SCHOOL

Contemporary State education policy requires the production/fabrication of a set of documents that attest to the school's effectiveness. Each South Australian school is required to produce a School Context Statement in which the population, location, curriculum and school structure is explained. They must also provide an annual report to parents which lists the school's achievements against the goals of an annual plan. The annual plan for school development must be derived in part from the overall system annual priorities and the links made explicit, thus creating the paper simulacrum of rational planning from top to bottom. Each school has been issued with computer software to conduct the administration and analysis of a parent satisfaction survey, which is to be included as part of the annual report. The annual report requires the production of a statement of purpose focussing on curriculum and pedagogy, and on school organisational matters.

The school is not required to provide any specific information about equity or justice in the annual report. This is left to the discretion of the school.

By and large most rustbelt schools have produced their annual reports and school context statements as required. Outright resistance is low. The weighting that principals attach to it, and the ways in which it is produced, vary. One principal decided that there would be no doubling up of information and that the annual report just meant business as usual. 'I give my annual report to the annual general meeting of the school council, it's the same one I send in—I don't do two . . .' (primary school principal). Some principals have decided that it should not be taken too seriously. The annual report is required by central office and is produced for that purpose alone. A few admit that their annual reports are sanitised documents that are not of much assistance in the everyday messy business of school change. 'A lot of the things we write are not for us in the school . . . I don't know that they mean that much, it's as if they've got flowers all round them and they smell nice' (secondary school principal).

One principal's tactic with such reporting/policy documents is to be seen to engage with them, but to go slow on those that are less immediately useful to the school. Others use all policy documents with some scepticism, encouraging staff to adapt and modify them: 'We've been curriculum mapping for some time. We do it critically, we do it politically, and we teach what we need to and if we have to, we can justify what we do' (secondary school principal).

Some principals find the annual report, and the model of school development it presumes, an imposition, part of the bureaucratic regime that intensifies work and redirects energies away from the local to central needs.

> Annual planning gets in the way, planning doesn't but Annual Planning does . . . I think annual reporting without any notion of it being for the benefit of the school gets in the way all the time. We've only done it once but I found it the most stressful piece of writing to do because there was no notion of what I was supposed to be writing about and I've heard people say that their reports are anywhere from between three and 70 pages long! (secondary school principal).

Yet some found them to be highly important and useful.

> What I tried to do is to report on progress or achievement—but I did realise I haven't got anything in place to let that happen, so it'll be a bit better this year. I think the impetus to be clearer about what we are doing and what impact we are having is good and that's that stuff about being a reflective school or teacher . . . (secondary school principal).

Rushbelt principal responses to audit requirements vary according to their overall philosophy of equity and their desire and practice of autonomy. One principal explained how he understood policy to be 'heteroglossic' (Bakhtin, 1981), full of different voices that would ultimately justify almost anything.

> We live in a world of policy contradictions. And I reckon we could really serve social justice if we could really put our energies into looking at the broad goals and coming up with some objectives and some programs and some strategies that we believe would really help our kids become global citizens . . . and what really would enable them to do that, maybe using technology differently, and it would be really exciting and make for a very exciting dynamic program and curriculum in a school (primary school principal).

This principal, like many others, finds it hard to get time to both fulfil the requirements, deal with the everyday, and do the developmental work. Despite the heteroglossic policy texts, the policy regime in action makes it more difficult to concentrate on the kinds of educational work that will make a difference for the children in the school. In the eyes of this particular principal, this means engaging actively with curriculum policies.

> But at the moment our time is literally consumed. I haven't had time to do the software for the annual report to get the client survey results in yet. And people are moaning about it and I don't join in those moans and the reality is that we do well here but people work very hard to do it. But I'd love more time away from that stuff to do the exciting bits. We've been a pilot school for the civics and citizenship materials. They're just absolutely disgusting really, and we're really pleased to be in there and to give feedback and I've co-taught them and we redesigned units of it and that's what we're sending in and that's what we're telling them (primary school principal).

This is not a principal who is a passive victim, but rather one who, like most rustbelt principals, looks for ways to make the current regime work in the interests of the students in their location.

Similar patterns of active principal agency can be seen in relation to the utilitarian performance-based agendas at the heart of the new curriculum. This has different emphases in primary and secondary schools. In primary it takes the form of dealing with literacy and testing. In secondary schools it carries a renewed emphasis on vocationalism.

STAYING ON AND WORKING

The late 1990s has seen a dramatic decline in apparent student retention rates (the number of students starting high school compared to the number in Year 12). This has been more acute in this city and State than in others, and significantly more in the State school system than in the non-government system. The figures for 1992 were: State school retention rate 87.6 percent; national average 73.8 percent. For 1999 they were: State school retention rate 58.1 percent; national average 66.4 percent; State non-government schools: 87.1 percent (Australian Bureau of Statistics, 2000b). These figures must be treated with caution, since this State has the highest number of part-time students (the figures are in full-time equivalents not bodies), and official statistics also show that the percentage of young people who are not working and not in full-time education has actually declined a little during the 1990s (Australian Bureau of Statistics, 2000a).

The retention rates of rustbelt schools are not officially published, but evidence from individual sites suggests that their retention rates are considerably lower than the State average of 58.1 percent. And, while there has been a bigger uptake of training programs by students from low-income families than middle-class families (Long, Carpenter & Hayden, 1999), early school leavers are predominantly from low-income homes and areas (determined by postcode) and have increasingly poor labour-market prospects (Dusseldorp Skills Forum & Curtain, 2000). There is, not surprisingly, a concentration of early school leavers in the rust belt, in the very places where youth unemployment is highest and where teenage jobs are scarce and becoming scarcer. Working-class girls, in particular, have very poor job prospects (Kenway, Collins & McLeod, 2000). While in other locations there has been a transfer of students from school to the technical and further education sectors, this is not the case in the rust belt. There, many young people just leave school and find what work they can, in both legal and illegal activities.

National (Brooks et al., 1997; Marks & Fleming, 1999; Marks et al., 2000) and local (Smyth et al., 2000) research suggests that inadequate school curriculum, pedagogy and disciplinary procedures have combined with student willingness to take any work on offer, to produce the downward retention graphs.

The retention and early leaving issue has sufficiently worried the State Government to the point where it has, after provocation from its political opposition, now raised the legal school-leaving age from fifteen to sixteen years. However, just as there is no simple explanation for the phenomenon of falling school retention rates there is no magic policy remedy to fix it. The policy on offer is a combination of coercion and vocational education. The policy rhetoric is a simple equation of vocational education and job acquisition and this creates credibility difficulties on the ground: 'Why would you assume that kids are so stupid—and when you tell them that they're doing all this work-place stuff and training and they say, "Yes, but will you get a job?" . . .' (secondary school principal).

Rustbelt secondary schools *must* engage with the vocational policy project pushed by both the State and national governments not just because it is policy. Education for productive employment is part of the promise and mandate of government schooling. This is what school communities want and argue is their due—an education that will be useful in getting work. In addition, vocational education is a major source of funding. Even if they do not believe that what is on offer as vocational education is the answer to falling retention, they still have to, and want to, take up the agenda (and the cash) and make of it what they can. Indeed many rustbelt schools undertake considerable curriculum innovation.

> We've got hospitality, tourism, office skills or procedures, they fitted in with what we were already offering in the school, and the passenger auto program. The most exciting one is music. It's creative, new . . . we're picking up national music modules, where students learn to manage a small business in music and learn the skill to organise small events, to be able to manage groups, learn how to manage a repair business or something associated with music and how to manage themselves so if they do the pub circuit or do performances then there is legal stuff, and contacts. By the time these kids finish their Year 12, they'll be credited with these music units as well, but will have cross accreditation with training programs (secondary school principal).

Some of the rustbelt schools also have a deliberate focus on the 'new economies' and youth cultures (c.f. Ball, Maguire & Macrae, 2000) as a way of keeping young people at school combined with some way of making a living after school.

Many school principals monitor post-compulsory students' learning very carefully, not to provide information to parents, but to see what other additional support and intervention is required. Some schools have established tutorial centres to provide specific assistance in the completion of assignments, and some provide online resources and take-home self-paced study guides. Principals personally spend a lot of time helping to create a culture in which students recognise that they will not simply follow a career 'pathway' when they leave school but need to be consistently working from the present towards a goal. Principals focus on dealing with the uncertainties of transition.

> Probably half of the kids understand that Year 12 will take them two years not one, and they plan around that. That's really useful because what I talk to them about is that it's quite likely that you will be able to do what you want but the way you choose to get there may well not be the same as those kids who come from these other kind of schools, so what you have to work out is how you can be successful when you're working 33 hours a week or when you're looking after a two-year-old. So it's about structuring into the school things that will help them do that (secondary school principal).

As this principal indicates, there are difficulties associated with establishing vocational programs that are specific to rustbelt schools. They include the following.

Many of the students already work

> I think about 42 percent of our school are in part-time employment and some of them up to 32 hours a week . . . so it's nearly full time . . . but a lot of them just get a few hours here and there . . . Friday night, Saturday morning, lots of fast food and supermarkets . . . lots of them are employed under-age . . . they are working when they are fourteen (secondary school principal).

Schools face the difficulty of trying to dragoon employers, who can easily find other employees and who often did not realise that they might be taking on a school when they took on the young person, into making the part-time job a work placement, with all its attendant paperwork and bureaucracy.

Work programs as they are currently constituted often fail to reach the most marginalised and alienated young people

When we are choosing kids, because we have a selection process involved in placements, we're not actually dealing with the students that perhaps the Federal Government imagines we're dealing with. They're not the ones who are at risk of not being employed, they are highly employable young people, and we have to do that—there are limited placements, anywhere you've got a work placement scheme there are limited placements, and . . . you're selecting the ones who are the best able to represent us, because the number of placements are limited . . . and why would you send off one of your males who might tell the employer to f*** off in the first half hour they are there and 'You can stick this job, what's this for?' We certainly wouldn't be sending them. So you're creaming off (secondary school principal).

What is required for the most marginalised young people is often something prior to and other than vocational education.

You have to actually look at how could you develop these skills, but then you're working against some of what they're thinking already, which is why would we be doing this anyway . . . And you start to try to find who actually it is that can work with that group in terms of work placements, or even work experience with that group and the kinds of things they might do, and that takes time and money to set up . . . (secondary school principal).

Some rustbelt schools have focussed specifically on the 'most at risk groups' and have eventually mustered sufficient funding to establish programs based on the students' interests and strengths. School administrators believe such projects cannot be at the cost of losing sight of those who can achieve.

We're going to define the outcome of all of our programs as being about students that can contribute to a holistic community, citizenship I guess . . . there are kids going off and getting the high stakes stuff . . . Saying that we offer maths 1 and 2 is as much a matter of social justice as offering the courses to at risk kids because if there is no option for those talented kids to win in what is the current system, then we're doing people out of it completely . . . and you measure the outcome as progressively more kids got to university and the ones that got there did more interesting courses . . . and by keeping kids that are homeless at school we stop their further degeneration to the street (secondary school deputy principal).

Vocational program funding is often inflexible

The difficulties of trying to look at having internal school choice, a way of catering for the diversity in the school population, is not taken up in simple policy prescriptions and measures of effectiveness.

> The attempt to try to coagulate everything into an answer . . . the one bureaucratic solution is a real problem. It's really messy to have 50 different things happening at once . . . but that's the way things work and you learn different lessons from all of them; some fail spectacularly but some of them get kids through a system that they never got through before . . . When you try to measure in terms of one kind of outcome . . . it's no good (secondary school deputy principal).

This flexible approach needs flexible resources, not tied grant programs with rigid outcomes. And it takes more to do more: '. . . if you've got a [disadvantaged] school with a high retention rate what you've got is a school with a lot more problems . . . if you've got fifteen- or sixteen-year-olds who don't want to be there you just need more resources and more flexibility' (secondary school deputy principal).

There are also geographical issues

Not all schools are close to viable businesses that will take students on placement. Some are also far from training colleges and the sheer cost of getting there can be a major deterrent to both students and staff. 'The college that we're working with is across town because they have a much more viable music set-up' (secondary school principal).

Schools in the wealthy eastern suburbs are more likely to have post-compulsory courses in the information industry and to focus on the work-related aspects of university-oriented courses in science and arts. Some privileged schools focus almost exclusively on generic work-related skills in junior high school, and others see accredited training as needed only by those students who are likely to be unsuccessful at a high prestige senior secondary course (Reid & Thomson, 1998). There is a spatial hierarchy of vocational education, with training modules associated with service and manufacturing industries concentrated in working-class and disadvantaged schools. However, a state information technology pilot project has enabled one rustbelt school to offer a full suite of information technology based vocational training programs.

By and large, rustbelt secondary principals still actively look for ways to make things better for their students, even as they worry about the Federal agendas, and how they will scrape by.

> Potentially as long as we've got resources coming in and you can employ some people you can do some things and occasionally be really adventurous but you've got to think what happens if that stops at some stage, how are we going to make sure these kids aren't going to miss out (secondary school principal).

This can-do-make-do attitude is also alive in the rustbelt primary schools, but there the policy agendas are around basic skills 'high stakes tests'.

TESTING TIMES

The concern with 'outcomes' in education has been noticeable for many years. At first, it was only special funding programs that were specifically evaluated. By the 1990s, however, both Federally and at the State level there was interest in 'indicators' of effectiveness, and this was followed almost immediately by the introduction of State quality assurance processes. Curriculum profiling was introduced in several States as a viable and better alternative to standardised tests (Boomer, 1999). However, the push for national and State testing continued, and by the mid-1990s, several States had introduced some form of standardised test of early literacy administered to at least two year levels.

The concern for testing is often sheeted home to conservative governments but it is also produced from the workings of new public management, which features the central determination of outcomes, declaration of targets for improvement, the specific allocation of policy and funds, and local implementation. 'Local results' can be measured, aggregated and tested against targets. This rational management works at a distance to contain, confine and control decentralised sites and limit debate about the designated 'outcomes'. These are now the conventions of all State and Federal funding programs including education. Because literacy has been first in line to be rendered 'measurable' and 'comparable', literacy has come to be a major performance indicator for almost all government school education initiatives, leading to what has been called the 'literacisation' of national policy (Comber & Hill, 2000).

Many rustbelt primary principals worry that the policy focus on basic skills, literacy, and narrow outcomes plotted on graphs in a game which their students cannot win will undermine their capacity to make a difference for students. They are committed to the priority of parent–school relationship building. They believe that this is integral to a broader set of neighbourhood processes and that rustbelt schools can play a positive part in the development of local social networks, can support social action and become sites in which decentralised democratic practice can be nurtured. Each of them fears that a politically induced testing process will undermine the trust that they have worked hard to win, and when children in disadvantaged schools are shown not to produce the same test results as their more middle-class peers, teachers will be blamed for their 'failure' by parents. They worry that grim days of unremitting hostility and despair will be the result.

Nevertheless most, but not all, primary school administrators have gone along with the Statewide standardised tests administered to Years 3 and 5, because they believed that it was not worth disputing. This was an approach adopted by their principals' association, but it was in conflict with the union position which was and is one of outright rejection. 'I have taken the approach that this is a battle I'm not going to fight, not this one, thank you very much, we're talking to staff here and I said, "We're not fighting this one, it's not worth it, we'll wait for a war to hit us"' (primary school principal).

Rustbelt primary principals and their staffs have taken a variety of actions and positions in relation to the testing regimes. Some have found that the testing is now a necessary aspect of the current institutional context of rustbelt schools, with large classes, harried teachers and transient populations creating possibilities for some students to be overlooked.

> With classes of 30, we're complex schools, with a complex range of ability, the behaviour management stuff and the teacher skills . . . I don't think we can just rely on teacher referral, teacher judgement. Now, I've always argued against standardised testing, but we've done testing across the school using a couple of reading tests and spelling tests and the State results, and 95 percent of the time the results are consistent with teachers. Now, I know the tests don't test stuff that the kids know . . . but I studied our results, and it did point up some stuff that wasn't being explicitly taught. I've argued against it as a diagnostic tool in the past . . . Now I think it's an indicator for some individual kids and it can give you some interesting stuff about your school (primary school principal).

This principal suggests that the testing agenda may not be unilaterally 'bad' and may well work as a 'safety net' provision. Other rustbelt principals have found that the testing agenda, far from creating problems with parents, actually assists relationships.

One of the things I've found is that the parents love it, they really love seeing what's happened, they want to know what differences there are, what are the changes, it doesn't matter to them where the child starts, what the base line data is, as long as they've seen that progress . . . And they come to see the teacher who manages the tests in the school and they come to see her all the time and say, 'Have you done that test yet, how did they go? Have they learned anything?' And that's quite apart from the reports that the teachers write, the nice reports with lots of descriptions and we have assessment portfolios where we explain the criteria of what's being assessed . . . they're more interested in: was there progress made between these two tests—because it's some thing they can actually catch hold of. It's something they can really understand . . . (primary school principal).

Others find that they face precisely the dilemma they feared. When the focus is on the individual child and their progress there are few concerns, but it is when the conversation turns to comparative results that difficulties arise.

The parents started to do the stuff about, 'Well if you taught better . . .' and 'We send our kids to you to teach them and why aren't they all brilliant?' . . . so I talked to them about different kinds of learning and what this test is measuring is a particular type of learning, and they understood that . . . but you're still left with how come the eastern suburbs primary kids are doing so much better . . . (primary school principal).

There are strong intimations here of the problems that will arise for rustbelt schools if league tables of test results were to be published, if single sites were to be apportioned blame for institutional practices and the social, economic, cultural and political relations that produce unequal societies and unequal schooling benefits. So far, there is a kind of semi-competition in which test scores are not made officially public, but some schools do publicise their own data if they think they are 'better than average'. Funding and internal system judgements about comparative school effectiveness are also based, in part, on basic skills test results.

Many rustbelt schools have introduced a range of tests and assessment practices of their own. Most have discovered that having a rich source of data about student achievement can be very useful. Three stories illustrate what happens when principals and their staffs have taken the opportunity to engage in formal inquiry focussed on students' learning, using teacher experiences and judgement and a range of 'evidence' of learning, and using the testing agenda as an impetus for local action.

Story one

We did literacy and numeracy audits and in year levels teachers got together and looked at whether a kid was at risk or not, and why and how and how you'd know that, and they got right into looking at what that all meant, and they found that really useful . . . and then they could see patterns across the school. We looked at year levels, we looked at boys and girls, kids of non-English speaking background, we looked at all the social factors that impinge on them, sort of a chart-mapping process . . . and that was good. We slotted in all the stuff that we actually used as useful information, there were student work samples, the audits we developed, the department tests, the curriculum profiles ascribing levels of outcomes, the ESL scales, the special education information . . . getting people to focus and have meaningful chats about teaching and learning was the most useful thing. We actually saw kids progress, you could actually see it . . . not just talk about it from memory, but be able to talk about it from all different points of view, using the work samples, you could do graphs about it . . . you could see the kids had got better at things because we'd actually taught it . . . well, that was our assumption . . . the fact was you could see that there was a better outcome and we could have debates about it and that was what I was hoping to do . . . (primary school principal).

Story two

The jump in kids' learning from Year 3 to Year 5 was amazing. It was incredible. It was a huge progression—for the kids who were here—there were only sixteen who'd done the State test in Year 3 and Year 5 . . . the development in those two years has been amazing . . . when you see how the kids come into junior primary and some of them don't know their colours and some of them don't know their name, and there's a whole range of learning that they still need to do . . . that junior primary time is their catching up—settling in, learning school language, understanding how school time works. Year 3 is still part of that, and then between the next two years there's this enormous jump, enormous development, they've learned school, suddenly they're into school because they understand it . . . The same is true for all our cluster schools, we've all talked about it, the change between Year 3 and Year 5 is quite dramatic and certainly above State average (primary school principal).

Story three

Everyone says, 'What about numeracy?', well our results showed that literacy was still scoring lower than numeracy even though we don't have any particular numeracy support programs and we've 'done literacy' for years ... so we looked within literacy. We looked at whether the strengths were in language or reading and basically the kids can read—in other words, they can receive information and texts, but they're scoring really low on language, that is in putting it out there ... in terms of oral or written language. There's a sort of a treadmill thing going on there. It's like some circuit breaking needs to go on—and teachers have to come in at different places so that kids know how to put it out there and understand they have things worth saying—and that's related to how the kids understand the complexities of the world and how it works, so consequently literacy programs that we set up are now about all those things (primary school principal).

There is certainly evidence in rustbelt schools that tests can provide new impetus for a systematic focus on learning. The rustbelt principals and teachers, who bring a range of information about student learning together with research literatures, who allocate time to discussion and work from a strong commitment to doing justice for their students, certainly seem to be far from beaten down under the semi-competition testing regimes that do not indulge in public league tables. To the contrary, if the schools are already committed to work as sites of inquiry, then the testing has become integrated into school-based research projects. What is required is that principals have the wherewithal to lead such processes.

ACTS OF PRINCIPLE

Disadvantaged schools are generally doing it tough in the current environment, much tougher than their more privileged counterparts on the other side of town. But many of them are still working for educational equity, they have not given up. In the post-industrial city, there are several rustbelt primary schools that are engaged in very innovative programs of reform. Some of the secondary schools are also working hard to deconstruct the grammar of schooling, although their sheer size, the effects of the external post-compulsory certificate and the push for vocational education, semi-competition and the rigidity of the time-space construction of timetable and subject specialisation constrain their movement.

In each of the schools where there is an explicit equity agenda for reform, it is the principal who 'gives permission' in the school. While individual teachers can take up questions of curriculum and pedagogy, if there is a passionate and committed principal then equity and 'doing justice' still matter across the institution. If that principal has a similarly committed administrative team; has taken advantage of the local selection of staff as much as possible to create leadership depth; has used combinations of professional development and imposed policy changes to stimulate local activity; operates collaboratively and with a strong pedagogical focus; then, provided that there are no overwhelming locality issues, the school is generally humming.

Taking up and taking on the current policy agendas to make them work in the long- and short-term interests of the children of the rust belt requires that school leadership teams have particular dispositions and knowledges. As one rustbelt principal put it, 'You have to have a really internalised sense of equity, and you have to tell yourself it's OK to use different words [from "policy"] and it's OK to go back and say it again, and do it again . . .' (primary school principal).

In conversation, rustbelt principals use a variety of theorisations of justice and equity. A handful talk extensively about social capital, a notion being actively pursued by one principal through personal connections with health reform projects. Some discuss literacies and their involvement with university-based teacher research projects, mentioning specific scholars whose approaches they use. A few mobilise a rights discourse drawn from involvement with indigenous education and Aboriginal activists. A minority speak of multicultural- ism and their connections with ethnic communities and events in Europe. There is talk of lifelong learning and much discussion of whole-school change drawing on language and ideas from previous equity policies. The principals of girls' schools in particular draw on feminism and poststructuralism and ideas gathered through reading and attendance at feminist conferences.

What is clear from these conversations is that rustbelt principals have intellectual resources about justice and equity that they draw on to design their everyday tactics. The retraction of schools' justice and equity policy has not left them high and dry with a diminishing sense of what they can do, or forced them to find directions only from within the discursive resources of conservative policies. While each school and school principal engages with the system agendas, they produce their own variations incorporating new songs along with the ongoing older justice and equity refrains.

Despite the difficulties of reducing resources, a hostile media and largely unsympathetic policy regimes, by and large the rustbelt schools and their principals are involved in more than mere policy response and passive implementation; they have taken an active stance and are working to critically and thoughtfully shape the agenda to particular situated circumstances, places and times.

9 | Discourses of equity

There are discussions of equity in funding and worries about stratification and the failure of urban school systems. It is, however, an argument mostly about measured gains in achievement, an argument waged by economists armed with regression equations. One thing that seems absent from these debates is a concern for caring or nurturance. Another is a concern for the shape of school communities (Strike, 1999, pp. 173–4).

In 1996, the long running Disadvantaged Schools Program (DSP) was abolished by the Federal Howard Government, and replaced by the Commonwealth Literacy Program (CLP). Given that the DSP had been in operation since the early 1970s, its demise was greeted with remarkably little public outcry, but considerable private/privatised regret.

REMEMBERING THE DSP

The DSP began in Australia as a result of considerable political agitation about economic and social inequities in Australia (see Henderson, Harcourt & Harper, 1970; Roper, 1970). In the early 1970s, the newly elected Whitlam Labor Government commissioned a series of social policy oriented inquiries (Fitzgerald, 1976; Henderson, 1975; Karmel, 1973) that resulted in a whole-of-government strategy to address poverty, The DSP, which specifically looked at education, was an integral part of an holistic reform and integration agenda for Federally supported government services. The DSP was designed to target 15 percent of Australia's school population and those schools in which there were the highest concentrations of students living in straitened financial circumstances. Funds were allocated by the Federal Government to States, which in turn distributed them to the targeted schools.

The DSP was initiated at roughly the same time as Head Start in the United States. However Head Start focussed primarily on early childhood, giving disadvantaged children access to preschool and remedial assistance in the first years of school, while their parents were involved in parenting groups. In the United Kingdom, similar family-based intervention programs were also undertaken. In stark contrast, the Australian DSP focussed on the whole school, and how it systemically produced disadvantage. The attention was not to be paid to individual deficit families, but to the operation of the institution.

While the Federal Government signalled some priorities for action, a key design element of the program was that local schools were to determine local needs and strategies using participatory processes that involved teachers, parents and students (Commonwealth Schools Commission Disadvantaged Schools Program, 1978). In addition, the Federal Government designated funding to States specifically to address very significant disparities and shortfalls in the condition of school buildings between poor and inner-city schools and others.

The DSP was not without its problems (Beasley, 1988; Schools Council, 1992). The funding was never a huge amount (some $100 per child), the Federal capital works contribution was often mysteriously swallowed up in State budgets, and almost as soon as the program began there were cries that the funds were completely inadequate to achieve major shifts in inequitable school results. The arbitrary statistical 'cut off' for the program and lack of formula transparency bewildered and angered schools that were deemed ineligible, even though they were only marginally different from those which received funding. In the beginning the DSP adopted onerous competitive submission processes in which some schools seemed to succeed handsomely, while others floundered. The latter became vocal cynics. Some of the projects that were funded had only vague connections with improved formal learning, and some, such as additional support for students to go on excursions or for performers to visit schools, became recurrent items that Federal policymakers tried in vain to get States to take up as part of their regular funding commitments.

Despite these well-publicised 'faults', the DSP had very considerable strengths. A veritable tsunami of school innovations resulted from the heady mix of money, time for discussion, professional development, and the opportunity to engage in practical classroom activities and school research (see Connell, White & Johnston, 1991). Many schools (often primary schools) established strong consultative networks and classroom participation programs with parents. In particular, the continuing Federal and State emphasis on literacy supported schools to undertake serious and long-term examinations of their literacy teaching practices. The twin notions of schools investigating their own practices and teachers as researchers became a significant aspect of the DSP commitment to local action. Schools undertook research projects that investigated how to improve teaching methods, varied approaches to classroom teaching, developed home–school reading projects, worked in partnership with researchers on systematic inquiries into learning, and invented technologies to help monitor 'improvement'. The DSP provided an important forum for significant development and debates amongst educators in and out of schools: but pragmatic yet selective adoption of 'anything that worked' was mostly the norm in classrooms. Many of the projects nurtured in DSP schools went on to influence Statewide policy, and many of the teachers who were responsible for them took up broader systemic roles.

The DSP was an important influence on the thinking of many current rustbelt school administrative teams. They remember the DSP as the Federal Government program which:

- made them part of a community of schools imbued with a worthwhile social mission, namely addressing poverty and advancing social justice;
- gave them permission to experiment and take risks and learn from experiences;
- fostered for the first time a school culture of creative and disciplined inquiry which stimulated the asking of useful questions, the systematic collection of evidence and the public recording and dissemination of 'findings';
- brought together university and school researchers to develop and debate theory and practice;
- regularly documented, disseminated and celebrated school-based 'successes';
- provided time for professional development, supported professional networks with regular conferences and newsletters and encouraged schools to share information and ideas;

- promoted diversity, democracy and the local, and valued and allowed space for the voices of parents and students;
- provided some security of funding and, particularly towards the latter stages of the program, encouraged whole-school planning and reporting.

Rustbelt principals both miss and mourn these contributions, while at the same time acknowledging that in its very last stages, the DSP (and the principals themselves and their schools) suffered from benign Federal Government neglect. They speak of the withering away of the ethos of national commitment to the alleviation of poverty and other social inequity(ies). They refer to 'manufactured crises' of il/literacy; these, they feel, imply that staff in DSP schools had been inactive and cavalier about the importance of reading, writing, speaking, listening and watching.

In the 1980s, South Australian schools were able to do more with their DSP funds than before. There were also new State social justice funds which, like the DSP, were directed to eligible 'poor' schools to be used at their discretion. DSP schools pooled the two sets of funds to maximise their effects. Many schools took up opportunities made available in newly decentralised staffing procedures to fund additional teacher leadership positions and realease time for teachers.

During the early 1990s this State social justice allocation dwindled dramatically, forcing DSP schools to rely once again on their Federal funds. State funding was being redirected towards special education, to support the costly integration of students with disabilities. Parents of children needing such provision, and special education self-help and advocacy groups, were increasingly vocal about their needs and rights. The ongoing possibilities of litigation against school systems for in-adequate care and instruction for students with disabilities provided a powerful motivator to swing attention and limited equity funds to meet these pressing needs.

From the inception of the DSP and other special purpose programs in the mid-1970s, there was continual tension around the locus of policy action—particular individual students, identified and targeted groups and/or the site. Federal policy documents spoke of the need for action in each arena, but this was as much a policy 'compro-mise' as it was a coherent argument about the need to work at each of three levels (individual, group and site) at the same time. The policy inclusion of individuals, groups and sites failed to placate those who saw and represented unmet needs. Limited funds were politely fought over by a range of equity advocates. In this competition for support, the anti-poverty and whole-school focus of the DSP was the eventual loser.

While the Clinton administration in the United States pledged more money for Head Start and the Blair Government in the United Kingdom initiated a new poverty program, Education Action Zones, the newly elected Howard Government in Australia declared that the DSP had run its course and that literacy, not poverty, was the issue. When the Commonwealth Literacy Program (CLP) replaced the DSP in 1996, there was relief that at least there would still be some funding for 'poor schools'. But there were misgivings too.

FROM DSP TO CLP: THE RISE OF 'RATIONAL' LITERACY POLICY

The CLP has retained some of the flavour of the DSP. Like its policy predecessor, CLP guidelines recognise that schools with high concentrations of students living in poverty are more likely to have concentrations of students who are 'less (school) literate' and thus require additional support. States are charged with directing at least some funding to targeted schools, and this is increasingly accomplished via 'global budgets' (e.g. Caldwell & Hayward, 1997). In most cases, States have retained some flexibility in their interpetation of Federal guidelines, allowing schools to determine at the local level what particular emphases and strategies will meet the literacy needs of their particular students.

Like the DSP, the CLP asserts the primacy of literacy learning as a key to school success, and as in the Hawke-Keating (Federal) policy period, links school literacy to the national goals of economic recovery made possible by a skilled (literate) workforce. But the DSP had embraced a wide range of possible 'outcomes', including improving attendance, reducing alienation from schooling, increasing retention rates, improving class participation, involving parents and students in decisionmaking, broadening teacher repertoires, changing what counted as school knowledge, altering school policies and structures . . . Because the DSP was broad in its scope and goals, it was notoriously difficult to evaluate: this indeterminacy was built into its decentralised, local decisionmaking structure. Such slipperiness was a source of great frustration to the new 1990s breed of managerial policymakers, who wanted to be 'sure' of the effects of their government funds. And DSP schools, it seemed, could never present their 'results' in ways acceptable to these policymakers.

It is important to remember that in the early 1990s, during the last stages of the DSP, there were no national literacy tests or benchmarks.

In the late 1980s, the national Schools Council commissioned a Macquarie University team (see Connell, Johnston & White, 1990) to evaluate the DSP, but its actual report was never officially published by the Federal Government. The talk at the time was that the authors had failed to provide 'hard' evidence of DSP effects, and 'perversely' argued for increased funding and a clearinghouse function for the Commonwealth. As the Macquarie University investigation began, the first work on educational indicators was undertaken: the exploratory work was conducted in State DSP organisations (e.g. Wilson, 1989) and at the national level (e.g. Wyatt & Ruby, 1989). Those who now hear policymakers suggesting that there is no evidence that the DSP led to improved learning outcomes, might well argue that the DSP was (and is) unfairly scapegoated for the overall lack of systemic national data. Such collection was the responsibility of States and the Federal Government to develop together, not that of a rather minor special needs funding program, which in reality had led the way in thinking about outcomes and indicators.

The CLP has substantially overcome these perceived 'problems' with the DSP. The CLP has coincided with (and has not been the impetus for) the development of national tests and benchmarks. These act as some way of monitoring improvements in some aspects of literacy and numeracy across all schools. It is tightly focussed and therefore much more amenable to the rationalist public management in vogue for much of the last decade (Taylor et al., 1997; Thomson, 1998b). But the CLP is positioned in part by the older and ongoing discourses around equity, and continues to speak of the 'proportional representation' of 'under-represented groups', that is whether the percentage of any targeted group's success in any educational activity is the same as their percentage of the total student population (Thomson, 1999b).

Rustbelt school administrators have mixed feelings about the CLP. They agree that literacy is a key issue in disadvantaged schools, but read into the heated discussions about literacy, often held via the print and electronic media, that policymakers think they were not concerned about literacy before. They argue that they devoted a great deal of school time and intellectual effort to the vexed nexus between socioeconomic status and apparent lack of student achievement in literacy. Their views have a basis in fact. According to a South Australian survey (Thomson & Wilkins, 1997) in the final year of the program, DSP schools devoted a considerable amount of time, money and effort towards improving literacy—between a quarter and a third of their curriculum budgets.

Rustbelt principals now feel as if they are being (mis)represented as leaders who have to be coerced and bribed into taking literacy learning and student outcomes seriously. One primary principal remarked bitterly, 'It's as if we have no data on literacy. We have heaps of data. We've collected it for years'.

Furthermore, school principals resent what they read to be their new category—that of a minority of schools who are 'bad' at teaching literacy, thus failing students and failing the nation. 'It's as if we're just one of a bunch of schools who are working on literacy, rather than having issues to do with poverty' (primary school principal). This is a far cry from feeling part of a supported minority who were doing important national work around a vexed social-economic-political question: that of equity and justice. According to one principal, this went further than just a warm glow: 'At least with the DSP you knew people and who was doing what, there were ways you could talk with each other about what seemed to work with your kids—best practice.'

The CLP and DSP programs are continually combined and contrasted in rustbelt principal narratives. While principals mourn the loss of the DSP, their responses to the CLP are not simply negative.

CLP: FOCUSSED EFFORTS

Many rustbelt school administrators of former DSP schools now targeted under the CLP actually feel that the shift from DSP to CLP has encouraged them to look again at literacy learning. Some suggest that the focus on literacy has encouraged a whole-school examination of classrooms and learning processes that was often missing from the DSP. Many also feel that their schools have benefited considerably from other State and national literacy initiatives that have accompanied the testing agenda. 'We know much more about linguistics and language than we did before' (primary school principal).

Unlike the DSP, the CLP is not a program with a unique mandate. All States, as well as the Commonwealth, have spawned a range of new literacy projects, predominantly focussed on early intervention and teacher training. In addition, most States have provided additional funding to schools on the basis of their students' literacy test 'failure'. A considerable number of 'new' and some 'old' CLP schools no longer focus on developing approaches to literacy based in local assessments of need and strategy, but put State funds together with those of the CLP in order to take up the vast number of new professional development packages and student remediation approaches available to schools.

A significant number of disadvantaged schools now take up literacy teaching approaches that are similar to those in schools in better off and privileged localities. Their additional funds become the means by which they participate in Statewide and/or national programs. There is thus considerable commonality around the expenditure of CLP funds.

The majority of rustbelt schools combine State and Federal funds to employ para-professional staff who work with small groups of children/young people on classroom teacher-designed literacy tasks. Some schools initially opted for specialist literacy teachers who withdrew students from classes (e.g. Reading Recovery), and some attempted to employ enough additional teaching staff to halve class sizes for at least one or two hours per day; they have largely had to abandon these strategies because of sheer expense. However, the details of what is actually happening is known only, it seems, to each school. One rustbelt principal says: 'I go to the office and I see that [other] schools are funding support staff, and I think well that's fine, but what's the program? What do these staff actually do? I'd really like to know more than just about my school' (primary school principal).

School administrators in schools receiving CLP funds generally agree that it is not the particular literacy 'package' that is used that seems to make a difference to student learning, but rather it is simply the additional time, specific focus and liaison with parents combined with greater teacher expertise and confidence that makes the difference. Some administrators, however, stress that they need to be attending to other issues, and mention the impact of new information and communication technologies as a pressing key concern and not unrelated to literacy.

Many principals construct a continuing narrative thread between their current work and that supported by the former DSP:

> I don't really do anything different now to what we did in the DSP. That's still the best way to work out what this particular school needs. Sure we look at literacy, we always did, and we look at our needs, collect our baseline data and do action research and design our own school programs (primary school principal).

Others see that very different circumstances now prevail: 'How much can you decide democratically in the school when it's already decided that you're doing literacy? I make more decisions about money now than I ever used to in the DSP when parents and staff could decide on priorities' (primary school principal). Many find themselves engaged in exercises of simulation, doing what they think is necessary while being seen to do what is required: 'We spend the money as we need to. So if the kids need help with transport to and from school, we spend the money and then try to measure their literacy improvement' (secondary school principal).

But if these school principals have mixed feelings about the CLP as a school change strategy, they are less sanguine about the capacity of the CLP, with its single focus and limited resources, to deal with what they experience as dramatically increasing poverty in their school populations.

CLP: CONTEXT BLIND

One of the key differences between the CLP and the DSP is that whereas the DSP was concerned with how socioeconomic contexts of education were both produced and reproduced through schooling, the CLP is solely concerned with what happens inside schools (cf. Lingard, 1997). By focussing only on literacy, numeracy and vocational education, current national policy agendas, of which the CLP is a part, marginalise discussions about schooling as an institution in which some stocks of knowledge, dispositions and ways of being in the world are privileged, while others—social and individual identities, cultures and literacies—are made liabilities. How the school is implicated in the construction of inequalities is rendered unproblematic: just do literacy and somehow educational outcomes will be equitable!

Ironically, current policy rhetoric positions schools as important contributors to society and particularly the economy, arguing that schooling is an institution that builds character and competencies that count for employment and citizenship. However, any discussion about how cultures, economies and politics contribute to schools, how they shape and position students, teachers, families, schools and neighbourhoods, is largely silenced. The national document *Literacy for All* (DEETYA, 1998), for example, selectively uses DSP literacy research to 'show' that when teachers discuss the home lives of their students, they are making excuses for inaction and rationalising their ineffectiveness. Freebody, Ludwig and Gunn (1995) did examine how deficit discourses at work in the classroom can shape teacher action. Their recommendations, however, were not that discussion of social context was irrelevant, rather they recommended *extensive* professional development and enhanced opportunities for debate about social and cultural issues and schooling. But the national policy remedy for this teacher 'excuse-making' is an unrelenting focus on 'core business', what it is that *can* be done in schools.

The contemporary educational policy focus on 'what can be done' translates into four allied processes:

1. the identification of those students who are 'failing', in order for individuals to become the objects of policy action;

2. training for teachers to improve their technical capacities to do better, thereby teachers becoming the agents of policy action; this simultaneously refocusses attention away from broader questions of the construction of class, gender and race;

3. identification of those schools and classrooms where improvement is (and isn't) occurring, in order that the schools can become sites of intervention;

4. systemic support for 'what works' with individuals, teachers and schools, which consolidates what counts as 'quality', 'good and bad' teaching and 'literacy'.

It is perhaps this simple-minded appeal to possible action and effect (do this, it works, and don't worry about what you can't control) that makes the linear discourses of effectiveness so seductive. But many who have worked in DSP schools and now work in CLP schools know only too well the frustrations of dealing with social injustices that are as hard to theorise as they are to make major headway against.

DSP: DISCOURSE(S) OF DISADVANTAGE

By looking at the corpus of texts produced during the life of the DSP—guidelines, reports, brochures and media articles—it is possible to see some prevailing narratives, 'truths' and 'ways of doing things'. Combined with a range of centrally determined priorities to direct local action and local discussions, it is helpful to formally consider the DSP as a discourse. The DSP discourse officially constructed:

• *A select group of schools categorised as disadvantaged*

This simultaneously ignored the production of privilege as the norm against which disadvantage was judged, while suggesting that the institutional processes that produced and reproduced disadvantage were unique, rather than it being the same system responsible for the re/production of both privilege and disadvantage. This idea was challenged by some of the key players around the DSP, notably Connell and assorted colleagues (Connell et al. 1982; Connell, 1993; Connell, White & Johnston, 1991).

- *A homogenising rhetoric of 'disadvantaged schools'*

The official text focussed on similarities between DSP schools rather than their differences. In practice, however, local differences were accommodated by local decisionmaking. This local particularity was never taken up at the rhetorical level where all DSP schools, parents and communities were assumed to be the same. And it is a simple move from the idea of 'disadvantaged schools' to 'like schools'.

- *A problematic of 'other' which was both a help and a hindrance*

Parents and students in schools and localities labelled as 'disadvantaged' and 'in poverty' were distressed and/or angered by the term: it is hardly surprising that they refused to 'feel good' about being categorised as somehow deficient. Staff who worked in the schools classified as disadvantaged on the basis of the socioeconomic status of their enrolments were pleased to argue that they needed more and different resources and support, but on the other hand, not pleased to be labelled lesser than other schools: a variety of euphemisms to stand for poverty and disadvantage were used (Comber, 1998). The difficult task of explaining face to face to families that their children were statistically less likely to get to university than those from wealthier families and that this did not mean that their school was worse than others, was something to be avoided, if possible.

- *A focus on the institutional site rather than on the individual*

DSP schools were discouraged from undertaking programs that focussed on particular students and their needs for remediation or specialised health and welfare services, in favour of 'whole school change'. Thus it was the DSP school and the social institution of schooling that did the disadvantaging, rather than individual students being disadvantaged. This was always difficult for DSP schools, many of whom were heartily relieved to obtain funding from various 'at risk' programs in the 1980s and 1990s so that they could attend to both the particular and the whole. In some States the focus on the single site also shifted to a locality and cluster, acknowledging the interrelated specificities of particular places.

- *A proliferation of categories*

While sites were homogenised, a proliferation of 'groups' were generated to recognise specific 'disadvantages', as identity politics collided with poverty intervention. Attempting to put together the proliferation of categories and expert knowledges led to clumsy rhetorics around 'multiple' and 'complex' disadvantages. Policy texts grounded firmly in the institutional avoided emerging understandings about the construction of particular classed, raced, gendered subjects, and multiple identities.

- *A binary of compensatory and transformative education*

This construction supported the separation of individual and institution. Welfare projects and remediation for individuals (bad) were juxtaposed against systemic pedagogical and organisational reform (good), rather than rhetorically and materially holding the two in tension.

- *A fuzzy and ineffective focus on learning and the classroom*

Very often DSP schools struggled with how to 'mainstream' smaller projects, rather than establishing the classroom as the centre of intervention.

- *A balance of local/central activity*

Local capacities to generate practice and theory were understood to be vital for systemic reform, and central activity was acknowledged as essential for aggregating ideas, connecting practitioners together in networks and bridging sectoral gaps between universities and schools (Lingard, Knight & Porter, 1993). The rhetoric of parent and student participation (or parent 'empowerment' and 'student voice', as it is often known) has recently been taken up in new neoliberal decentralised structures, while the practices of top-down bottom-up commitment to democratic principles and networked learning that characterised the DSP have been abandoned.

- *Literacy as a set of practices that were understood to 'work' across the curriculum and thus underpinned school success*

The DSP emphasis was on whole-school approaches to literacy: those students experiencing most 'difficulty' were not seen as individuals needing remediation, but rather the place to begin local research into specific local issues and practices.

The strengths of the DSP were its whole schools focus, the latitude it allowed for local schools to determine their own priorities, the emphasis on research and the production of new professional knowledge and practice and its networked collaborative sense of moral purpose.

CLP: DISCOURSE(S) OF INDIVIDUAL IMPROVEMENT

Looking at the texts that make up the CLP—guidelines, reports and ministerial media releases—it is possible to see a different set of prevailing narratives, 'truths' and 'ways of doing things'. The CLP's singular focus both problematises and addresses a set of 'difficulties' largely ignored by the DSP, and might be seen as a further iteration of equity policy. But in many ways, the CLP is the direct policy opposite of the DSP. The CLP officially constructs:

- *Literacy as a 'sign' for poverty*

As a one-shot explanation for the highly complex ecologies of uneven distribution of educational credentials and advantages associated with poverty, 'literacy' is a necessary partial 'solution', but hardly sufficient. Furthermore, the equation of illiteracy and poverty obscures the lived reality of the 'literate poor' students who also experience the processes of the re/production of class via the school system.

- *Illiteracy as a substitute for illiterate 'poor boys'*

There is substantive evidence (Kenway et al., 2000; Lamb & Ball, 1999; Teese, 2000) that by far the biggest 'group' of literacy 'failures' are specifically classed and gendered. Attempting to understand and intervene in the production of illiteracy is thus not simply a matter of focussing on literacy learning, as the CLP proposes, because it is tangled up in the production of particular kinds of working-class masculinities. A simplistic approach focussing only on literacy, for example, may well do little, whereas more nuanced, gender- and class-aware, situated interventions might be more productive.

- *A binary between particular students who are 'failing' in literacy (as measured by systemic tests) and their 'other' who 'succeed'*

This construction fails to recognise how the same system(at)ic educational practices are responsible for both successes and failures. This blindness leaves available for action only those teachers, schools, classrooms and pedagogical processes that are 'failing students'.

- *A focus on technique at the expense of knowledge*

What counts as literate practices, how these might be implicated in the production of 'success and failure' and how they might be changed are sidelined. What are foregrounded are how well students are learning the prescribed outcomes and the efficacy of teachers.

- *A homogenisation of 'literacy'*

Specificities relating to schools ('subject' discipline, [multi]media, and textual genre), students' cultures and ethnicities (dialect, lexicon, access to formal English tuition) and locality (local literacies, narratives and knowledges) are diminished in importance. What *is* regarded as important is what is deemed 'transferable', 'general' and able to be measured.

- *A separation of the formal curriculum from environment*

The formal curriculum in/through which literacy is learned is understood as distinct from the classroom as a holistic environment. Learning to 'do school' by adhering to classroom conventions and disciplinary processes is carved off and labelled 'behaviour management' and made oppositional to literacy rather than seen as the one process and learning experience.

• *A separation of the school from its context*
Evidence about the delimiting effects of systemic policy on what it is possible for students and teachers to do (e.g. through the provision of equipment, class sizes, and public examinations) is not taken into account. Similarly, as already discussed earlier, sociocultural issues, for example, poverty, unemployment and transience, are ignored or dismissed as 'excuse making', 'union activism' or 'political correctness'.

• *A diagnostic approach*
There are regimes to diagnose and apparatus to 'explain' individual student 'failure' (since social explanations are unacceptable) and a resulting proliferation of time-consuming and costly negotiated plans, expert systems, specialist programs and training packages. Once individual students are categorically isolated, they can then be physically removed from the classroom for short (e.g. the New Zealand program Reading Recovery) or long (e.g. the US program Head Start) periods of time for specialised assistance. It is worth noting that one of the major critiques of such 'pull out' programs is that they can have deleterious long-term consequences on both formal and social learning (Ellsworth & Ames, 1998). There are various alternatives, such as using additional staff to reduce class size, now favoured by many former 'individual support' policymakers.

• *A shifting of responsibility for 'failure'*
Failure to learn is the fault of particular students, teachers and schools who become the site for further policy action. This aspect of the CLP has comparable variations in the allocation of designated time for literacy (UK) and in the 'naming and shaming' via competitive inter- and intra-school league tables (US & UK).

• *A compensatory narrative*
The CLP story suggests that teachers and schools must remedy individual deficiencies. At the same time there is also a story of transformation in which 'all children succeed', because they have all been 'fixed up'. This is the epitome of 'wishful rationality' (Simola, 1998).

DSP AND CLP AS A BINARY

The DSP and the CLP have different, but related stories to tell. Some of the key differences are summarised in the table on p. 178.

Table 9.1 Comparison of aspects of the DSP and CLP

Focus	DSP	CLP
Mission	Schools contribute to improving social justice.	Schools improve educational outcomes, specifically literacy.
Policy rationale	Schools are active agents of the re-production of social inequities. It is in the national interest for this to be changed.	Australia must have a literate workforce.
Policy preferred mode	Schools, systems and universities must find out together how to do better.	School systems will improve if they are given targets for and access to expertise and best practice.
Local scope for action	Local determination of needs and strategies within central guidelines.	Local implementation of centrally determined priority, local adoption of centrally developed strategies.
Site of action	Whole school.	Individual.
Focus of action	Diverse aims, including broad view of literacy(ies).	Literacy, and a dominant view of literacy as reading, writing and spelling.
Mode of change	Curriculum reform; action research.	Improvement of teacher knowledge and teaching techniques; diagnosis of student 'failures' and remediation.

This diagram is not meant to suggest that working beyond these simplistic dualities did and does not happen in schools and systems, but rather that it is and always was work 'against the grain'. Indeed, many rustbelt principals suggest that their efforts in both the DSP and CLP were and are often directed towards combining aspects of what these policy discourses attempt to separate and divide.

Despite being an artificial and necessarily limited heuristic, taking the two policy discourses together offers the possibilities of seeing how and where they are constructed as oppositional. This is an important activity because, as Pam Gilbert (2000, p. 33) explains:

> Oppositional paradigms . . . can be dangerous: not only are they limiting in the perspectives they allow us to generate, but they are potentially naive in their capacity to support exploration of social contexts and social values. Situations, issues, contexts, people, events can all be more sensitively and perceptively explored if we acknowledge and accept their inevitable complexity and plurality, rather than attempt to bracket such diversity out of our considerations.

The DSP and the CLP together reflect such oppositional logic. Where the DSP focussed on the social, the CLP focusses on the individual. Where the DSP fostered notions of curriculum, the CLP focusses on instruction—and neither produce a robust conceptualisation of pedagogy or knowledge. While the DSP fostered discussion on school change, and the CLP on changing teaching and classroom processes, debates about what might be required of schooling in and for changing times was not a prime concern. Where the DSP focussed on the local, the CLP focusses on the central and comparative—and neither allows for the variable specificities of local/central relationships that this-ness implies. Where the DSP focussed on school-based inquiry and teachers generating theory/practice, the CLP relies on teachers learning 'state of the art' theory/practice—and neither allows for a rich and diverse mix of theory-generated practice and practice-saturated theory. Neither the DSP or the CLP made/make strong connections with other areas of public policy. Only the DSP supported robust debate about justice and equity, and neither the DSP nor the CLP have foregrounded issues around identities.

Any new equity policy might well begin by refusing simple binary logic to embrace complexities and ambiguities. It could focus on both sides of the column at once, even though they are in substantial tension. Such tension is productive.

Policymakers might also look around to see what can be learned from the vernacular practices and everyday experiences of rustbelt schools.

10 | Doing justice

Policy making is inevitably a process of bricolage: a matter of borrowing and copying bits and pieces of ideas from elsewhere, drawing upon and amending locally tried and tested approaches, cannibalising theories, research, trends and fashions and not infrequently flailing around for anything at all that looks as though it might work (Ball, 1998a, p. 127).

The stories told in this book point to a renewed policy framework to better support rustbelt schools, families and neighbourhoods. This is neither the time nor place to go into detail, but rather to gesture towards some broad principles for action and attention. There are many policy matters that have arisen in different sections of this text, but most of them fit under the following eight broad principles. These are intended to be invitations to a discussion, not principles for adoption. They are, however, principles that might be used to judge equity policy as it continues to shift and change.

These principles sit together with the understandings of reform scholars who suggest that education policy must:

- give attention to engaging students and parents as active participants;
- expand the teaching and learning repertoires of teachers and students;
- adopt a systemic perspective with coherence and contingency inbuilt across the policy agenda;

- take a school-development perspective, informed by the research on school change (Hopkins & Levin, 2000, p. 20–1).

PRINCIPLES OF JUSTICE

(1) SCHOOLS AND 'THE SOCIAL' ARE INTERWOVEN

This book demonstrates connections between the social and schools.

Rustbelt schools are enmeshed in the totality of the globalised nation–state policy relations. Wholescale economic, cultural and social changes and economic, cultural, social and even foreign policy can be seen in the day-to-day life of schools. The dismantling of the Australian welfare assistance state and the erosion of the social wage that enabled nearly all Australians to have a relatively good standard of living are marked by the rise of market principles, self-insurance, privatisation and cuts in public expenditure. In new and hard times, families are made vulnerable because parents either cannot get ongoing and secure work or, if they are engaged in so called unpaid work such as raising children, their welfare benefits are now increasingly likely to be tied to work obligations. Even though there is no absolute border between 'rich and poor', as is suggested by the aerial views of planners and demographers and sociological terms like 'rustbelt', there is never-theless a non-synchronous common 'class' terrain on which multiples of different gendered, aged, raced and hard lives are lived.

Teachers and principals deal with the results of inequalities—but they also play their part in the production of social inequalities through the institutional mediation of policy and the broader social context, and the distribution of the cultural capital that counts. If schooling is to be changed to become fairer, then it is vital that policymakers acknowledge the permeability of schools as well as their institutional capabilities and the relationship between the two.

If education policy is based on and in understanding the convo-luted and shifting imbrication of schools and society then expectations of schools, the amount and distribution of funds and staffing, quality assurance practices, administrative procedures, and guidelines and infra-structures to support teacher learning and everyday operations will be organised differently. The histories of changing social, political, cultural, technological, economic and educational arrangements can come into view. The systemic production of privilege and disadvantage will be opened up to debate, together with more nuanced discussions about what kind of education might be needed in and for the future.

(2) IDEALISM AND REALISM ARE IN PRODUCTIVE TENSION

As has often been said, schools cannot create an equal society. Anyon (1997, p. 170), in discussing inner urban schools in the United States, puts it this way: 'Any educational initiatives that are chosen for inner city schools and districts will need to be combined with attempts to improve the economic and political milieus in which the schools are located.'

Seen in this broader context, 'doing justice' is a daunting task. The very idea seems to require extraordinary tenacity and capabilities, to demand efforts beyond the possible. It is easy to understand how the discourse of 'core business' and making a difference by focussing on only a few topics (like literacy) are so seductive. It is easy to understand how, when resources become increasingly stretched and other cooperating agencies harder to find, schools do the things that they have the capacity to achieve rather than disperse their scant time across an ever increasing set of options and needs. It is easy to empathise with those who can no longer do the task, who have just run out of emotional will to keep plugging away against the odds.

A reasonable and achievable set of expectations of rustbelt schools should be adopted, not as a 'second best', but in recognition of their particular social place and conflicting tasks. It is not the case in rustbelt schools that nothing can be done, nor is it the case that everything can be done. Even holding to common goals for schooling and national reporting, there must be a way found to shift from 'one best', standardised policy and accountability requirements to recognising the specific issues specific rustbelt schools face. It is not reasonable to expect schools where, for example, there are highly mobile populations and the major issue for teachers is to establish relationships and learning continuity, to have the same emphasis on improving literacy test results as other schools with more stable populations. It *is* a matter of making a positive difference—but rustbelt staffs cannot pretend that there is an impermeable barrier between the school and the 'outside', and as if institutional practices and policies are not at issue (cf. Thrupp, 1999).

At the same time, realism should not translate into lowered expectations for individual children and young people. Teachers and schools must act as if every Vicki and Thanh can learn what matters for them to have equal life chances, as well as take up the things that interest them. And while teachers and schools might be disappointed when this does not miraculously occur within the time frame of the annual or three-year plan, they should not be regarded or regard themselves as failing—they are engaged in an ongoing intellectual and emotional struggle against the odds. Nor should realism equate with the abandonment of the imaginary of a just and caring society. It is these dreams that provide us with hope and with ways of being (ontologies) and ways of understanding the world (epistemologies) and how it might be (axiologies): it is with and from this standpoint that we interrogate and make judgements about our everyday practices as well as that of the school system.

Realism and idealism are in tension with each other, and it is a tension that is productive if recognised rather than ignored.

(3) CONTINGENCY AND UNCERTAINTY ARE ACKNOWLEDGED

The notion of a contingent curriculum and school might replace the 'distributive curriculum' and the 'effective school' with their fixed and unquestionable outcomes. The notion of contingency allows for change and for the production of new understandings about schooling. Not only would this allow rustbelt schools to explore and innovate at the local level to develop the kinds of pedagogy and curriculum that might better meet the needs, interests and knowledges of their particular students, but it would provide legitimacy for such activity. Contingency permits experimentation at the edges of schooling— with its institutional gridlock of time, age-grade promotion and discipline. It encourages thinking about how changing life worlds, popular cultures and local and indigenous knowledges connects to schools. It allows for teachers and principals to work with new partners and new technologies. Embracing contingency also requires continual conversation and examination of what is happening and whether it is of benefit to students or not, whether there are other options and alternatives, whether important things are being lost or damaged.

(4) THE LOCAL AND 'THISNESS' ARE THE BASIS OF POLICY

Complexity matters. What is common to rustbelt schools is that the majority of their students come from families who are currently 'doing it tough', who have been made vulnerable by de-industrialisation and who are not well placed to get the benefits of the re-industrialisation that is occurring in the city. However, it is not a simple matter of the rustbelt schools being poor and irrevocably divided from more privileged locations and schools. There are differences between schools based on sector—primary or secondary, and on school enrolment.

There are also substantive differences between each rustbelt school. Each of them is unique as well as occupying a similar socio-institutional place (see Appendix for a thisness checklist). Thisness also offers possibilities for allowing school-by-school modifications to global budgets using transparent and defensible criteria. It offers a set of issues that schools might use to present a case for particular funding. Some, such as student mobility, are already included in global budget allocations in some States. If rustbelt schools were able to systematically document what issues were delimiting their capacity to make a difference, and if the education system were able to 'see' those factors amenable to systemic policy response, then some ongoing and intractable issues might be put on the agenda in different ways. For example, one of the more common but not universal issues in the rustbelt schools, as noted, has to do with staff turbulence. This may not be resolved by placing responsibility for staffing at the local level and may well require other forms of systemic policy response. If the school administrators in rustbelt schools are right, then a policy priority of stabilising staffing may well do more for students' literacy attainment than many other interventions. Similarly, student transience, which adversely affects only a few schools, may be moderated by differential finding and counselling support, but might be additionally improved through some cooperative activity between the education system and public housing agencies. This would become apparent by systematically 'looking' at thisness, rather than acting as if such factors can be screened out.

(5) A HOLISTIC, INTEGRATED AND REGIONAL POLICY FRAMEWORK IS DEVELOPED AND MAINTAINED

Acknowledging the society–school relationship and thisness means that policies for rustbelt schools ought not to be treated separately from other related government policies that impact on neighbourhoods. An overall policy framework is needed, one that seeks to manage markets and equity together, that holds in balance the private and social benefits of education, and that has as its focus the growth and development of financial, physical, human and social capitals. A combined (State and Federal) policy approach that integrates, coordinates and allows for pooling of funds to support job creation, labour market and business development, public housing, transport, health and welfare may profoundly improve aspects of the context of local neighbourhoods and their schools.

Because globalisation and neoliberal policies have combined to produce new and deeper inequalities and polarisation between urban and rural regions, as well as between and within regions, such an integrated policy approach needs to have a regional focus. An approach which allows for regional decisionmaking, and increased participation in discussion as well as regional action is important.[1] Crucially and unlike regional policies focussed on social exclusion in the United Kingdom, economic policy should not be separated from social policy, nor should the interests of any one sector dominate decisionmaking bodies. It is important too to avoid the kind of decentralisation that binds the local tightly with guidelines, unreasonable and unrealistic accountability measures and impossible time lines. An enabling State framework may be able, for example, to tackle 'the uneven development in incomes and high-paying jobs' (Fincher & Saunders, 2001a, p. 33) in ways that regional communities cannot, so the relationship between State and region is also important.

A holistic policy framework must get below the level of the region to smaller and more sensitive geographies. The creation, support and strengthening of vertical and horizontal social, economic, cultural and political networks is important. Community development processes that link together the local and the region are necessary. At the same time, steps must be taken to avoid the tyrannies of localism. A neighbourhood-based policy that supports work from and with local assets and capabilities, without spending huge sums of time-money on coordination and meetings, is something to which rustbelt schools can importantly contribute.

Social and economic policies must be flexible and responsive for those localities most pushed to the limits. When there are local crises, such as in one small neighbourhood and school suddenly beset with a significant number of new families with substance-abuse problems, then sufficient coordinated resources need to be locally mobilised without huge bureaucratic fanfare and time-consuming performance requirements. Where there are concentrations of families in crisis, with schools and charities extended beyond their limits, there must be provision for continuing intensive support coordinated at the local level.

Additional professional development should be available to all staff, including those in schools, who work in hard-pressed rustbelt locations. Such professional learning should be locally geared to building 'leadership depth' and local networks and should be based in specific issues and needs. The emotional toll of working with families at the end of their patience and optimism needs to be taken into account and a variety of support mechanisms put into place, including immediate transfer without personal or professional stigma.

(6) ADEQUATE RESOURCES ARE PROVIDED

There must be adequate financial resourcing by governments for disadvantaged schools. If they are to do more, then they need more.

Rustbelt schools simply must have *more* staff. The task of catering for the very diverse range of students and the specific sets of issues that they bring with them to school requires significant expertise, for example, counsellors, as well as lower class sizes. Just dealing with the volume and level of stress, grief, anger and alienation of some children is a task that more advantaged schools do not have. Any formula that treats all students and all schools the same will discriminate in favour of the already advantaged. Nor will it be the case that there will be two groups of schools—'disadvantaged' and the others. A differential mechanism that also recognises differences is necessary.

An urgent priority for rustbelt schools is achieving staffing stability with well-trained committed staff. This does not necessarily mean local hire or fire, nor even local selection. It is often automatically assumed that the answer to poor central performance is to move the task to the local level rather than improve the central processes. Further experimentation with mixes of central and local staff selection are needed.

The centre must develop formulas for redistribution that take into account discipline, order and curriculum change. The formulas must be more finely tuned to individual schools and their capacity to raise additional funds, their specific enrolments and neighbourhood assets.

(7) DEMOCRATIC WORK BUILDS LOCAL ASSETS

Working with the local and contingent opens up possibilities for schools to become significant neighbourhood assets. The World Bank (1999) argues that:

> Family, community and state involvement (in education) helps to increase the relevance and quality of education by improving ownership, building consensus, reaching remote and disadvantaged groups, mobilising additional resources and strengthening institutional capacity.

Example one: local school management means that schools have control of larger sums of money and relative autonomy in expenditure. Local schools *might* look to see what this could do in their neighbourhoods—getting not necessarily the cheapest deal from any source, but buying and hiring local in order to benefit the neighbourhood, and in the longer term, the students. This is an idea that is gaining currency in the United States where schools are increasingly seen as central to urban renewal projects. Driscoll and Kerchner (1999) argue:

> In most poor city and suburban neighbourhoods, relatively little of the school's funds find their way into the immediate community. The multiplier effect of school expenses on the local micro-economy is severely attenuated and so too are the social capital-generating activities associated with incomes and prosperity.

Schools that wish to direct their resources to such multiplying effects might decide to hire local people and contractors. They could decide to patronise local enterprises rather than go to big chains and multi-national distribution agents. Given the often considerable funds at the disposal of some schools at particular times, such approaches might, while not necessarily getting the immediate cheapest 'deal', have considerable spin-offs for local employment and wellbeing, as well as plugging the school into local assets/neighbourhood networks.

Example two: in de-industrialised and rural localities where social networks are emptying out and public infrastructure increasingly underfunded and scarce, children and young people are often left, as Nespor (1997) writing of a rust belt in the United States suggests, 'without a locus of embodied, locally meaningful activity'. His descriptions of the solitary pursuits of young people 'spinning round skating rinks, dreaming of roller coasters, ogling commodities in the mall or sitting in front of their televisions' have considerable resonance with similar Australian studies. Hasluck and Malone (1999), for example, report that young unemployed, underemployed and school students are spending increased amounts of time at home because, despite their keen interest in sport, '. . . lack of access to sports and leisure activities, regulation and representation of spaces, and restricted mobility are all issues young people must deal with before participation' (p. 195). Indeed, they say, '. . . the only option for many working class kids is to maintain involvement passively through television content, dress style, video games and informal sporting pursuits' (p. 195).

The lack of active and accessible recreation is an agenda which city rustbelt and isolated schools could certainly take on (and indeed a few of them have), since the everyday lives of children and young people, and planning and providing for their futures, are the chief concern of schools. Furthermore, because the boundaries between the school and its neighbourhood are highly porous, what happens to children and young people outside school has considerable impact on what does and can happen at school. Acting to support local families

and the young people themselves to improve access to, and participation in, local recreational activities could easily be argued as being in
the educational interests of schools and their students.

School systems can make it difficult or easy for schools to support
neighbourhood projects and broaden their focus to include what is
happening outside the school gate. At the very least, school systems
committed to supporting socially productive neighbourhood–school
relations would:

- redistribute funds through the global budget processes so that
  local school management did not contribute to increased
  differences between neighbourhoods;
- develop protocols and processes for the provision of additional funds
  for the use of school facilities by local communities and for the use
  of local facilities for educational purposes (cf. Bentley, 1998);
- support local schools who make local community development a
  priority by providing them with sufficient resources for the
  employment of people with particular community expertise, for
  example, parent liaison, bilingual community workers, indigenous
  education workers;
- build social and economic capital-generating activities, such as
  cooperative activities between schools and contributions to
  neighbourhood networks and infrastructure, into quality
  assurance and official recognition processes;
- increase civic engagement by parents and students and develop
  curriculum approaches that promote understanding of the
  complexities of communities to the same level as that accorded
  vocational education.

(8) SUPPORT FURTHER RESEARCH

Rustbelt school administrators are looking for three things from the
academy:

- *Research that provides evidence for equity and justice policymaking*

While this has been the intent behind this book, given the current
predilection for quantitative research, different methods might well be
used to re-examine many of the issues raised. For example, while
rustbelt principals are prepared to make percentage claims about the
amount of time they spent on disciplinary matters, a systematic study
to follow up the situation in disadvantaged and privileged schools

might be very instructive, provided it did not adopt a 'blame the student, families, neighbourhoods or cultures' approach. Similarly, international and local studies of school funding, not unlike that of Townsend (1998) in Victoria, would provide evidence for the argument that disadvantaged schools do more with less.

• *Research that assists schools to identify places and practices where they need to do justice*
It is important to research how it is that students 'fail' and 'succeed' and how it is that teachers as mediators and resource providers produce inequities. It is helpful to continue to deconstruct policy and the textual practices of schools as institutions. (It is even more helpful if these do not become what Fine and Weiss [1998] aptly call 'texts of despair'.) Narratives of the real life of schools attempting to change, narratives based on empirical study that do not seek to create 'best practice' and models, but rather tell particular stories that exemplify potentially useful principles for ways of working, have some hope of connecting with the reform efforts of other real life schools (Clandinin & Connelly, 1998). Such research would be mutually constructed and conducted.

• *Sharing mutual stories*
There is a pressing need to continue to support teachers and schools making efforts to 'do justice'. It is evident in the conversations of school administrators that the scholarly community of peers in universities and professional associations can be very important—sharing concepts, language and connections that become resources on which schools can draw as they work to make local sense and actions from imposed policies.

While there are, of course, many other possibilities for research these are the ones that schools would find most immediately useful.

NO NEW IDEAS AFTER ALL?

As I write this conclusion and attempt to make some headway towards a new policy framework, I am struck by how similar this list is to the vision of the Henderson Poverty Inquiry (1975). In the schools' volume of the inquiry a year later, Fitzgerald wrote:

> People who are poor and disadvantaged are victims of a societal confidence trick. They have been encouraged to believe that a major goal of schooling is to increase equality, while in reality, schools reflect society's intention to maintain the present distribution of status and power.

Henderson, Fitzgerald and their poverty commission colleagues did not, however, think that this analysis was final. They developed an integrated, locality-based policy and planning approach to redressing social division, a hopeful picture of what schools might do to benefit students and the wider community and a recognition that schools needed to change.

Connell and his various colleagues (Connell et al., 1982; Connell et al., 1990; 1991) made much the same analysis and quoted Fitzgerald. They also argued for a local curriculum focus, democratic processes at the local school and central levels, programs tailored to specific local situations, and greater integration of education, health and welfare. These recommendations were written in the light of already obvious long-term and high youth unemployment and the weakening faith of working-class parents and students in the capacity of schools to lead to a good life and/or social mobility. Connell and his colleagues (1991, p. 33) suggested that there were two goals for a social justice program in education:

- to work to eliminate the contribution that the education system makes to the production over time of social inequity in general; and
- to maximise the positive contributions that the education system makes to social equality.

The strength of these interconnected goals is that they eliminate the separation of welfare work from education work and the separation of disadvantaged schools from the wider education system.

Since Fitzgerald and Henderson wrote in the 1970s and Connell and colleagues in the 1980s and early 1990s, both poverty and wealth have arguably changed—more people are economically vulnerable; more of the economically vulnerable are concentrated in particular parts of the city; young people have less optimistic life options; and both State and Federal Governments have less money and even less will to address the issues.

But like Henderson, Fitzgerald and Connell, I would argue that education policy cannot be separated from other public policies and that working for social justice is inevitably linked to working for economic justice and working to eliminate the new and old geographies of distinction.

I cling to imaginings of a more just school system. The ongoing challenge is how to move from where we are to a more equitable and civil society. After all, Vicki and Thanh's future depends on it.

Appendix

DOING JUSTICE—WHAT SCHOOLS NEED

Schools find the current annual report process tedious. By and large they do find the statistics they are now collecting useful. The question seems to be how to put these in a frame that makes more sense at the local level. If we have a systemic outcomes framework which not only relied on the normal statistics such as retention, attendance and test scores, but added a richer set of questions which schools could deal with as well . . .

Some questions drawn from analysis of principals' conversation and school documents follow. These might be a useful framework for school reviews and reports.

ACCESS

Are children and young people able to take up educational programs that meet their specific and collective needs and interests? Are there particular patterns of attendance, health and welfare issues, lack of English language instruction, particular physical facilities, ways of doing things that are working to limit student and family access? Are there school structures and cultures that act as barriers? Are the knowledges that count, and the information about why they count, equally available to all children and young people?

DISCOURSE

Is family, culture and/or neighbourhood used as an explanation for inequity? Do children, young people and their families have a say in how they are named and categorised? Have all children and their families heard their story? Can they tell their story, and where necessary act on it?

OPPORTUNITY

Do all children and young people get quality support in making choices about the programs and knowledges they will take up? Is there an explicit monitoring of and intervention in systematic patterns of inequitable choices? Are all children and young people able to build positive identities in the school? Can and do all children and young people engage in the productive individual and collective work they and others value?

PARTICIPATION

Can all children and young people meaningfully engage with the curriculum and life in the school? Can they get pleasure and reward from their participation? Do they have a part in making decisions about what they need and want? Are all children and young people able to achieve the knowledges and repertoires of practice that will enable them to be active contributors to families, communities and economies?

THISNESS

We also need a way to think past the simplistic accountability discourse of 'like schools', to actually get to grips with why things happen as they do in particular places . . . In order to begin to get a grip on 'thisness', the following list and questions are a starting point:

NEIGHBOURHOOD MATTERS

School mix

How are students in this school affected by:

- changes in the labour market—levels of unemployment/ underemployment/tenuous employment? Is this a long term trend? How is this connected to changes in the global and national economy?
- changes in families—what combinations of separated, blended and extended families are there in this school?
- changes in public policy—what health issues are there in this neighbourhood? Who can get to school on public transport? How have public housing decisions affected who comes to this school?
- concentration of families in crisis—how many families are pushed to the edge in their current circumstances? How is this playing out in the school? How many students and families are transient? What effects is this having in the school?
- patterns of migration and diaspora—what immediate language and cultural support needs are in the school? Are there families that are dealing with the traumas of persecution and forced migration? Are there families and children who are the victims of racism?
- changing enrolment—is this neighbourhood growing or declining? Is there a concentration of any particular gender, religious, ethnic or cultural group in the school?

Resources available to the school in the neighbourhood

What resources are there, for example:

- community infrastructure—what services are available in the neighbourhood? What local funds of knowledge, locally managed infrastructures and institutions are there?
- employment and employment networks—what work is available in the local area? What businesses are there? How are local enterprises affected by globalisation and microeconomic reform? How are students connected to employment networks? Is there competition between local schools for access to work placements?
- availability of voluntary labour—how many parents have time to donate to the school? What opportunities does the school provide for parents? Are school expectations of parent time congruent with their everyday life worlds?
- age of locality—age of school facilities. Is the school rundown and in need of repair? Does it need upgrading? What influence can the school exert on decisionmakers about the condition of

plant? What capacity does the school have to pay for some renovation and repair themselves?

- income based on parent contribution and fundraising—how much can the school depend on funds other than that given by the government? Are there particular local circumstances that enable the school to raise funds? Is this in competition with other local school?

Neighbourhood issues

What is going on locally that impacts on the school, namely:

- specific local events—are there local acts of racism, a culture of lighting fires and vandalism against school properties, events that have garnered unwelcome media attention, murders and tragedies?
- neighbourhood change—is the neighbourhood in the process of redevelopment? Is the school undergoing external review or targeted for closure or amalgamation because of population decline?
- history of the school—what place does this school have in the regional hierarchy of schools? What local stories circulate about it?

There are also differences in schools that are related to systemic policy, so:

EDUCATION MATTERS

System support

- school administration—were people appointed because of and with a commitment to and understanding of justice and equity?
- staffing turbulence—what is the turnover of teachers? How many reluctant placements are there? Can the school get the staff it wants and needs? Is there casualisation of support staff? How much turnover is there in the leadership team?
- staffing 'fit'—are there staff who can 'do justice' as their professional work? Is there a spread of leaders in the school staff? Are there enough teacher-leaders?
- income—is there sufficient systemic redistribution to compensate for locality factors? How does this school's budget compare with

that of wealthier localities? What extra expenses are there in this school?

- 'fit' between system quality assurance and school needs and level of documentation required—is the accountability culture one of blame and performativity? Do principals feel that they have to simulate plans and performance to meet systemic requirements? How much time is spent on accountability and documentation? Is there a culture of inquiry in the school?

- professional development—is the school able to do research into more equitable schooling practices? Is there support for networks of schools, teachers and administrators? Are schools able to connect with universities and get access to current research as well as work in partnership with them? Is there a rigorous debate around pedagogies and practices that do justice?

- Support for school-based democratic practices—are schools expected to implement policy without discussion at the same time as they are judged on how consultative they are?

Using these questions, one can begin to imagine a school system beginning to develop a more sensitive approach to resourcing, and a more supportive approach to accountability.

Notes

1 VICKI AND THANH

1   See Bourdieu & Passeron (1977) for a specific commentary on schooling, and Bourdieu's *Distinction* (1984) for the theorisations of difference, differentiation and distinction itself.

2 THE CITY

1   The 1996 Census of Population and Housing (Australian Bureau of Statistics, 1997b) set the mean average personal weekly income for the State in which our city is located at $267. When these figures are broken down into smaller units, some of the differences come into view. The city and inner city enjoyed an average personal weekly income of $522, with two inner eastern areas following on $492 and $417 respectively. By contrast, the 1996 Census showed that the lowest average weekly personal incomes were found in the northwest with $177 and $192 in the outer north (Australian Bureau of Statistics, 1998).

2   Eagle eye maps showing these pictures can be found in the South Australian Social Atlas (Australian Bureau of Statistics, 1997a) and the Social Health Atlas (Glover et al., 2000).

3   For example, single parents are poor, not because they are single parents but because of particular government decisions about levels of income support available to single parents. In Australia, as in the United States and the United Kingdom, governments have regarded welfare benefits as a minimum living allowance, whereas in Scandinavian countries, by contrast, such income support payments are closely linked to average wages and subsequently in those countries the correlate of single parents and low income would not apply (UNICEF, 1996).

4   These figures are from Spoehr (1998b). It is important to note that the figures are now substantially reduced by a combination of narrowing eligibility criteria for unemployment benefits, an increase in part-time employment and some economic recovery.

5   Eighty-one weeks as compared to the national average of 53 weeks.

6   From a taped conversation cited with permission.

7   Accessible introductions to debates about globalisation can be found in Allen and Hamnett (1995) and Wiseman (1998). Populist accounts of changes in work and organisations can be located in any airport bookshop—see Handy (1994), Reich (1991) and Rifkin (1996), for example. More detailed scholarly accounts can readily be found—to get a sense of the field see Appadurai (1996) on localisation of global cultural shifts; Castells' *Information Age* trilogy (1996; 1997; 1998); edited collections by Balakrishnan (1996), Cvetkovitch and Kellner (1997), Jameson and Myoshi (1998); and Big Theory, such as Bauman (1998), Beck (1992) and Lash and Urry (1994).

8   See, for example, Massey (1995) and Swyngedouw (1997).

9   For the argument for government policy directions, see journalist Paul Kelly's account (1994). For the case against, see Bell (1997), Carroll and Manne (1992), the seminal Pusey (1991), and Rees and Rodley (1995). On education policy, see Lingard, Knight and Porter (1993), Marginson (1993; 1997a & b), and Taylor et al. (1997).

10 For information on poverty in Australia start with Bryson and Winter (1999), Fincher and Nieuwenhuysen (1998), and Troy (1995; 1999). For discussion about the particular state of South Australia, see Spoehr (1999).

11 See Eckersley (1998) for a range of perspectives on the idea of the 'good life'.

12 In this state, the reducing capacity of the state to raise revenue for public services, such as schools, hospitals, roads and public transport, was compounded by the Federal Government's decision to

relax monetary policy in order to sustain economic activity after the 1987 share market collapse. The availability of funds encouraged rampant speculation and lending for property investment. The subsequent Federal Government-induced recession through the raising of interest rates in 1989 meant that property debts were unable to be realised and many financial institutions found themselves with significant difficulties. In one Australian state a merchant bank and an entire network of investments collapsed, leaving thousands of investors, big and small, suddenly without savings and security. In this state, the State Bank suffered massive debt. One estimate puts its losses at $3000 million (Walmsley & Wernard, 1997, p. 73). The spectacular collapse of the State Bank resulted in its sale and the rejection of the state's long-term Labor Government.

13 For details about this state, see Spoehr (1999a); about Victoria, Webber and Crooks (1996) and for the nation, Troy (1999).

3 PLACE OF TROUBLE/TROUBLED PLACES

1   These scenes are constructed from interview data and one is taken from printed material.
2   This deconstruction is informed by critical ethnographies of the working of 'risk' discourse (e.g. Fine, 1995; Fine & Weis, 1998; Gitlin, Margonis & Brunjes, 1993; Swadener, 1995).

4 BRINGING PARTICULARITY INTO SITE

1   This was one of my oversights when I was a principal in the north.

5 RHETORIC AND RESOURCES

1   The credit allowance is allocated when the parents can demonstrate, by means of an income declaration, their poverty (generally this means their receipt of income assistance due to unemployment, illness and disability or sole parenting). This line of credit is a marginal improvement on the previous scheme, known as 'Free Books' (and the students as 'Free Book kids'), by which the family had no discretion over the expenditure.

6   STAFFING MATTERS

1   These short-term appointments have a complex genesis. The metropolitan surplus of teachers and the shortage of staff in the country was resolved for some time by the combined policy of guaranteed return to the city for country teachers after four years and the 'ten year rule', which makes compulsory a move every ten years for all classroom teachers. Merit-based selection procedures that go on late in the year and require short-term back-fill also create temporary jobs. Industrial negotiations now play their part, too, in creating the need for short-term staff positions in schools, as state-funded special needs salary has become a bargaining chip. Short-term vacancies are filled by PATs—Permanent teacher Against a Temporary vacancy. PATs can be placed in short-term vacancies from one term to one year.

2   There are still two affirmative staffing strategies that remain in the system. The two single-sex girls' schools in the system choose *all* of their staff according to specific criteria and this works better for the middle class school than for the disadvantaged school. One cluster of schools in Elizabeth offers long-term contracts, some of which become permanent, to unemployed, often young, teachers. These are relatively successful and do provide some stability in the handful of schools involved. P21, the state devolution scheme, may offer staffing advantages, but details of this are not public knowledge and are subject to a parliamentary inquiry.

7   THE POLICY TERRAIN

1   See Kenway et al. (1997); Marginson (1993; 1997a; 1997b); Taylor et al. (1997); and Thomson (1999b).

2   See Davis (1997); Dunant and Porter (1996); and Feldstein (1997) for accounts of the 'political correctness' ideology, its adherents and tactics.

3   Patterns of unpredictable voting and the rise of 'independent' politicians regularly produced the decline of public confidence in government analysis. Headlines such as 'The loss of trust' (*Weekend Australian*, Review, 13–14 November 1999, p. 5), 'Let's rebuild a tribal Australia' (the *Age*, 17 June 1999), and 'Why we love to be governed' (*Weekend Australian*, 21–22 February 1998, p. 26) and 'Why voters are bitter' (the *Age*, 23 July 1998) suggest the tenor of the public debate.

4   The distinctions between vocationalist and generalist approaches, as opposed to what are more commonly regarded as 'vocational' and 'general' subjects, were originally devised by Carr and Hartnett (1996) and I have placed them in the Australian context elsewhere (Thomson, 1997).

5   See, for example, Jack Dusseldorp's (1998) speech to Victorian principals in which he leaps to the conclusion that a critique of the instrumentalism of vocational education equates to support for an elite university-oriented curriculum, rather than seeing that there are positions other than a simple for/against binary.

6   The works of UK and US educational writers of various persuasions were influential in Australia—from school ethnographers such as Jackson and Marsden (1966), reproduction theorists such as Bowles and Gintis (1975), resistance theorists (Willis, 1977), deschoolers such as Illich (1973), and progressives such as Holt (1972).

10   DOING JUSTICE

1   There is a significant rekindling of Australian policy interest in regions, for example, Latham (1998), Martin (2000), Spierings (2000) and Fincher and Saunders (2001b).

References

Achilles, C. (1999), *Let's Put Kids First, Finally,* Corwin Press, Thousand Oaks.

—— (2001), 'Class size research', Paper presented to the Australian Education Union (SA Branch) conference, Adelaide, March.

Achilles, C. & Finn, J. (2000), 'The varieties of small classes and their outcome', Paper presented at the Taking Small Classes One Step Further Conference, Temple University, Philadelphia.

ACTU/TD (1985), *Australia Reconstructed: Report of the Joint ACTU-Trade Department Mission to Europe,* Australian Council of Trade Unions, Melbourne.

Allen, J. & Hamnett, C. (eds) (1995), *A Shrinking World? Global Unevenness and Inequality,* Oxford University Press, Oxford.

Allen, J., Massey, D. & Cochrane, A. (2000), *Rethinking the Region,* Routledge, London.

Ames, L. & Ellsworth, J. (1997), *Women Reformed, Women Empowered: Poor Mothers and the Endangered Promise of Head Start,* Temple University Press, Philadelphia.

Angus, M. (1996), 'The integration of the public and private schooling sectors in Australia', in B. Lingard & P. Porter (eds), *A National Approach to Schooling in Australia? Essays on the Development of National Policies in Schools Education,* Australian College of Education, Canberra.

Angwin, J., Henry, C., Laskey, L., McTaggart, R. & Picken, N. (1998), *Paths to Pathway: Vocational Education and Training for Educationally Disadvantaged Groups of Young People*, Deakin Centre for Education and Change, Deakin University, Geelong.

Anyon, J. (1980), 'Social class and the hidden curriculum of work', *Journal of Education*, vol. 162, no. 1, pp. 67–92.

—— (1997), *Ghetto Schooling: A Political Economy of Urban Educational Reform*, Teachers College Press, New York.

Appadurai, A. (1996), *Modernity at Large: Cultural Dimensions of Globalisation*, University of Minnesota Press, Minneapolis.

Armitage, C. (1999), 'Brightest and best', *Weekend Australian*, 23–24 Jan., p. 25.

Australian Bureau of Statistics (1997a), *Adelaide—A Social Atlas. 1996 Census of Population and Housing*, ABS, Canberra.

—— (1997b), *Census of Population and Housing—Selected social and housing characteristics for statistical local areas*, ABS, Canberra.

—— (1998), *Australia in Profile—A Regional Analysis*, ABS, Canberra.

—— (1999), *Education and Training in Australia*, catalogue no. 4224.0, ABS, Canberra.

—— (2000a), *Australian Social Trends 2000*, catalogue no. 4102.0, ABS, Canberra.

—— (2000b), *Labour Force Australia, February 2000*, catalogue no. 6202.0, ABS, Canberra.

—— (2000c), *Labour Force, Teenage Employment and Unemployment Australia, Preliminary*, catalogue no. 6202.0.40.001, ABS, Canberra.

—— (2000d), *Schools, Australia 1991–1998 and 1999*, ABS, Canberra.

Australian Government (1997), *Not a Level Playground*, Senate Standing Committee on Employment, Education and Training, Canberra.

Ayers, W. (2000), 'The standards fraud', in J. Cohen & J. Rogers (eds), *Will Standards Save Public Education?*, Beacon Press, Boston, pp. 64–9.

Bagshaw, D. (1998), *What adolescents say about conflict and peer mediation in secondary schools*, unpublished paper, University of South Australia.

Bakhtin, M. (1981), *The Dialogic Imagination: Four Essays* (trans. M. Emerson), University of Texas Press, Austin.

Balakrishnan, G. (ed.) (1996), *Mapping the Nation*, New Left Review & Verso, London.

Ball, S. (1993), 'What is policy? Texts, trajectories and toolboxes', *Discourse*, vol. 13, no. 2, pp. 3–11.

—— (1997), 'Good school/bad school: Paradox and fabrication', *British Journal of Sociology of Education*, vol. 18, no. 3, pp. 317–36.

—— (1998a), 'Big policies/small world: An introduction to international perspectives in education policy', *Comparative Education*, vol. 34, no. 2, pp. 119–30.

—— (1998b), 'Educational studies, policy entrepreneurship and social theory', in R. Slee & G. Weiner (eds), *School Effectiveness for Whom? Challenges to the School Effectiveness and School Improvement Movements*, Falmer Press, London, pp. 70–83.

Ball, S., Maguire, M. & Macrae, S. (2000), *Choice, Pathways and Transitions Post-16: New Youth, New Economies in the Global City*, Falmer Press, London.

Ball, S. & Vincent, C. (1998), '"I heard it on the grapevine": "hot" knowledge and school choice', *British Journal of Sociology in Education*, vol. 19, no. 3, pp. 377–400.

Bascia, N. & Hargreaves, A. (eds) (2000), *The Sharp Edge of Educational Reform: Teaching, Leading and the Realities of Reform*, Falmer Press, London.

Batten, M. & Russell, J. (1995), *Students at Risk: A Review of Australian Literature 1980–1994*, Australian Council for Educational Research, Melbourne.

Baum, S., Stimson, R., O'Connor, K., Mullins, P. & Davies, R. (1999), *Community Opportunity and Vulnerability in Australia's Cities and Towns*, Australian Housing and Urban Research Institute, Melbourne.

Bauman, Z. (1993), *Postmodern Ethics*, Blackwell Publishers, Oxford.

—— (1998a), *Globalisation: The Human Consequences*, Columbia University Press, New York.

—— (1998b), *Work, Consumerism and the New Poor*, Open University Press, Buckingham.

Beasley, B. (1988), *A Critical Review of the Priority Projects Program*, Priority Projects, South Australian Department of Education, Adelaide.

Beck, U. (1992), *Risk Society: Towards a New Modernity*, Sage, London.

Bell, S. (1997), *Ungoverning the Economy: The Political Economy of Australian Economic Policy*, Oxford University Press, Melbourne.

Bentley, T. (1998), *Learning Beyond the Classroom. Education for a Changing World*, Demos & Routledge, London.

Bessant, J. & Hil, R. (eds) (1997), *Youth, Crime and the Media: Media Representation of and Relation to Young People in Relation to Law and Order*, National Clearinghouse for Youth Studies, Hobart.

Bhaba, H. (1984), 'Of mimicry and man: The ambivalence of colonial discourse', *October*, vol. 28, pp. 125–33.

Birrell, B., Maher, C. & Rapson, V. (1997), 'Welfare dependence in Australia', *People and Place*, vol. 5, no. 2, pp. 68–77.

Bishop, R. & Glynn, T. (1999), *Culture Counts. Changing Power Relations in Education*, Dunmore Press, Palmerston North.

Blatchford, P., Mortimore, P. & Edmonds, S. (2000), 'Symposium on the effects of class size and pupil–adult ratio differences on teaching and learning and educational progress over Key Stage One', Papers presented at the British Educational Research Association, University of Cardiff, 7–10 Sept.

Boomer, G. (1999), 'Curriculum and teaching in Australian schools, 1960–1990: A tale of two epistemologies', in B. Green (ed.), *Designs on Learning: Essays on Curriculum and Teaching by Garth Boomer*, Australian Curriculum Studies Association, Canberra, pp. 127–46.

Bourdieu, P. (1984), *Distinction: A Social Critique of the Judgement of Taste* (trans. R. Nice), Harvard University Press, Boston.

—— (1990), *In Other Words: Essays Towards a Reflexive Sociology*, Stanford University Press, Stanford.

—— (1991), *Language and Symbolic Power*, Polity Press, Oxford.

—— (1998), *Practical Reason: On the Theory of Action*, Blackwell, Oxford.

—— (1999a), 'The order of things', in P. Bourdieu et al. (eds), *The Weight of the World: Social Suffering in Contemporary Society*, Stanford University Press, Stanford, pp. 60–76.

—— (1999b), 'Site effects', in P. Bourdieu et al. (eds), *The Weight of the World: Social Suffering in Contemporary Society*, Stanford University Press, Stanford, pp. 123–9.

Bourdieu, P. & Passeron, V. C. (1977), *Reproduction in Society, Education and Culture*, Sage, London.

Bourdieu, P. & Wacquant, L. (1992), *An Invitation to Reflexive Sociology*, University of Chicago Press, Chicago.

Bowles, S. & Gintis, H. (1975), *Schooling in Capitalist America*, Basic Books, New York.

Brooks, M., Milne, C., Paterson, K., Johansson, K. & Hart, K. (1997), *Under-age School Leaving: A Report Examining Approaches to Assisting Young People at Risk of Leaving School Before the Legal School Leaving Age*, National Clearinghouse for Youth Studies, Hobart.

Brotherhood of St Lawrence (1998), 'State schools: costs and dilemmas', *Changing Pressure Project, no. 2*, Melbourne, http://www.bsl.org.au/cp21.htm, accessed 5 May 1998.

Brown, S. G. (2000), *Words in the Wilderness: Critical Literacy in the Borderlands*, State University of New York Press, Albany.

Bryson, L. & Winter, I. (1999), *Social Change, Suburban Lives: An Australian Newtown 1960s to 1990s*, Australian Institute of Family Studies & Allen & Unwin, Sydney.

Buckby, M. & Woolford, G. (1998), 'Parents behaving badly', *Advertiser*, 28 Mar., p. 48.

Bullen, E., Kenway, J. & Hay, V. (2000), 'New Labour, social exclusion and educational risk management: The case of "gymslip mums"', *British Educational Research Journal*, vol. 26, no. 4, pp. 441–56.

Caldwell, B. (1999), 'Markets, choice and public good in school education', *Australian Journal of Education*, vol. 43, no. 3, pp. 257–72.

Caldwell, B. & Hayward, D. (1997), *The Future of Schools*, Falmer Press, London.

Caldwell, B. & Spinks, J. (1998), *Beyond the Self Managing School: Student Outcomes and the Reform of Education*, Falmer Press, London.

Carr, W. & Hartnett, A. (1996), *Education and the Struggle for Democracy: The Politics of Educational Ideas*, Open University Press, Bristol.

Carroll, J. & Manne, R. (eds) (1992), *Shutdown: The Failure of Economic Rationalism and How to Rescue Australia*, Text Publishing, Melbourne.

Carson, E. & Martin, S. (2001), *Social Disadvantage in South Australia*, Social Policy Research Group, University of South Australia & South Australian Council for Social Services, Adelaide.

Casey, E. (1998), *The Fate of Place: A Philosophical History*, University of California Press, Berkeley.

Castells, M. (1996), *The Rise of the Network Society*, vol. 1, The Information Age: Economy, Society and Culture, Blackwell, Oxford.

—— (1997), *The Power of Identity*, vol. 2, The Information Age: Economy, Society and Culture, Blackwell, Oxford.

—— (1998), *End of the Millennium*, vol. 3, The Information Age: Economy, Society and Culture, Blackwell, Oxford.

Castles, F. (1985), *The Working Class and Welfare: Reflections on the Political Development of the Welfare State in Australia and New Zealand, 1890–1980*, Allen & Unwin, Sydney.

—— (1994), 'The wage earners' welfare state revisited', *Australian Journal of Social Issues*, vol. 29, no. 1, pp. 120–45.

Clandinin, D. J. & Connelly, F. M. (1998), 'Stories to live by: Narrative understandings of school reform', *Curriculum Inquiry*, vol. 28, no. 2, pp. 149–68.

Class Size Reduction Research Consortium (2000), *Class Size Reduction in California: The 1998–99 Evaluation, Final Report*, http://www.classsize.org/summary/98-99/index.htm, accessed 20 Dec. 2000.

Collins, C., Kenway, J. & McLeod, J. (2000), *Factors Influencing the Educational Performance of Males and Females in School and their Initial Destinations After Leaving School*, Department of Education, Training & Youth Affairs, Canberra.

Comber, B. (1998), 'The problem of "background" in researching the student subject', *Australian Educational Researcher*, vol. 25, no. 3, pp. 1–21.

—— (1999), 'Doing schooling, literacy and curriculum work', in B. Johnson & A. Reid (eds), *Contesting the Curriculum*, Social Science Press, Sydney, pp. 43–58.

Comber, B., Green, B., Lingard, B. & Luke, A. (1998), 'Literacy debates and public education: A question of "crisis"?', in A. Reid (ed.), *Going Public: Education Policy and Public Education in Australia*, Australian Curriculum Studies Association, Canberra.

Comber, B. & Hill, S. (2000), 'Socioeconomic disadvantage, literacy and social justice: Learning from longitudinal case study research', *Australian Education Researcher*, vol. 27, no. 3, pp. 151–66.

Commissioner for Public Employment (1997), *Annual Report*, South Australian Government, Adelaide.

Commonwealth Schools Commission (1978), *Disadvantaged Schools Program*, Commonwealth Schools Commission, Canberra.

Connell, R. W. (1993), *Schools and Social Justice*, Our Schools/Ourselves Foundation & Pluto Press, Toronto.

—— (1995), 'Social justice in education', in M. Kalantzis (ed.), *A Fair Go in Education*, Australian Curriculum Studies Association & Australian Centre for Equity in Education, Canberra, pp. 4–10.

Connell, R., Ashenden, D. J., Kessler, S. & Dowsett, G. W. (1982), *Making the Difference: Schools, Families and Social Divisions*, Allen & Unwin, Sydney.

Connell, R. W., Johnston, K. M. & White, V. M. (1990), *Measuring Up: Assessment of Student Outcomes and Evaluation of Program Effectiveness and the Educational Implications for Child Poverty in the Disadvantaged Schools Program*, Schools Council, National Board of Employment, Education and Training, Canberra.

Connell, R., White, V. & Johnston, K. (1990), *Poverty, Education and the Disadvantaged Schools Program (DSP): Project Overview and Discussion of Policy Questions*, Poverty, Education and the DSP Project, Macquarie University, Sydney.

—— (1991), *Running Twice as Hard: The Disadvantaged Schools Program in Australia*, Deakin University Press, Geelong.

Coorey, M. (1998), 'Call for merged schools system', *Australian*, 9 Oct., http://www.theaustralian.com.au/national/4351167.htm, accessed 9 Oct. 1998.

Crouch, B. (1998), 'Schools face more lawsuits', *Sunday Mail*, 11 Oct., p. 9.

Cummings, S. (1998), *Left Behind in Rosedale: Race Relations and the Collapse of Community Institutions*, Westview Press, Boulder.

Cvetkovich, A. & Kellner, D. (eds) (1997), *Articulating the Global and the Local: Globalisation and Cultural Studies*, Westview Press, Boulder.

Datnow, A. (1998), *The Gender Politics of Educational Change*, Falmer Press, London.

—— (2000), 'Power and politics in the adoption of school reform models', *Educational Evaluation and Policy Analysis*, vol. 22, no. 4, pp. 357–74.

Davis, M. (1997), *Gangland: Cultural Elites and the New Generationism*, Allen & Unwin, Sydney.

de Certeau, M. (1988), *The Practice of Everyday Life* (trans. S. Randall), University of California Press, Los Angeles.

DEETYA (1998), *Literacy for All: The Challenge for Australian Schools. Commonwealth Literacy Policies for Australian Schools*, vol. 1, AGPS, Canberra.

Dempster, N. (2000), 'Guilty or not: the impact and effects of site-based management on schools', *Journal of Educational Administration*, vol. 38, no. 1, pp. 47–63.

Denzin, N. K. (1997), *Interpretive Ethnography: Ethnographic Practices for the 21st Century*, Sage, London.

Devine, J. (1996), *Maximum Security: The Culture of Violence in Inner-City Schools*, University of Chicago Press, Chicago.

Dimmock, C. (1999), 'Principals and school restructuring: conceptualising challenges as dilemmas', *Journal of Educational Administration*, vol. 37, no. 5, pp. 441–62.

Dorn, S. (1996), *Creating the Dropout: An Institutional and Social History of School Failure*, Praeger, Westport.

Driscoll, M. & Kerchner, C. (1999), 'The implications of social capital for schools, communities and cities', in J. Murphy & K. S. Louis (eds), *The Handbook of Research on Educational Administration: A Project of the American Educational Research Association*, Jossey Bass, San Francisco, pp. 385–404.

Du Gay, P. (1996), *Consumption and Identity at Work*, Sage, London.

Dunant, S. & Porter, R. (eds) (1996), *The Age of Anxiety*, Virago, London.

Dunstan, D. (1998), 'Economic promise and political will', in E. Carson, A. Jamrozik & T. Winefield (eds), *Unemployment: Economic Promise and Political Will*, Australian Academic Press & Social Policy Research Group, University of South Australia, Adelaide, pp. 290–6.

Dusseldorp, J. (1998), Keynote address to Victorian secondary principals, Paper presented at the VASSP Leadership Conference, Melbourne, 18 Aug.

Dusseldorp Skills Forum & Curtain, R. (2000), *How Young People are Faring: Key Indicators 2000*, Dusseldorp Skills Foundation, Sydney.

Dyson, A. H. (1997), *Writing Superheroes: Contemporary Childhood, Popular Culture, and Classroom Literacy*, Teachers' College Press, New York.

Eckersley, R. (ed.) (1998), *Measuring Progress: Is Life Getting Better?*, CSIRO, Collingwood, Vic.

Ellis, C. & Bochner, A. P. (eds) (1996), *Composing Ethnography: Alternative Forms of Qualitative Writing*, Alta Mira Press, London.

Ellsworth, E. (1989), 'Why doesn't this feel empowering? Working through the repressive myths of critical pedagogy', *Harvard Education Review*, vol. 59, no. 3, pp. 297–324.

Ellsworth, J. & Ames, L. (eds) (1998), *Critical Perspectives on Project Head Start: Revisioning Hope and Challenge*, State University of New York Press, Albany.

Fairclough, N. (1994), *Language and Power*, Longman, Singapore.

Fecho, R. (1998), personal communication.

Feldstein, R. (1997), *Political Correctness: A Response from the Cultural Left*, University of Minnesota Press, Minneapolis.

Fincher, R. & Nieuwenhuysen, J. (eds) (1998), *Australian Poverty: Then and Now*, Melbourne University Press, Melbourne.

Fincher, R. & Saunders, P. (2001a), 'The complex contexts of Australian inequality', in R. Fincher & P. Saunders (eds), *Creating Unequal Futures? Rethinking, Poverty, Inequality and Disadvantage*, Allen & Unwin, Sydney.

—— (eds), (2001b), *Creating Unequal Futures? Rethinking Poverty, Inequality and Disadvantage*, Allen & Unwin, Sydney.

Fine, M. (1995), 'The politics of who's "at risk"', in B. B. Swadener & S. Lubeck (eds), *Children and Families 'At Promise': Deconstructing the Discourse of Risk*, State University of New York Press, Albany.

Fine, M. & Weis, L. (1998), *The Unknown City: The Lives of Poor and Working Class Young Adults*, Beacon Press, Boston.

Fitzgerald, R. (1976), *Poverty and Education in Australia*, National Commission of Inquiry into Poverty, AGPS, Canberra.

Flecha, R. (1999), 'New educational inequalities', in M. Castells, R. Flecha, P. Freiere, H. Giroux, D. Macedo & P. Willis (eds), *Critical Education in the New Information Age*, Rowman & Littlefield, Lanham, pp. 65–82.

Fordham, S. (1996), *Blacked Out: Dilemmas of Race, Identity and Success at Capital High*, University of Chicago Press, Chicago.

Forster, C. (1986), 'Economic restructuring, urban policy and patterns of deprivation in Adelaide', *Australian Planner*, vol. 24, no. 6, pp. 6–10.

Freebody, P., Ludwig, C. & Gunn, S. (1995), *Everyday Literacy Practices In and Out of Schools in Low Socio-economic Urban Communities*, vol. 1, Commonwealth of Australia & Curriculum Corporation, Canberra.

Freeland, J. (1998), 'Future security amidst uncertainty: young people in a changing world', Paper presented at the VETNET National Conference: Changing Work, Changing Society, Adelaide, 19–21 Aug.

Fullan, M. (1999), *Change Forces: The Sequel*, Falmer Press, London.

Galton, M., Hargreaves, L. & Pell, A. (1996), *Class Size, Teaching and Pupil Achievement*, National Union of Teachers & School of Education, University of Leicester, Leicester.

Gerwitz, S., Ball, S. & Bowe, R. (1995), *Markets, Choice and Equity in Education*, Open University Press, Buckingham.

Gibson, R. (1998), 'Free education too expensive for some', *Age*, 3 Mar., http://www.theage.com.au/daily/980319/news/news980317.html, accessed 3 Mar. 1998.

Giddens, A. (1991), *Modernity and Self Identity*, Stanford University Press, Stanford.

Gilbert, P. (2000), '"The deepening divide": choices for Australian education', *Australian Educational Researcher*, vol. 27, no. 1, pp. 31–45.

Gillbourn, D. & Youdell, D. (2000), *Rationing Education: Policy, Practice, Reform and Equity*, Open University Press, Buckingham.

Gitlin, A., Margonis, F. & Brunjes, H. (1993), 'In the shadow of the excellence reports: School restructuring for at-risk students', in R. Donmoyer & R. Kos (eds), *At-risk Students: Portraits, Policies, Programs, and Practices*, State University of New York Press, Albany, pp. 265–90.

'Give us a choice, say parents of disabled children' (1999), *Advertiser*, 29 Jan., http://www.news.com.au/sa/4336130.htm, accessed 29 Jan. 1999.

Glover, J., Shand, M., Forster, C. & Woollacott, T. (2000), *A Social Health Atlas of South Australia*, 2nd edn, South Australian Health Commission, Adelaide.

Gore, J. (1993), *The Struggle for Pedagogies: Critical and Feminist Discourses as Regimes of Truth*, Routledge, New York.

Green, B. & Bigum, C. (1993), 'Aliens in the classroom', *Australian Journal of Education*, vol. 37, no. 42, pp. 119–41.

Haberman, M. (1991), 'The pedagogy of poverty vs good teaching', *Phi Delta Kappan*, vol. 73, no. 4, pp. 290–4.

Hall, V. (1996), *Dancing on the Ceiling: A Study of Women Managers in Education*, Paul Chapman Publishing, London.

Hamnett, S. & Freestone, R. (eds) (2000), *The Australian Metropolis: A Planning History*, Allen & Unwin, Sydney.

Handy, C. (1994), *The Empty Raincoat: Making Sense of the Future*, Hutchison, London.

Harding, A. & Szukalska, A. (1999), 'Trends in Child Poverty 1982 to 1995', Paper presented at the Australian Association for Social Research annual conference, University of New South Wales, 12 Feb.

Hasluck, L. & Malone, K. (1999), 'Location, leisure and lifestyle:Young people's retreat to home environments', *Contemporary Perspectives on Family Research*, vol. 1, pp. 177–96.

Hattam, R. (1999), 'School reform and "Howard's way"', in J. Spoehr (ed.), *Beyond the Contract State: Ideas for Social and Economic Renewal in South Australia*, Wakefield Press, Adelaide, pp. 244–64.

Henderson, R. (1975), *Poverty in Australia*, AGPS, Canberra.

Henderson, R., Harcourt, A. & Harper, R. (1970), *People in Poverty: A Melbourne Survey*, Institute of Applied Economic and Social Research & Cheshire, Melbourne.

Hill, S., Comber, B., Louden, B., Reid, J. & Rivalland, J. (1998), *100 Children Go to School: Connections and Disconnections in Literacy Development in the Year Prior to School and the First Year of School*, vols 1–3, Department of Employment, Training, Education and Youth Affairs, Canberra.

Holt, J. (1972), *How Children Fail*, Penguin, Harmondsworth.

Hopkins, D. & Levin, B. (2000), 'Government policy and school development', *School Leadership and Management*, vol. 20, no. 1, pp. 15–30.

Howard, J. (1999), 'The Australian way', Paper presented at the Federation Address to the Queensland Chamber of Commerce and Industry, Brisbane, 28 Jan.

Hugo, G. (1999), 'South Australia's population at the turn of the century', in J. Spoehr (ed.), *Beyond the Contract State: Ideas for Social and Economic Renewal in South Australia*, Wakefield Press, Adelaide, pp. 55–91.

Illich, I. (1973), *Deschooling Society*, Penguin, Harmondsworth.

Jackson, B. & Marsden, D. (1966), *Education and the Working Class*, Penguin, Harmondsworth.

Jameson, F. & Miyoshi, M. (eds) (1998), *The Cultures of Globalisation*, Duke University Press, Durham.

Jensen, B. & Seltzer, A. (2000), 'Neighbourhood and family effects in educational progress', *Australian Economic Review*, vol. 33, no. 1, pp. 17–31.

Johnson, B. (1998), personal communication about ongoing research project into bullying.

Johnson, M. (1999), *Failing School, Failing City*, Jon Carpenter Publishing, Charlburg.

Karmel, P. (1973), *Schools in Australia*, Interim Committee of the Schools Commission, Canberra.

Kelly, P. (1994), *The End of Certainty: Power, Politics and Business in Australia*, Allen & Unwin, Sydney.

Kenway, J. (1990), 'Education and the right's discursive politics: Private versus state schooling', in S. Ball (ed.), *Foucault and Education: Disciplines and Knowledge*, Routledge, London, pp. 167–206.

Kenway, J., Kelly, P. & Willis, S. (2001), 'Manufacturing the global locality, customising the school and designing young workers', in J. Demain (ed.), *Sociology of Education Today*, Macmillan, London, pp. 119–41.

Kenway, J., Willis, S., Blackmore, J. & Rennie, L. (1997), *Answering Back: Girls, Boys and Feminism in Schools*, Allen & Unwin, Sydney.

Kerr, B. (2000), 'Optimism and reality in disadvantaged schools', *Teachers Journal*.

Kozol, J. (1991), *Savage Inequalities: Children in America's Schools*, Harper Perennial, New York.

—— (1996), *Amazing Grace*, Harper Perennial, New York.

Kress, G. (2000), 'A curriculum for the future', *Cambridge Journal of Education*, vol. 30, no. 1, pp. 133–45.

Kretzmann, J. & McKnight, J. (1993), *Building Communities from the Inside-Out*, Asset-Based Community Development Institute, Chicago.

Kuehn, L. (1998), 'Globalisation made me do it', Paper presented at the VETNET conference, Adelaide, 19–21 Aug.

Ladson-Billings, G. (1994), *The Dream-Keepers: Successful Teachers of African American Children*, Jossey Bass, San Francisco.

Lamb, S. & Ball, K. (1999), *Curriculum and Careers: The Education and Labour Market Consequences of Year 12 Subject Choice*, Longitudinal Surveys of Australian Youth Research Report 12, Australian Council for Educational Research, Melbourne.

Lash, S. & Urry, J. (1994), *Economies of Sign and Space*, Sage, London.

Latham, M. (1998), *Civilising Global Capital*, Allen & Unwin, Sydney.

—— (2001), What Did You Learn Tod@y?, Allen & Unwin, Sydney.

Lather, P. (1991), 'Deconstructing/deconstructive inquiry: The politics of knowing and being known', *Educational Theory*, vol. 41, no. 2, pp. 153–73.

Lawn, M. (1886), *Modern Times? Work, Professionalism and Citizenship in Teaching*, Falmer Press, London.

LeFebvre, H. (1971), *Everyday Life in the Modern World* (trans. S. Rabinovitch, 1994 edn), Transaction Publishers, London.

Levin, B. (2001), *Reforming Education: From Origins to Outcomes*, Falmer Press, London.

Levin, B. & Young, J. (1998), *Understanding Canadian Schools: An Introduction to Educational Administration*, 2nd edn, Harcourt Brace & Company, Toronto.

Levinson, B. & Holland, D. (1996), 'The cultural production of the educated person: An introduction', in B. Levinson & D. Holland (eds), *The Cultural Production of the Educated Person*, State University of New York Press, New York, pp. 1–54.

Levitas, R. (1998), *The Inclusive Society? Social Exclusion and New Labour*, pp. 1–54, Macmillan, Basingstoke.

Lingard, B. (1997), 'The disadvantaged schools program: Caught between literacy and local management of schools', *International Journal of Inclusive Education*, vol. 1, no. 3.

Lingard, B., Knight, J. & Porter, P. (eds) (1993), *Schooling Reform in Hard Times*, Falmer Press, London.

Lingard, B. & Mills, M. (2000), 'Teachers, school reform and social justice: Challenging research and practice', *Australian Education Researcher*, vol. 27, no. 3.

Lipman, P. (1998), *Race, Class and Power in School Restructuring*, State University of New York Press, Albany.

Lloyd, N. (1998), 'Principals want fee subsidy lift for needy', *Advertiser*, 24 Apr., p. 14.

—— (1998b), 'Threat to fine abusive parents: Teachers' plea for help', *Advertiser*, Mar. 23, p. 1.

Long, M., Carpenter, P. & Hayden, M. (1999), *Participation in Education and Training 1980–1994: Longitudinal Studies of Australian Youth*, Research Report 13, Australian Council for Educational Research, Melbourne.

Luke, A. (1999a), 'Education 2010 and new times: Why equity and social justice still matter, but differently', Paper presented at the Education Queensland on-line conference, 20 Oct.

—— (1999b), *The 'New Basics' Technical Papers*, Education Queensland, Brisbane.

Luke, A. & Luke, C. (2000), 'A situated perspective on cultural globalisation', in N. Burbules & C. Torres (eds), *Globalisation and Education: Critical perspectives*, Routledge, New York, pp. 275–98.

Luke, C. (ed.) (1996), *Feminisms and Pedagogies of Everyday Life*, State University of New York Press, Albany.

—— (1999), 'What next? Toddler netizens, playstation thumb, techno-literacies', *Contemporary Issues in Early Childhood*, vol. 1, no. 1, pp. 95–100.

Mac An Ghaill, M. (1996), 'Sociology of education, state schooling and social class: Beyond critiques of the new right hegemony', *British Journal of Sociology of Education*, vol. 17, no. 2, pp. 163–76.

McDonald, F. & Siemen, D. (2001), 'Families, work and welfare', in P. Saunders (ed.), *Reforming the Australian Welfare State*, Australian Institute of Family Studies, Melbourne, pp. 206–23.

MacDonald, R. (ed.) (1997), *Youth, the 'Underclass' and Social Exclusion*, Routledge, London.

McDowell, L. (1999), *Gender, Identity and Place: Understanding Feminist Geographies*, University of Minnesota Press, Minneapolis.

Mackay, H. (1998), 'Why voters are bitter', *Age*, 23 Jul., http://www.theage.com.au/daily/980723/news/news980727.htm, accessed 23 Jul. 1998.

McKnight, J. (1995), *The Careless Society: Community and its Counterfeits*, Basic Books, New York.

Manicom, A. (1995), 'What's health got to do with it? Class, gender, and teacher's work', in M. Campbell & A. Manicom (eds), *Knowledge, Experience, and Ruling Relations: Studies in the Social Organisation of Knowledge*, University of Toronto Press, Toronto, pp. 135–48.

Marcuse, P. (1993), 'What's new about divided cities?', *International Journal of Urban and Regional Research*, vol. 13, pp. 697–707.

Marginson, S. (1993), *Education and Public Policy in Australia*, Cambridge University Press, Melbourne.

—— (1997a), *Educating Australia: Government, Economy and Citizen Since 1960*, Cambridge University Press, Melbourne.

—— (1997b), *Markets in Education*, Allen & Unwin, Sydney.

Marks, G. & Fleming, N. (1999), *Early School Leaving in Australia: Findings from the 1995 year 9 SLAY cohort*, Longitudinal surveys of Australian youth, Research Report 11, Australian Council for Educational Research, Melbourne.

Marks, G., Fleming, N., Long, M. & McMillan, J. (2000), *Patterns of Participation in Year 12 and Higher Education in Australia: Trends and Issues*, Longitudinal surveys of Australia youth Research Report 17, Australian Council for Educational Research, Melbourne.

Martin, R. (2000), 'Regional educational disadvantage: Towards a new approach', *Australian Educational Researcher*, vol. 27, no. 3, pp. 167–84.

Massey, D. (1994), *Space, Place and Gender*, University of Minnesota Press, Minneapolis.

—— (1995), 'The conceptualisation of place', in D. Massey & P. Jess (eds), *A Place in the World? Places, Cultures and Globalisation*, Open University Press, Milton Keynes, pp. 45–88.

Meier, D. (1995), *The Power of Their Ideas: Lessons for America from a Small School in Harlem*, Beacon Press, Boston.

Miller, D. W. (2001), 'Poking holes in the theory of "broken windows"', *The Chronicle of Higher Education*, vol. 47, no. 22, 9 Feb., http://chronicle.merit.edu/ (by subscription only).

Ministerial Council on Education, Employment, Training and Youth Affairs, (1999), *The Adelaide Declaration on National Goals for Schooling in the Twenty-First Century*, http://www.deetya.gov.au/schools/adelaide/text.htm, accessed 6 Dec. 1999.

Mink, G. (1998), *Welfare's End*, Cornell University Press, Ithaca.

Miron, L. (1996), *The Social Construction of Urban Schooling: Situating the Crisis*, Hampton Press, Cresskill, N.J.

Moll, L., Tapia, J. & Whitmore, K. (1993), 'Living knowledge: The social distribution of cultural resources for thinking', in G. Salomon (ed.), *Distributed Cognitions*, Cambridge University Press, Cambridge, pp. 139–63.

Morris, L. (1994), *Dangerous Classes: The Underclass and Social Citizenship*, Routledge, London.

Nankervis, D. (1999), 'Aussies "miracle workers"', *Sunday Mail*, 31 Oct., p. 38.

Neilsen, A. (ed.) (1999), *Daily Meaning: Counternarratives of Teachers' work*, Bendall Books, Mill Bay, Canada.

Nespor, J. (1997), *Tangled up in School: Politics, Space, Bodies, and Signs in the Educational Process*, Lawrence Erlbaum Associates, Mahwah, N.J.

Newman, K. (1999), *No Shame in My Game: The Working Poor in the Inner City*, Russell Sage Foundation & Alfred Knopf, New York.

Newmann, F. & associates (1996), *Authentic Achievement: Restructuring Schools for Intellectual Quality*, Jossey Bass, San Francisco.

Nye, B., Hedges, L. & Konstantanopolous, S. (1999), 'The effects of small class sizes in academic achievement: The results of the Tennessee class size experiment', *Education Evaluation and Policy Analysis*, vol. 21, no. 2, pp. 127–42.

Pascoe, S. (1996), *Broadening Our Horizons*, Australian Council for Educational Administration, Melbourne.

Pate-Bain, H., Fulton, D. & Boyd-Zaharias, J. (1999), *Effects of Class-size Reduction in the Early Grades (K–3) on High School Performance*, National Education Association, http://www.nea.org/issues/class size/bain.html, accessed 3 Jul. 2000.

Pech, J. & McCoull, F. (1998), 'Intergenerational poverty and welfare dependence: Is there an Australian problem?', Paper presented at the Institute of Family Studies annual conference, Melbourne, 25–27 Nov.

Pedder, D. (1999), 'Pupil and teachers' professional knowledge and practices in large and small classes: A methodological report', paper presented at the British Educational Research Association, University of Sussex, Brighton, 2–5 Sept.

Peel, M. (1995a), *Good Times, Hard Times: The Past and Future in Elizabeth*, Melbourne University Press, Melbourne.

—— (1995b), 'The urban debate: From "Los Angeles" to the urban village', in P.Troy (ed.), *Australian Cities: Issues, Strategies and Policies for Urban Australia in the 1990s*, Cambridge University Press, Melbourne, pp. 39–64.

Phillips, A. (1999), *Which Equalities Matter?*, Polity Press, Cambridge, Mass.

Popkewitz,T. & Lindblad, S. (2000), 'Educational governance and social inclusion and exclusion: Some conceptual difficulties and problematics in policy and research', *Discourse*, vol. 21, no. 1, pp. 5–44.

Powell, D. (1993), *Out West: Perceptions of Sydney's Western Suburbs*, Allen & Unwin, Sydney.

Pudney, J. (1998a), 'Stay away from school, Dad told', *Advertiser*, 12 May, p. 3.

—— (1998b), 'Dad fights school bans', *Advertiser*, 30 May, p. 45.

Pusey, M. (1991), *Economic Rationalism in Canberra: A Nation-building State Changes its Mind*, Cambridge University Press, Cambridge.

—— (1998), 'The middle Australia project', Paper presented at the VETNET national conference, Adelaide, 19–21 Aug.

Rees, S. & Rodley, G. (1995), *The Human Cost of Managerialism: Advocating the Recovery of Humanity*, Pluto Press, Sydney.

Rees, S., Rodley, G. & Stillwell, F. (1993), *Beyond the Market: Alternatives to Economic Rationalism*, Pluto Press, Sydney.

Reich, R. (1991), *The Work of Nations: A Blueprint for the Future*, Simon & Schuster, New York.

Reid, A. & Thomson, P. (1998), Survey of vocational offerings in principal association members' schools, unpublished paper for South Australian Secondary Principals Association.

Richardson, L. (1994), 'Writing: A method of inquiry', in N. Denzin & Y. Lincoln (eds), *The Handbook of Qualitative Research*, Sage, Thousand Oaks.

—— (1997), *Fields of Play: Constructing an Academic Life*, Rutgers University Press, New Brunswick.

Riessman, C. K. (1993), *Narrative Analysis*, vol. 30, Sage Publications, California.

Rifkin, J. (1996), *The End of Work: The Decline of the Global Labour Force and the Dawn of the Post Market Era*, Putnam, New York.

Riseborough, G. (1993), 'Primary headship, state policy and the challenge of the 1990s: An exceptional story that disproves total hegemonic rule', *Journal of Education Policy*, vol. 8, no. 2, pp. 155–73.

Robertson, R. (1995), 'Glocalisation: time-space and homogeneity-heterogeneity', in M. Featherstone, S. Lash & R. Robertson (eds), *Global Modernities*, Sage, London, pp. 91–107.

Roper, T. (1970), *The Myth of Equality*, National Union of Australian Students, Canberra.

Rose, G. (1995), Place and identity: A sense of place', in D. Massey & P. Jess (eds), *A Place in the World? Places, Cultures and Globalisation*, Open University Press, Milton Keynes, pp. 87–132.

Saunders, P. (1998), 'Defining poverty and identifying the poor: Reflections on the Australian experience', Paper presented at the conference to mark the centenary of Seebohn Rowntree's first study of poverty in York, University of York, 18–20 March.

Schools Council (1992), *Consultation Paper: Consultation on the Development of a Broadbanded National Equity Program for Schools*, Schools Council, National Board of Employment, Education and Training, Canberra.

Sen, A. (1992), *Inequality Reexamined*, Harvard University Press, Cambridge, Mass.

Senate Standing Committee on Employment, Education & Training (1997), *Not a Level Playground*, Australian Government, Canberra.

Sharp, R. & Green, A. (1975), *Education and Social Class*, Routledge & Kegan Paul, London.

Shirk, M., Bennett, N. & Aber, J. L. (1999), *Lives on the Line. American Families and the Struggle to Make Ends Meet*, Westview Press, Boulder.

Short, J. R. & Kim, Y.-H. (1999), *Globalisation and the City*, Longman, Harlow.

Simola, H. (1998), 'Firmly bolted into the air: Wishful rationalism as a discursive basis for educational reforms', *Teachers College Record*, vol. 99, no. 4, pp. 731–57.

Sizer, T. (1985), *Horace's Compromise: The Dilemma of the American High School*, Houghton Miflin, Boston.

Smyth, J., Hattam, R., Edwards, J., Cannon, J., Wurst, S., Wilson, N. & Shacklock, G. (2000), *Listen to Me, I'm Leaving*, Department of Education, Training and Employment, Senior Secondary Assessment Board of South Australia & Flinders Institute for the Study of Teaching, Flinders University, Adelaide.

Smyth, P. & Cass, B. (eds) (1998), *Contesting the Australian Way: States, Markets and Civil Society*, Cambridge University Press, Melbourne.

Soja, E. (2000), *Postmodern Geographies: The Reassertion of Space in Critical Social Theory*, Verso, London.

South Australian Business Vision 2010 (2000*)*, *Indicators of the State of South Australia 1999*, Executive Summary, SA Business Vision 2010 Inc., Adelaide.

Southworth, G. (1999), 'Continuities and changes in primary headship', in T. Bush, L. Bell, R. Bolam, R. Glatter & P. Ribbins (eds), *Educational Management: Redefining Theory, Policy and Practice*, Paul Chapman Publishers, London, pp. 29–42.

Spierings, J. (2000), 'Developing a new regional education, employment and training agenda: Early lessons from Whittlesea', Dusseldorp Skills Forum, http://www.dsf.org.au.

Spoehr, J. (1997), *South Australian Labour Market Briefing*, December, Centre for Labour Studies, Adelaide University, Adelaide.

—— (1998a), *A Future that Works: Tackling the jobs crisis. Policy options for the South Australian Government*, Public Service Association of South Australia & Centre for Labour Research, University of Adelaide, Adelaide.

—— (1998b*)*, *South Australian Labour Market Briefing*, September, Centre for Labour Studies, University of Adelaide, Adelaide.

—— (1999a), *Beyond the Contract State: Ideas for Social and Economic Renewal in South Australia*, Wakefield Press, Adelaide.

—— (1999b), 'A labour market in crisis?', in J. Spoehr (ed.), *Beyond the Contract State: Ideas for Social and Economic Renewal in South Australia*, Wakefield Press, Adelaide, pp. 92–106.

Spring, G. (1997), 'Is there a crisis in government schools? Of course not!', Paper presented at the Issues in Public Sector Change conference, Centre for Public Policy, University of Melbourne, 12 May.

—— (1998), 'The role of positive welfare policies in helping each student achieve their full potential at school', Paper presented at the VASSP annual leadership conference, Melbourne.

Spring, J. (1998), *Education and the Rise of the Global Economy*, Lawrence Erlbarm & Associates, Mahwah, N.J.

Stasz, C. & Stecher, B. (2000), 'Teaching mathematics and language arts in reduced size and non-reduced size classrooms', *Educational Evaluation and Policy Analysis*, vol. 22, no. 4, pp. 313–29.

Strachan, J. (1999), 'Feminist educational leadership in a New Zealand neo-liberal context', *Journal of Educational Administration*, vol. 37, no. 2, pp. 121–38.

Street, J. (1997), *Politics and Popular Culture*, Polity Press, Cambridge.

Stretton, H. (1980), 'Future patterns for taxation and public expenditure in Australia', in J. Wilkes (ed.), *The Politics of Taxation*, Hodder & Stoughton, Sydney.

Strike, K. (1999), 'Three pictures of justice and caring', in M. Katz, N. Noddings & K. Strike (eds), *Justice and Caring: The Search for Common Ground in Education*, Teachers College Press, New York, pp. 167–78.

Stronach, I. & MacLure, M. (1997), *Educational Research Undone: The Postmodern Embrace*, Open University Press, Buckingham.

Swadener, B. B. (1995), 'Children and families "at promise": Deconstructing the discourse of risk', in B. B. Swadener & S. Lubeck (eds), *Children and Families 'At Promise': Deconstructing the Discourse of Risk*, State University of New York Press, Albany, pp. 17–49.

Swyngedouw, E. (1997), 'Neither global nor local: "Glocalisation" and the politics of scale', in K. Cox (ed.), *Spaces of Globalisation: Reasserting the Power of the Local*, Guilford Press, New York, pp. 137–66.

Szkudlarek, T. (1993), *The Problem of Freedom in Postmodern Education*, Bergin & Garvey, Westport.

Tattam, A. (1999), 'Governments on trial', *Australian Educator*, vol. 23, pp. 12–15.

Taylor, S., Rivzi, F., Lingard, B. & Henry, M. (1997), *Educational Policy and the Politics of Change*, Routledge, London.

Teese, R. (2000), *Academic Success and Social Power*, Melbourne University Press, Melbourne.

The New London Group (1966), 'A pedagogy of multi-literacies: Designing social futures', *Harvard Educational Review*, vol. 66, no. 1, pp. 363–76.

The Smith Family (1998), *Free Education: Who Can Afford It?*, The Smith Family, Melbourne.

Thomson, P. (1994), *Local Decision Making and Management*, Joint Principals Associations, South Australia, Adelaide.

—— (1997), 'Learning [not] to labour. How [some] working class kids get [some] working class jobs [some of the time]', in E. Carson, A. Jamrozik & T. Winefield (eds), *Unemployment: Economic Promise and Political Will*, Australian Academic Press, Brisbane, pp. 205–17.

—— (1998a), *The Changing Role of the Principal* (CD-ROM), South Australian Secondary Principals Association, Adelaide.

—— (1998b), 'Thoroughly modern management and a cruel accounting: the effect of public sector reform on public education', in A. Reid (ed.), *Going Public: Education Policy and Public Education in Australia*, Australian Curriculum Studies Association, Canberra, pp. 37–46.

—— (1999a), *Doing justice: Stories of everyday life in disadvantaged schools and neighbourhoods*, unpublished PhD thesis, Deakin University, Geelong.

—— (1999b), 'How doing justice got boxed in: A cautionary tale for policy activists', in B. Johnson & A. Reid (eds), *Contesting the Curriculum*, Social Science Press, Sydney.

—— (1999c), 'How stopping it makes us go blind', *Education Links*, vol. 59, pp. 10–12.

—— (1999d), 'Some observations from a failed, but no longer disappointed, school reformer: A response to Fielding, Hargreaves and Little', *Australian Education Researcher*, vol. 26, no. 2, pp. 45–66.

—— (2001), 'From Here to Where? "Disadvantaged" Schools, Literacy and Policy', *English in Australia*, in press.

Thomson, P. & Wellard, S. (1999), *Get a Grip on Research: Critical and Postcritical Approaches*, Deakin University Press, Geelong.

Thomson, P. & Wilkins, P. (1997), *Survey of Spending of DSP Schools*, Joint Principals Associations, South Australia, Adelaide.

Thrupp, M. (1998), The caring role of schools: Teachers' and children's perspectives', Paper presented at the Children's Wellbeing at School conference, University of Otago, Dunedin, 1–2 Dec.

—— (1999), *Schools Making a Difference: Let's Be Realistic! School Mix, School Effectiveness and the Social Limits of Reform*, Open University Press, Buckingham.

Tittle, D. (1995), *Welcome to Heights High: The Crippling Politics of Restructuring America's Public Schools*, Ohio State University Press, Columbus.

Townsend, T. (1998), 'School self-management and effective education—compatible?', Paper presented at the Effective School Self-Management—What's Ahead? conference, Wellington, Oct.

Travers, P. & Richardson, S. (1993), *Living Decently: Material Well-being in Australia*, Oxford University Press, Melbourne.

Troy, P. (ed.) (1995), *Australian Cities: Issues, Strategies and Policies for Urban Australia in the 1990s*, Cambridge University Press, Melbourne.

—— (1999), *Serving the City: The Crisis in Australia's Urban Services*, Pluto Press, Sydney.

Tyack, D. & Cuban, L. (1995), *Tinkering Toward Utopia: A Century of Public School Reform*, Jossey Bass, San Francisco.

UNICEF (1996), *Solo Poverty*, Luxembourg Income Study, Working Paper 127, http://www.unicef.org/pon96/insolo.htm, accessed 20 Nov. 1997.

US Department of Education (September 2000), 'The class size reduction programme: Boosting student achievement in schools across the nation', http://www.ed.gov/offices/OESE/ClassSize. Accessed 3 December 2000.

Valencia, R. (ed.) (1997), *The Evolution of Deficit Thinking: Educational Thought and Practice*, Falmer Press, London.

Vincent, C. (2000), *Including Parents? Education, Citizenship and Agency*, Open University Press, Buckingham.

Wade, M. (2000), 'Jobs to go as manufacturing hits 8-year low', *Sydney Morning Herald*, 18 Dec., http://www.smh.com.au/news/0012/0018/national/national0011.html, accessed 18 Dec. 2000.

Walmsley, D., & Wernard, H. (1997), 'Is Australia becoming more unequal?', *Australian Geographer*, vol. 28, no. 1, pp. 69–88.

Webber, M. & Crooks, M. (eds.) (1996), *Putting the People Last: Government, Services and Rights in Victoria*, Hyland House, Melbourne.

Wexler, P., Crichlow, W., Kern, J. & Martusewicz, R. (1992), *Becoming Somebody: Toward a Social Psychology of School*, Falmer Press, London.

Wheatley, K. (2000), 'Fifth of state's families live in poverty', *Advertiser*, 12 Dec., http://www.theadvertiser.com.au/common/story_page/0,451101529017.html, accessed 12 Dec 2000.

Whitty, G., Power, S. & Halpin, D. (1997), *Devolution and Choice in Education: The School, the State and the Market*, Open University Press, Buckingham.

Willis, P. (1977), *Learning to Labour: How Working Class Kids Get Working Class Jobs*, Saxon House, London.

Wilson, B. (1989), *Evaluating Outcomes: A Paper Prepared for the Victorian Disadvantaged Schools Program*, Youth Research Centre, University of Melbourne, Melbourne.

Wilson, W. J. (1997), *When Work Disappears: The World of the New Urban Poor*, Alfred A. Knopf, New York.

Wiseman, J. (1998), *Global Nation? Australia and the Politics of Globalisation*, Cambridge University Press, Melbourne.

World Bank Social Capital Initiative (1999), Working Paper Five, *Social Capital: Conceptual Frameworks and Empirical Evidence. An annotated bibliography*, World Bank, http://www.worldbank.org/poverty/scapital/wkrppr/index.htm, accessed 10 Dec. 1999.

Wyatt, T. & Ruby, A. (1989), *Education Indicators for Quality, Accountability and Better Practice, Papers from the Second National Conference at Surfers Paradise, Australia*, Australian Conference of Directors General of Education.

Yandell, J. (2000), 'Measure for measure, or inspecting the inspectors', *Changing English*, vol. 7, no. 2, pp. 119–28.

Zukin, S. (1997), 'Cultural strategies of economic development and the hegemony of vision', in A. Merrifield & E. Swyngedouw (eds), *The Urbanisation of Injustice*, New York University Press, New York, pp. 223–43.

Last words

The doctoral research on which this book is based was supervised by Richard Bates at Deakin University, and supported by other faculty members, most particularly Jane Kenway and Jill Blackmore. My current colleagues at the University of South Australia, Barbara Comber, Helen Nixon and Phillip Cormack, were willing readers and tea drinkers. Bob Lingard (series editor) and Elizabeth Weiss and Rebecca Kaiser from Allen & Unwin were inordinately patient as I struggled to write a short and up-to-date text. At home, Randy Barber was always supportive and supremely confident I would write to completion. My thanks to all of these people. Finally, this book was only possible because my colleagues willingly talked for hours about everyday life in rustbelt schools: thankyou.

Index